Symbolic Childhood

Toby Miller
General Editor

Vol. 5

PETER LANG
New York • Washington, D.C./Baltimore • Bern
Frankfurt am Main • Berlin • Brussels • Vienna • Oxford

Symbolic Childhood

EDITED BY
Daniel Thomas Cook

PETER LANG
New York • Washington, D.C./Baltimore • Bern
Frankfurt am Main • Berlin • Brussels • Vienna • Oxford

Library of Congress Cataloging-in-Publication Data

Symbolic childhood / Daniel Thomas Cook, editor.
p. cm. — (Popular culture & everyday life; vol. 5)
Includes bibliographical references and index.
1. Children—Social conditions. 2. Children in popular culture.
3. Children—Cross-cultural studies. I. Cook, Daniel Thomas. II. Series.
HQ767.9 .S94   305.23—dc21   2001038446
ISBN 0-8204-5580-6
ISSN 1529-2428

Die Deutsche Bibliothek-CIP-Einheitsaufnahme

Symbolic childhood / ed. by: Daniel Thomas Cook.
–New York; Washington, D.C./Baltimore; Bern;
Frankfurt am Main; Berlin; Brussels; Vienna; Oxford: Lang.
(Popular culture and everyday life; Vol. 5)
ISBN 0-8204-5580-6

Cover photo (protesters demonstrating against the NATO bombing of Serbia
at the Canadian Parliament in Ottawa, March 1999) by Daniel Thomas Cook
Cover design by Dutton & Sherman Design

The paper in this book meets the guidelines for permanence and durability
of the Committee on Production Guidelines for Book Longevity
of the Council of Library Resources.

© 2002 Peter Lang Publishing, Inc., New York

Printed in the United States of America

To my grandparents, Josephine and John Cook, and to my mother, Josephine, who loved me as a person even when I tried to impose myself as a symbol.

Table of Contents

Illustrations

Note: Every effort has been made to secure permission for usage of copyrighted material. Any rights holder who feels that material was used improperly should contact the publisher.

Acknowledgments

The idea for *Symbolic Childhood* came to me as I was writing my dissertation on the history of the children's wear industry in United States. As I culled through industry trade materials, I began to realize that "the child" was essentially nonexistent—i.e., that retailers, marketers, and store designers had created and traded among themselves a particular, commercially motivated image of their child customer. This "child" took on different hues at different historical times. It stood for various needs, wants, and social relations. It served as a symbol.

Immediately after completing the dissertation, I began soliciting manuscripts for *Symbolic Childhood*—something which only could have been done at that juncture by someone governed by a kind of blind enthusiasm borne of naiveté about the arduous task facing an editor. Early in the process, Jean Comaroff offered encouragement and gave insight about the tricky process of creating something out of nothing.

Throughout this time, for this project and others, Jessica Clark has been my inspiration and strength, always at the ready with ideas, encouragement, and enthusiasm.

Yu-Ling Chen provided extraordinary editorial assistance, including managing the difficulties in coordinating the manuscripts and designing the layout. I greatly appreciate her efforts.

Finally, I extend my appreciation to the Contributors, many of whom exhibited great patience as I struggled to bring this project together. I feel confident that they have made good company for one another each other in this volume.

Introduction

Interrogating Symbolic Childhood

Daniel Thomas Cook

Childhood resides in a semantic domain distinct from most others. Those who speak for childhood are rarely children. Unlike women, ethnic/racial minorities, sexual minorities and the economically marginalized, those occupying the "age of minority" must move out of their socially assigned subordinate position to speak with any authority to a public. When adults—those "outsiders"—act and speak in the name of *children*, they offer an emblem, a representation, of *childhood*.

The contributors to *Symbolic Childhood* engage directly with the politics of representation by scrutinizing the connection between portrayals of children and childhood and the exercise of power. The authors share a general outlook that comprehends childhood not as a given, natural category transparently understood, but as a thoroughly social artifact infused with contradictory and inexact meaning. As a social construction, childhood is thus a production that can be taken apart and reconstructed in a variety of ways for a variety of purposes. Each contributor to this volume takes pains to specify the key actors and institutions active in the making and remaking of childhood, and thus of children's identities.

Symbolic Childhood builds on and extends an impressive body of research and thought, emergent mainly in the 1990s, that understands childhood foremost as a social construction. Allison James, Alan Prout, and Chris Jenks have spearheaded a "new paradigm" for the sociology of childhood by debunking the notion that childhood is merely a prelude to adulthood (James and Prout 1990; Jenks 1996; James, Jenks, and Prout 1998). They advocate that children and childhood cultures are worthy of study in their own right. Ethnographic studies foreground children's active involvement in the negotiation of gender relations (Thorne 1993), uses of technology (Buckingham 2000; McNamee 1998), and peer relations generally (Corsaro 1997; Adler and Adler 1998). Central to this view is a model of the "child" as a competent social actor who makes meaning and actively interprets the world like anyone else.

Sociologist Jens Qvortrup frames the social construction of children and childhood in a different, complementary way, arguing that childhood as an age-defined social station must be distinguished from children as social actors. Every individual loses child status, Qvortrup (1987, 1993) observes, but childhood is retained collectively as a permanent structural element regardless of how many individuals enter or leave it at any one time. When approached in these terms, childhood resembles a minority category, akin to social class (Oldman 1992) or gender (Oakley 1993; Alanen 1994), and is thereby subject to systemic discrimination, marginalization, and paternalizing tendencies.

The chapters that make up *Symbolic Childhood* interweave through these approaches and themes, favoring the structural view a bit more than, but not at the expense of, a focus on agency. Without denying children's ability to interpret and construct the world in which they inhabit, the following studies investigate institutional, historical, and structural factors and actors that give shape and definition to various articulations of childhood in politically meaningful ways.

Why *Childhood*? Why *Symbolic*?

Children are born not into a "society" *per se* but into a childhood, that is, a particular configuration of ongoing relations that give social shape and cultural meaning to their initial membership in the human world. Childhood thus precedes and frames any specific child, socially and temporally speaking. Like other social institutions, it has a presence and a history larger than any of its members. Unlike other institutions, its members have little ability, opportunity, or power to (re)define it in ways which survive beyond local and episodic contexts, like the school yard, the play group, or the family. Childhood, as social institution, preauthorizes biographies that perform the cultural work of outlining the timing and movement through the early life course in ways considered appropriate for the young to follow and for adults to monitor.

No child is ever as naked socially as the bare body of a newborn suggests. "The child" comes into the world already implicated in, and somewhat prefigured by, specific kinds of cultural practice. It has been subjected to nutritional regimens and medical directives. Ongoing kinship, class, gender, and race relations provide ways to structure interaction with an infant as well as to structure its future access to resources. Those born into the consumer-media societies of post-industrial capitalism will have toys waiting and rooms already furnished and decorated prior to their arrival. Indeed, many newborns will not be an "it" upon arrival, but a "she" or a "he," with a name picked out and perhaps "appropriate" colors and garments at the ready so as to anchor the child in a milieu.

Self-awareness and self-understanding also require interpretive work. Children become aware that they *are* children in a language acquired under the canopy of imperfectly shared articulations of what it means to be a child at a particular time, in a particular place. Children encounter, acquire, and negotiate descriptions of and prescriptions for how to be a child from parents and from school influences that draw upon and make use of any number of cultural categories and narratives (see Adler and Adler 1998). Never completely reproductive, these encounters and meaning systems nevertheless provide a standard, an extant structure of meaning, against which children position themselves and their peer cultures. Dependency (Hockey and James 1993), innocence (Kincaid 1998; Higonnet 1998; Giroux 2000), gender relations (Thorne 1993; Eder, Evans, and Parker 1995), the tension between instrumental and sentimental values (Zelizer 1985), a romanticism and nostalgia for a desired, imagined past (Lears 1983; Steedman 1994), the promise of the future (Jenks 1996), and the relationship between humans and the cosmos (Calvert 1992) are among the signs and signifiers populating the life space of children. Children don't leave home without childhood. It walks with them to school. It is there at recess, encoded in the rules and structures of their games. It accompanies them to the mall.

"Childhood," as a moniker, encodes any and all these meanings and associations without having to make reference to a single existing child in support of its claims. The very presence of a living, breathing child can challenge the larger meanings of childhood because he or she cannot completely represent such encompassing, contradictory, and poly-morphous sets of signs. Only children who somehow remain frozen in time seem to successfully stand for some version of childhood. Examples include children of the cinema, like the enduring childhood embodied by the 1930s' version of Shirley Temple (Cook 2000a); Lewis Hine's early twentieth-century photographs of working and poor children; and famous children who are no longer living, such as Polly Klaas and JonBenet Ramsey. Fictional children of literature, such as Little Lord Fauntleroy, Rousseau's Emile or Nabokov's Lolita, can also endure as icons of childhood as can children of advertisements including Buster Brown, the Gerber Baby, or the Campbell Soup Kids.

These "children" do not have childhoods *per se*; instead, they represent childhood. Their existence is totemic, in the Durkheimian sense. A totem, Durkheim reminds us, is "not an individual, but a species or variety: it is not such and such a kangaroo or crow, but the kangaroo or crow in general" (1915, 125). In this vein, the chapters in this book variously illustrate how no depiction of a child is singular, how every image or representation of a child at once invokes a version of a more generalized childhood. "The child" stands for childhood, which itself is symbolic of other constellations of meaning.

Childhood often stands in contrast to adulthood in ways which are not the simple inverse of adulthood's relation to childhood. Any particular child "stands" for childhood in ways that any particular adult doesn't represent adulthood. We research children because they are children, thereby actively contributing to the construction of childhood by such practices as taking their statements and recording their behavior as indicative of a *child's* point of view or life world. As adults, we are seen as, and often understand ourselves as, moments of less global identities. Often, we are seen and see ourselves as more thoroughly specified—i.e., gendered, raced, and classed—than children, having traversed life's defining phases. The only time adults seem to be investigated *as* adults is when the subject matter is children/childhood. Our "adultness" as researchers or observers then becomes a basis of contrast with the particularity of the "childness" being sought.

It is worth noting that to render childhood symbolic, to situate it discursively in a field of signs, is not to negate the "real," biographical children we all know and love (and hate), but to affirm them as thoroughly social configurations. One cannot comprehend that wriggly, now-crying-now-asleep-now-hungry mass of flesh without making recourse to some discourse—to some universe of semantic relations— about what a child *is*. This child is surely unlike us adults who look upon it, comment upon it, and thereby impart, share, and negotiate its meaning. This child will not read these words and will not be able to act upon them until such time that it is no longer a child—or, at least, less of a child than an infant, or toddler, or preadolescent, or adolescent, for that matter.

The phrase "less of a child" gestures toward seeing childhood as a continuum rather than a state of being. Transience is essential to what a child *is*. A child is a child only at any given moment—a moment that is fleeting—and is reasonably expected to occupy a qualitatively different phase or part of life in some foreseeable, tangible future. Family photograph albums record these changes. Developmental psychology, intelligence testing, and age-graded school systems define and institutionalize the "proper" movement through them in historically specific ways (see Rawlins, this volume; Chudacoff 1989). The great change or paradigmatic shift in the study of childhood, noted above, can be located in the strides made by those who rightly insist on capturing the lived situatedness of children and their understandings. The point of the new childhood studies is to dismantle the epistemological hegemony that has regarded children as being *merely* in transition, as nothings and nobodies in the here and now. A counterbalance position, represented in part by the contributions to this volume, seeks to keep "children" astride with "childhood," to re-recognize how structure and agency co-create each other.

The contributors to *Symbolic Childhood* share a basic conviction that children, in addition to being subjects, also arise as objects in the social world. They become objects, that is, in G. H. Mead's (1934) sense of being subjected to the gaze and scrutiny of others. A person, in this view, is never completely self-authoring, but emerges in the dynamic interplay between self and other, between the I and the Me. Children become acutely aware of their symbolic, subordinate status when, at an early age, they speak of what they will be when they "grow up," oftentimes differentiating themselves from babies by making a "baby" of their own doll. Reclaiming children's agency in social theory need not be done at the expense of turning a blind eye to their status as social objects—a status which, to be sure, serves as fodder for a variety of interests and ends.

Power, Agency, and Moral Authority
in Representing Childhood

There is a ubiquitous politics to childhood not because individual children have much to do with it—and not only because of *what* childhood may represent at any one time—but because childhood is eminently and multiply represent*able*. No one group "owns" childhood in the same way that no one group "owns" the institution of the family or of marriage. People can be in charge of, responsible for, and even "own" individual children in various degrees. No one, however, has exclusive proprietary rights over the concept of childhood, thus rendering it a pre-eminent site for political contestation and ideological conflict.

Childhood stands as a site of contestation also as a result of the relative powerlessness of children, which enables images and depictions of children—and, by extension, their identities—to be quite malleable. Adults/parents dress their children when they are young, care for their appearance, and fight with them over their modes of self-presentation for many years afterward (see Flusser 1992; Kaiser and Chandler 1991). The sailor suit, sports team uniforms, tie-dyed toddlers outfitted by Grateful Deadhead parents, his-and-her Harley Davidson leather togs for tots, and infant T-shirts displaying sayings like "shit happens" are instances of imputing identity to young children who *seem* like blank slates. They seem like they can don almost any garb, portray almost any persona, play with most any identity. In U.S. advertising, there is a century-long tradition of depictions of children serving as vehicles for the personification of commodities (Cook 1999; see also Alexander 1994). Aside from sexual issues that surfaced in the Calvin Klein controversy in 1995[1] and concerns about the violent content of films and video games, the general absence of protest about portrayals of children (or of childhood) in advertisements and other media testifies, I believe, to a general absence of agreement as to what is essential about "child-ness."

Children may never be able to successfully counter "stereotypes" about childhood and to expound their "rights" as women and sexual and ethnic minorities continue to do because such action ultimately requires adult intervention (in everyday life, in media portrayals, in schools). Children did not pass the 1989 United Nations statement on the rights of the child, nor did they draft antigun legislation proposed to protect them, nor did they write and copyright the jingle about being a "Toys 'R' Us Kid" (although children sing it in the commercial). Children clearly "have" agency as well as a right to exercise it, but this agency is rarely sufficient to move the adult world—unless it is accompanied by a gun, as in the recent rash of school killings (see Jacobs this volume; Cook 2000b)—without making use of another kind of agency, i.e., someone else serving as an agent.

The infant or young child cannot exercise the autonomy of choice and the volition of action that is implied in the idea of a "rights-bearing" subject (McCall 1992, 69–84; Stephens 1995, 35–41), the rise of "fetal personhood" notwithstanding (Newman 1996). This structure of child personhood—i.e., supposedly "having" rights but unable to fully realize them—always contains a void, a void of agency whereby an adult agent is needed to represent and act on the child's behalf. Adults, most often mothers, serve as agents on behalf of their children thereby committing a profoundly moral act on a daily basis. To commit this moral act requires an agent who explicates or assumes to determine the child's place in the order of things. That is to say, any act performed on behalf of an unknowing, relatively powerless being—in this case a child—necessarily invokes a set or system of moral beliefs.

Childhood designates a distinctly moral arena—indeed a hypermoral arena—unlike any other. Tensions of voice, of persona, and of the locus of decision-making are present in every personal interaction with a child, in every depiction of a child, in every iteration of childhood, and in every gesture made by, toward, and about children. Each word to a child seems like a directive; each decision made on its behalf or in response to a request favors some aspects of the world over others; every lifestyle choice is potentially didactic. This is the contemporary world of supposedly open, democratic, be-all-you-can-be childhood. No word or deed related to children can be morally neutral because everyone must position herself or himself in relation to the power/agency void inherent in this intensely overdetermined moral space.

Children, in some contexts, may have become ghettoized into their own spaces and times (see Holloway and Valentine 2000), but childhood remains engaged in the world, always standing for something more than itself—for futures and pasts, for hopes and anxieties, for strengths and weaknesses. The chapters to follow give substance to these claims. They bring historical, ethnographic, and discursive evidence to bear upon the power dynamics immanent in the various constructions of the childhoods at issue.

Outline of the Volume

Symbolic Childhood is divided into four parts, each providing a different point of entrée into "the child" and its multiplicity. As the construction of the child is always political, with power involved every step of the way, the place to start is at home. Part I looks at *The Child as Subject/Object of Research* with three chapters interrogating the researcher as well as those under the research gaze.

In Chapter 1, Harriet Strandell opens with quotes from children at a Finnish daycare center who are questioning her as she takes field notes. They want to know how they will be represented to the adult world. It is a question that turns out to be generative for Strandell. Instead of seeing these questions as intrusive, she wisely understands them as children's interventions into the research act. They move her to question such things as the boundaries and the content of "the field." In so doing, she tackles the problem of how to bring children's narratives into an institutional context—where adult constructs pervade and often prevail—in ways that do not reproduce their routine subordination. Working through these questions and issues, Strandell offers grounded insight as to how researchers create their objects, even when these objects are children.

Mary Lorena Kenny, in Chapter 2, looks at how Brazilian street children come to be defined as a "problem" by experts, including researchers. Her fieldwork in Recife, Pernambuco in the northeast region of Brazil brings the painful descriptions of these children concerning their daily existence into the context of the "problem industry" that has been built up around street children. Kenny skillfully illuminates the ways in which "being studied" is an important aspect of street children's understanding of themselves and of their place in symbolic and monetary markets. Their acute awareness of their market value as fodder for researchers, reporters, and others, is revealed in their questions to her about her own source of funding. In the semiotic crowding of street children through photographs, news stories, Michael Jackson videos and social science research, Kenny poignantly exposes how many of these youngsters are implored to perform their status as a "street" child in a manner convincing enough to garner attention and, possibly, resources. She concludes by suggesting that attempts at rescuing street children and restoring an "authentic" childhood among them are misguided.

Children assume a different order of scientific use in Adriana Benzaquén's intriguing discussion of "wild children" in Chapter 3. Benzaquén argues that wild (or feral) children—i.e., those said to have been brought up in the wild, or those who suffered extreme social isolation or neglect—"became the targets of a long-standing, deep-seated will to know and the unwitting receptacles of adult anxieties and projections." The stories of three isolated children, John, Genie, and Kaspar, bring into relief how "scientific" curiosity about the unique renders these unfortunate human beings as "cases" to be studied, analyzed and, in some cases, popularized. Each "child," or construction thereof, posed opportunities for scientists to explore problems of categorization—savagery/civilization, normalcy/retardation, extraordinary existence/child abuse. Benzaquén reads these attempts at "knowing" children as exercises in the reinscription of power, explaining and exposing the position of the knower rather than that of the object of knowledge—that is, the child.

In Part II, *The Child in and of History*, three chapters invite a look at the ways in which anxieties about change, nationhood, and morality find expression through historically situated and strategically deployed childhood imagery.

In Chapter 4, Roblyn Rawlins offers an important analysis on the changing view of children in the American context between the late nineteenth and early twentieth centuries. Focusing on published prescriptions for the development of self-control and the management of aggression among children, she traces how the social meaning of early intellectual development transformed over the period between 1870 and 1920. During this time, the dominant figure was that of the "precocious child," which was seen to be plagued by pathologies ranging from physical debilitation to death. Rawlins details how the intellectually precocious child encoded other types of precocity—sexual, economic, and social—and gave expression to the anxieties of a white, middle-class social stratum facing uncertainty in the wake of historical change. In the place of the precocious child arose the "gifted child," whose "early" intellectual development gained social approval and scientific adjudication in the form of intelligence testing, which helped to legitimize claims about racial and class superiority.

Kathryn Libal, in Chapter 5, theorizes the connections between nationalism, modernity, and childhood in her reading of the "robust Turkish child" in the context of early republican Turkey in the 1920s and 1930s. Libal untangles how ideas about children and childhood become instrumental to the processes of nation-state building. She deftly demonstrates how the figure of the child plays a dynamic role in the imaginative labor of Turkish nationalism, as both a symbol of future strength and an object of state-centered programs. She details how Turkey's quest to gain inclusion in the group of nation-states considered to be "developed" or "civilized" in the 1920s and 1930s was linked to notions of modernity and progress, notions largely embodied through the image of the "robust child" (*gurbuz cocuk*). In this setting, what came to be defined as *gurbuz*, or robust, is revealed in the visual imagery of advertising, poster art, and photographs of robust child contest winners. The images blended notions of health, class, and race ascribed to by nationalist elites.

In Chapter 6, Janice Hill explores the interplay between imperialist and religious discourses in the moral regulation of children during a crucial time in the visioning of Canadian nationhood, 1880 to 1920. Hill examines the burgeoning of the Boy Scouts and Girl Guides organizations at this time as sites where children were cultivated as national resources and made into projects to be "improved" through bodily practice. Reproducing gender relations while producing the next generation of soldiers, mothers, workers, and leaders, scouting and guiding sought to enhance national growth by directing children's social and moral development as well. In this light, Hill calls into question the strict division often made between sacred and secular organizations, focusing instead on the making and governing of children's subjectivities in the service of God and Nation. She encourages us to "rethink traditional liberal and Marxist treatments of childhood that tend to ignore children altogether, allocate their concerns to the private sphere of the family, or append them to their mothers."

Contributors to Part III, *The Social Value of Children*, confront endemic tensions posed by contemporary iterations of childhood in three different contexts: the market value of children in adoption procedures, the moral value of children as encountered in discourses on school shootings, and the symbolic value of children as encoded in anxieties about gender display and sexuality.

In Chapter 7, Sara Dorow insightfully pursues parallels in the tensions evident between care and consumption and between persons and markets in her ethnographic piece on the transnational adoption of Chinese children. Drawing on interviews with adoption agency personnel and with potential adoptive parents, Dorow explores how market and nonmarket sensibilities interrelate through interlocking discourses. She teases out how these discourses construct "the child" at once as something into which various kinds of needs can be read. As formulated by agency workers and adoptive parents, children's "needs" provide a moral lubricant that helps to ease the passage of the child from the status of an unwitting item of exchange to that of a daughter or son. Care and consumption in this context, argues Dorow, cannot be seen as opposing tendencies but as mutually constituted ones.

Mark Jacobs challenges us, in Chapter 8, to confront the recent rash of school shootings as a ritual of sacrifice tied closely to the changing social world of children. Examining the famous Columbine High School incident, Jacobs finds social psychological explanations unsatisfying partly because the killers did not fit any profiles of risk offered by experts and partly because these explanations tend to individualize their actions. The moral ecology of the high school, according to Jacobs, is undergoing profound change that is acutely localized in the rearrangement of cliques—the structures through which high schoolers place themselves vis-à-vis others. Approached from a cultural perspective, the killings begin to make sense as a form of ritual sacrifice, the function of which is to restore a moral order to social arrangements. Instead of moral order, however, moral panic has ensued. The overwrought media attention and the mutual finger-pointing of the "no fault society" surrounding these incidents, Jacobs claims, have only served to exacerbate the pain of those dealing with such tragedy.

In Chapter 9, Susan Kaiser and Kathleen Huun investigate the intense gender coding and sexualizing of children's appearance increasingly present in public discourses and imagery. Examining a fundamental shift that has occurred in the representation of young children in the United States over the last century, they ask: Why are images of young children so heavily gender coded now, when adults are experiencing a rearrangement of gender relations in dominant middle-class culture? How and why does the gender symbolism in young children's clothing become co-constructed with sexuality and fashionability? Kaiser and Huun argue that young children have become cultural figures who bear the weight of a whole host of tensions and anxieties regarding the complex interplay among gender, sexuality, and fashionability. Children's bodies bear the weight of ambiguities that adults may sense in their own lives, and thus become the vicarious repositories of dominant cultural anxieties regarding the future.

In Part IV, *Making Childhoods with and Through Media*, the authors examine quite different ways in which electronic media become involved in the shaping of childhoods.

Jeffery P. Dennis unpacks the recent appearance of the sexually precocious heterosexual preadolescent boy on prime-time situation comedies in chapter 10. These characters boast of sexual prowess and actively pursue heterosexual liaisons. Through a series of sharp readings of television sit-coms, Dennis sketches the contours of the aggressively heterosexual preteen boy. He finds that this persona usually appears in dramatic contexts where adult heterosexual desire—implicitly defined as inevitable and universal—has been challenged. Dennis discusses how this symbolic/dramatic figure serves to defuse male homophobic panic by essentializing heterosexual desire—i.e., by pushing back the "discovery of girls" to infancy, or even to the womb.

In Chapter 11, Chandra Mukerji and Tarleton Gillespie observe that cartoons are an extraordinarily flexible medium. When developed for children, there is a presumption that the audience does not know enough about the world to think "realistically" or have the mastery of language to fully comprehend the cultural categories in which they are already implicated. In a memorable analysis of the cartoon *Animaniacs*, Mukerji and Gillespie show how the ambiguity available in cartoons provides a means for children to make sense of their contradictory, unclear place in relation to the adult world without having to provide them with a consistent set of meanings. In cartoons, children can see "cultural themes that describe the child's nature, and how childhood works as a site of cultural conflict." Cartoons, the authors assert, provide children with tools to negotiate childhood by allowing them a way to play with it.

Stephen Kline and Greig de Peuter complete the volume with a deep, visual-thematic analysis of late-1990s video-game television advertising. Interweaving descriptions of the framing of commercials, portrayals of the almost exclusively male gamers, and narratives of fantasy and isolation, the authors illustrate how game marketers' thinking becomes "encoded in the ad's design." Inviting the viewer to enter an ecstatic state of suspended disbelief, the video hyperreality of these commercials simulates the experience of playing the game, all the while promoting branding, positioning product, and targeting consumers. Kline and de Peuter conclude by urging cultural analysts to read the intensified fantasy and fragmentation of postmodern childhood as a "structure of feeling" inseparable from the ongoing strategic commodification of children's culture.

* * *

The essential work of ideology is to present invented and therefore pliable social arrangements as natural and beyond the realm of human action. The task of critical engagement is to counteract ideology by demonstrating the constructedness of so-called immutable facts and, in so doing, lay bare the power dynamics thereby involved in maintaining their existence as facts. It is my hope and belief that this volume accomplishes the latter task. [2]

NOTES

1   See *Advertising Age*, September 4, 1995, and September 11, 1995, for an advertising trade view of the incident.
2   I thank Mark Jacobs and Jessica Clark for helpful suggestions on this chapter.

REFERENCES

Adler, Patricia A., and Peter Adler. *Peer Power: Preadolescent Culture and Identity.* New Brunswick, N.J.: Rutgers University Press, 1998.

Alanen, Leena. "Gender and Generation: Feminism and the 'Child Question.'" In *Childhood Matters*, edited by Jens Qvortrup, Marjatta Bardy, Giovannia Sgritta and Helmut Wintersberger, 31–42. Aldershot, UK: Avebury Press, 1994.

Alexander, Victoria. A. "The Image of Children in Magazine Advertisements from 1905–1990." *Communication Research* 21 (December 1994): 742–765.

Buckingham, David. *After the Death of Childhood.* Cambridge: Polity, 2000.

Calvert, Karin. *Children in the House.* Boston: Northeastern University Press, 1992.

Chudacoff, Howard. *How Old Are You?* Princeton: Princeton University Press, 1989.

Cook, Daniel Thomas. "The Visual Commodification of Childhood: A Case Study from a Children's Wear Trade Magazine, 1920s–1980s." *Journal of Social Sciences* 3, no. 1–2 (1999): 21–40.

———. "The Rise of 'the Toddler' as Subject and as Merchandising Category in the 1930s." In *New Forms of Consumption*, edited by Mark Gottdiener, 111–130. Lanham, Md.: Rowman and Littlefield, 2000a.

———. "Childhood Is Killing 'Our' Children: Some Thoughts on the Columbine Shootings and the Agentive Child." *Childhood* 7, no. 1 (2000b): 107–117.

Corsaro, William. *The Sociology of Childhood.* Thousand Oaks, Calif.: Sage, 1997.

Durkheim, Emile. *The Elementary Forms of the Religious Life.* New York: The Free Press, 1915.

Eder, Donna, Catherine Evans, and Stephen Parker. *School Talk: Gender and Adolescent Culture.* New Brunswick: Rutgers University Press, 1995.

Flusser, Marilise. Party Shoes to School and Baseball Caps to Bed: The Parents' Guide to Kids, Clothes and Independence. New York: Simon and Schuster, 1992.

Giroux, Henri. *Stealing Innocence.* New York: St. Martin's Press, 2000.

Higonnet, Anne. *Pictures of Innocence.* London: Tames and Hudson, 1998.

Hockey, Jennifer., and Allison. James. *Growing Up and Growing Old: Aging and Dependency in the Life Course.* London; Newbury Park: Sage, 1993.

Holloway, Sarah L. and Gill Valentine, ed. Children's Geographies. London: Routledge, 2000.

James, Allison and Alan Prout, ed. *Constructing and Reconstructing Childhood.* London: Falmer Press, 1990.

James, Allison, Chris Jenks, and Alan Prout. *Theorizing Childhood.* New York: Teacher's College Press, 1998.

Jenks, Chris. *Childhood.* New York: Routledge, 1996.

Kaiser, Susan B. and Joan L. Chandler. "Gender Socialization, Appearance, and Stone's Ubiquitous Mother—A Feminist Critique and Revision." Paper presented at the Society

for the Study of Symbolic Interaction: Gregory Stone Symposium, San Francisc
February 1991.

Kincaid, James. *Erotic Innocence*. Raleigh, N.C.: Duke University Press, 1998.

Lears, Jackson. *No Place of Grace: Antimodernism in American History*. Chicag
University of Chicago Press, 1983.

McCall, Catherine. *Concepts of Person*. Aldershot, UK: Avebury Press, 1992.

McNamee, Sara. "Youth, Gender and Video Games: Power and Control in the Home."
Cool Places, edited by Tracey Skelton and Gill Valentine, 195–206. Londo
Routledge, 1998.

Mead, George Herbert. *Mind, Self and Society*. Chicago: University of Chicago Press, 1934.

Newman, Karen. *Fetal Positions*. Stanford, Calif.: Stanford University Press, 1996.

Oakley, Ann. "Women and Children First and Last: Parallels and Differences betwee
Children's and Women's Studies." In *Childhood as a Social Phenomenon*, edited b
Jens Qvortrup, 51–70. Vienna: European Centre, 1993.

Oldman, David. "Adult-Child relations as Class Relations." In *Childhood Matters*, edited b
Jens Qvortrup, Marjatta Bardy, Giovannia Sgritta, and Helmut Wintersberger, 43–5
Aldershot, UK: Avebury Press, 1992.

Qvortrup, Jens. "Introduction." *International Journal of Sociology* 17, no. 1 (Fall 1987): 1
26.

Qvortrup, Jens. "Nine Theses About 'Childhood as a Social Phenomenon.'" In *Childhoc
as a Social Phenomenon*, edited by Jens Qvortrup, 11–18. Vienna: European Centr
1993.

Steedman, Carolyn. *Strange Dislocations*. Cambridge, Mass.: Harvard University Pres
1994.

Stephens, Sharon. "Introduction." In *Children and the Politics of Culture*, edited b
Sharon Stephens, 3–48. Princeton: Princeton University Press, 1995.

Thorne, Barrie. *Gender Play*. New Brunswick, N.J.: Rutgers University Press, 1993.

Zelizer, Viviana. *Pricing the Priceless Child*. New York: Basic, 1985.

PART ONE

The Child as Subject/Object of Research

Chapter 1

On Questions of Representation in Childhood Ethnography

Harriet Strandell

What are you writing? What did you write just now? Have you written that we are playing football? Have you written that I'm playing with Antti? Why do you always write when I say something? Are you writing a book? Read all that...(looks at the page) What kind of book are you writing? Are you going to sell it? (HS: Guess so...) Hih, then we can buy it too. Yes, then dads and mums can see how children play, that we are not teasing at all (ironically)...

These are some of the questions children in a daycare center asked me and my co-researcher Helena Kupiainen when we conducted ethnographic research on children's activities and social relations in the early 1990s. As part of the process of letting us into their social world, they asked questions about who we were, what we were doing in the daycare center and why, and more precisely, how we conducted our work. In addition, some of them were also curious about how they were going to be talked about to dads and mums, aunts and uncles—that is, how they were going to be represented to the adult world. At least to some degree they were aware that the researcher was in a strategic position because she was able to decide how and what she was going to tell about them to people outside their world. Their comments and questions can be understood as a signal that the telling was, for them, problematic, because they were subjected to social control and definition from adult society.

The children's questions provided the impetus for us to think about how children are represented in research reports, and of how the question of representation in childhood research has been dealt with. It was after the report was written and published and the findings presented to interested audiences that I seriously started to reflect on the question of representation as an important part of the research process.

There has been growing interest in the last decade in childhood ethnography. New approaches to children as social agents who are active in the construction of their own social lives and worlds have found a welcome home in ethnography (Prout and James 1990, 8). Ethnographic approaches have made visible the multiplicity and complexity of children's activities and the richness of their social understanding, as well as the diversity of lived childhoods. Scholarly interest in children's everyday worlds and social experiences has produced ethnographic research on questions of participation and social order in children's daily lifeworlds, their activities, their social relations with peers and adults, and their forms of knowledge and use of knowledge (Corsaro 1985; Deloache and Brown 1987; Goodwin 1990; Thorne 1993; Mayall 1994; Strandell 1994; Brannen and O'Brien 1996; Hutchby and Moran-Ellis 1998).

Much methodological effort has been invested in how to make the entry into and the participation in children's worlds possible, and in how to look more "from the inside" at what is going on there and at what the children are doing and experiencing. New and more sensitive research practices have been developed; these are less objectifying and thus allow children more voice and participation in research. Efforts to reduce "othering" children (James, Jenks, and Prout 1998), that is, treating them in research as if they were very different from "us," have also been characteristic for these new childhood ethnographies. Another theme that has been discussed is how to design one's research role in order to cope with the inequalities in the relationship between children and adults.

My aim in this chapter is to contribute to the discussion about children and childhood ethnography by commenting on a few themes that perhaps have not received nearly the attention that the questions mentioned above have. I will draw on my own experiences of doing fieldwork in an institutionalized childhood setting—daycare centers in Finland—and especially on my experiences of what happened *after* the study was finished and published, in the encounters with interested readers and users of the research results. The focus will lie more on the end of the process, on how children are discussed or represented as research subjects.

The first theme addresses *what constitutes a field*, because the question of "field" has implications for how children can be represented in research. A widely debated question about the question of field in more recent anthropology (Clifford and Marcus 1986; Marcus 1998) is here approached from the perspective of how the children's actions and the meanings they attach to them relate to the social order and structure of the institutional context of which they are part—including the discursive construction of that context. What does seeing actions as structured and discursively constructed mean concretely when being in the field and in textual representations of the children? How should structure be approached *in doing* the fieldwork?

That children are social actors in their own right has been stressed in childhood research, but what kind of actors are they? How should their actions be conceptualized? What attributes do we attach to children and childhood? How do we tell the story? What stories do we tell? To what end? For whom do we tell them? These kinds of questions frame another theme of the chapter. I reflected seriously on these questions after the study had been published (Strandell 1994), and after I had discussed the findings with interested audiences and users of research. In that process I learned that there are very different ways—sometimes quite opposite—of seeing and interpreting what is going on in social interaction between children. In what follows, I relate the different interpretations to different knowledge interests and different discursive constructions.

Studying Children in an Institutional Context

At the end of the 1980s, in connection with a comparative project on Nordic childhood, I became curious about what children do in daycare centers. There were many small children gathered together for many hours every day—what were they doing? Occasional stays at daycare centers had given me an impression of a considerably social density. The children seemed to be very intensively directed toward other children. However, existing research at that time focused mainly the actions of adults—the professionals of the institutions—and on what they do or should do in order to make the children's stay at the center "beneficial." In Finland, daycare centers play a central role in the life of many children under school age (ages one to six). Most of the children attend their center for seven to nine hours a day. In addition to "free play" and organized activities, the children take part in many different routines of everyday life, including having breakfast, lunch (a hot meal), and snacks; being outdoors; and resting or sleeping.

In the beginning of the 1990s, I conducted, together with Helena Kupiainen, a student of social psychology, ethnographic research in daycare centers in the Helsinki region. The groups we studied each consisted of eighteen to twenty children ages three to six. During a five-month period we followed the children in their everyday lives at three daycare centers: We listened to their discussions and observed how they organized their activities and social relations. The focus of observations was on the *social interaction* of the children. We did not focus on individual children, but on the characteristics of the interaction itself. This led us to consider questions of social participation and organization, of how the child group functioned as an interpretive frame for the children's actions and of the meaning they attached to those actions. All kinds of activities occurring during the day, as well as situations in which the children seemed to be doing nothing at all, were studied.

The study, which takes an interactionist and constructionist approach, regards social life as an *interpretive* process. The children's encounters with the world are made in their participation in social interaction, where they attach meaning to actions. Talking about meaning production through "negotiation" means that meaning cannot be decided upon intrasubjectively; instead, it has to undergo a process in which actions and the intentions behind them are interpreted and reacted to by others. (Bruner 1986, 1990). Storytelling is a powerful instrument for negotiation on meaning, a central way of creating possible worlds, possible courses of action (Bruner 1990, 67–97; 1986, 11–19). Narrating is a human way of functioning that is in no way child-specific. Children do, however, get involved in it extensively, because they are active at telling stories. The structure of what is often called symbolic play, or role playing, is narrative; it is based on developing a plot and telling a story (Strandell 1997, 448–49).

The study is also characterized by an ambition to regard children as not so different from adults: I was interested in trying out the limits of a research approach that did not build too much on childhood as a specialty, but instead approached questions of social participation and social order in much the same way as they are approached in sociological research on adults (Strandell 1997).

What Is the Field in Childhood Ethnography?

What is special about children and childhood as a field of research ? Childhood ethnography does of course share a lot of characteristics, as well as problems, with ethnographic research in general, regardless of the specific subject of research. The "crisis of representation" has been widely debated, especially inside anthropology, and there has been rethinking concerning what constitutes an ethnographic field (e.g., Clifford and Marcus 1986; Atkinson 1992; Marcus 1998). However, the position of childhood in modern or postmodern society also points to some specialties that children do not share with other groups in society, which set questions of representation in a slightly different manner.

Children's activities and social interaction cannot be studied "as such"; they do not occur in a social vacuum. They are generated in historically specific social and institutional contexts. The relationship between childhood and adulthood in Western countries is in our time characterized by a considerable distance between childhood and adult society, leading to a need for new forms of social control and governing of children (Rose 1990; James, Jenks, and Prout 1998). Childhood has become institutionalized, and in the process of increasing institutionalization, daycare of children under school age represents a new form of governing.

Reflection on the relation between childhood and adulthood, and on how that relationship models children's social position in modern society, have constituted some of the central themes in recent childhood sociology. One of the assumptions to be discussed in this chapter is that the position of children—in relation to professionals—has consequences for possible research strategies and for representations of childhood.

Children have become the *object of work* for groups of adults, for *child professionals*. In most institutionalized childhood settings such as daycare centers, children and their development are projects to be worked on. According to David Oldman (1994), children create many jobs for adults; thus, childhood has a considerable economic value for society. In writing about children's activities in schools, Oldman regards the relation between teacher and pupil as a *relation between activities*— the children's and the adults'. *Child work* is, according to Oldman, "work done by adults on the organization and control of child activities" (1994, 45).

Naturally, professionals do not only have children as their object of work. When people are sick or handicapped, they sometimes need professional help. What is distinct about children and childhood, however, is that the organizing criteria for becoming the object for another's work is age and not having a "disability." Children become objects in a totalizing sense through the age-based institutions that are developed to govern childhood and that also control and regulate children's bodies and minds through spatial and temporal arrangements (see, for example, James, Jenks, and Prout 1998; Rose 1990; Mayall 1996; Gordon and Lahelma 1996). Whatever space in society children occupy (e.g., daycare centers, schools, sports), they are almost always closely surrounded by adults who work with "the best interest of the child" in mind and who are adjudicated to "know" what children need and how they develop. Being a teacher in a daycare center requires being very close to children in their everyday lives and using expert knowledge as the basis for the relationship with the children.

What, then, does the extensive "governing" of children mean for what constitutes the "field" and for doing fieldwork? At the least it means including the institutional context and the forms of governing in the notion of the "field" so as to avoid the tendency to exoticize and essentialize childhood and children's culture, thereby cutting them off from their institutionalized contexts. The "field" is not just that of the separate children's world; it also encompasses the adult professional world of work, which is strongly framed.

Including the forms of governing that shape the activities of, and the relations between, the actors operating in the field into the notion of "field" has consequences for how to position oneself as researcher. If children's activities are to be regarded and analyzed in relation to social order and structure, what does that actually mean in fieldwork practice? Research reports and methodologies in the field (e.g., Fine and Sandstrom 1988; Mandell 1988; Corsaro 1981) give some good advice about how to design one's "researcher" position in relation to the children, including how to avoid using adult authority in the interaction with the children. The question of how to do fieldwork in childhood settings has largely been addressed as a question of how to relate to the children. But what about the role of the researcher *in relation to the child workers* who uphold and transmit the institutional structures and discursive constructions with which the children engage? My own research report (Strandell 1994) says but little on this matter. But I can clearly remember my ambiguity on this point. How should the researcher keep in social contact with the adults at the institution and communicate with them without starting to look at things through their eyes, and without using their concepts and their naming of events as means of understanding what is going on? While doing fieldwork I felt a need to distance myself from the daycare professionals' understanding of what was going on between the children and of why things happened. Ann-Carita Evaldsson also comments on this question briefly in an appendix to her research report. Toward the end of her stay in after-school centers, she began to talk to the staff more. She states: "[W]hen I began to spend more time with the staff, I became part of their ways of talking and thinking about the children. This made it difficult to participate in peer activities without talking with the staff. I was gradually disconnected from the children's peer activities, feeling transformed into an adult again" (Evaldsson 1993, 276).

In ethnographic research, we are used to talking about gatekeepers in the field: people who have power to regulate outsiders' access to the field and to knowledge about it. In my case, getting access to the field in the sense of being allowed to be present in the daycare center and follow the children's doings posed no problem. I was given a free hand to be present whenever I wanted and to look at whatever I wished.

Conceptual Gatekeeping: The Example of Play

There is, however, another form of "gatekeeping" that is far more penetrating and difficult to grasp. It is hidden and it works through *conceptual* governing of the field. Conceptual gatekeeping is related to field-owning. It gives the gatekeeper power to define and to label the children's doings as well as the meanings of their doings. Conceptual gatekeeping strongly influences what one sees, coloring empirical observations. Empirical facts do not exist "out there"; they are theoretically constructed. They intersect with theoretical discourses, which are in a way built into empirical data (Tyler 1986, 130–31). The naming of certain empirical phenomena, for example, "play," is loaded with references to specific discourses and knowledge interests. It is important to include the concepts and discourses operating in and shaping the field in the discussion, as empirical facts as it were.

The concept of *play* is a good example of conceptual gatekeeping. Play has become a dominating concept in modern Western childhood, a kind of archetypal child activity. Play and child activity have become more or less synonyms. Play has such a self-evident and normative position whenever children's activities are discussed that it is hard to get around it. In Western cultures, children are expected to play so as to have a "good" childhood, and play is used by adults as a working method in governing childhood in institutions for preschool children. The problem then is not about a lack of knowledge about children's activities. It is that the answers are too readily available from dominant, normative beliefs and discourses. Playing is so "good" for children that it is hard even to imagine that their doings could be conceptualized in terms other than play.

The longer I spent in the daycare centers, however, the more confused I became about the possibility of using the play concept at all. It seemed much too narrow, and at the same time all-encompassing and non-differentiating. The more I have reflected on children's activities and social relations in the daycare centers I studied, the more critical I have become of the ideological and separating character of the play concept, at least in its widely used pedagogical version (for a critical discussion on the play concept, see Strandell 1997). I have more and more begun to think that the play concept is not very useful in trying to understand children's activities in daycare centers.

Built into the notion that what children do is play is a separateness from the adult world. Play as a concept separates children and positions them in a fictive world where real life is only simulated (Strandell 1997). The sociological challenge, however, in conceptualizing children's actions and the ways in which children create meaning in their actions is to see them in relation to the social order and the social structure of the institutional contexts of which they are part. James, Jenks, and Prout (1998) penetrate the problems inherent in the concept of "children's culture" as a concept, which separates children's actions from questions of social order and structure.

The concept of children's culture situates children in an autonomous world of their own, apart from adult society. There are many similarities in this respect between the concepts of "children's culture" and "play." James, Jenks, and Prout (1998, 88) stress the systematic exploration of the formative materiality in childhood, paying attention to the intersection between ordering properties and subjective experience. They would like to see the concept of children's culture as "a form of social action contextualized by the many ways in which children choose to engage with the social institutions and structures that shape the form and process of their everyday lives."

The following sequence of interaction is taken from transcribed field notes. The episode is neither a very typical one nor a rarity. These kinds of interactional sequences exist, and an ethnographic approach that has the ambition to regard all kinds of social interaction between the children as equally interesting easily gains sight of them. As such, the episode provokes clear definitions of activities and situations, and it's not easy to say what the children are actually doing in it.

"Free play"[1] in the big room, 8.25—9.00

Participants: Marko (age six) and Jussi (age four), boys; Mari (age three), girl

Marko and Jussi are in the big room. The boys are romping on a mattress.

Jussi to Marko: *Let's start... (?)*
              (Aletaan...(?))
Marko to Jussi: *No, not that.*
              (Ei aleta sitä.)

Jussi runs here and there about the room. Then he steams into the dining room. Marko runs after him, shouting:

I know what we can do, Jussi.
(Mä tiedän mitä aletaan, Jussi.)

The boys return a moment later and continue romping on the mattress.

***

Marko pushes a soft toy up his sweater, jumps again, does a somersault, stands up and says:

I'm going to show Hanna.[2]
(Mä meen näyttää HANNAlle.)

Marko goes off to the dining room with Jussi following. Jussi is giggling all the time. Marko goes and shows Hanna his big tummy. The boys then return to the big room. Jussi leaps off a bench onto the mattress. Marko gets up on the swing and swings backward and forward.

***

After jumping and swinging for a moment, Jussi says:

I don't want to be with you anymore.
(Mä en oo enää mukana.)

I'm going to be with Aki.
(Mä oon Akin kans.)

Jussi goes out into the entrance hall.

Marko to Jussi: No, stay with me, you can... (?)

(Ei ku oo mun kanssa, saat...(?))

Jussi has gone out into the entrance hall, Marko running after him. A moment later the boys return to the big room.

Marko to Jussi: *Let's shut the door.*
                 (Laitetaa ovi kiinni.)

Jussi goes and closes the door to the hall. Marko shuts the sliding door to the dining room. The boys resume their jumping and swinging.

***

A buzzing sound can be heard in the entrance hall.

Jussi to Marko: *I'm going to see...*
                 (Mä meen katsoo...)

Jussi runs into the hall, then comes back. After a while, Mari enters the room. Jussi says to her, "Don't come in here." She collects a piece of cloth and leaves the room. Marko suggests to Jussi that they should clean up; they discuss what they each should do. They put things into proper places and leave the room.

When daycare teachers have been shown this episode, many have seen a bad quality of play in it. When (role) play is used as a working method and a normative concept, the episode looks like playing that is continuously disturbed and never has a real chance to develop. It seems just to confirm that children cannot concentrate on what they are undertaking. Symbolic play, or role play, which three- to six-year-old children are supposed to engage in according to psychological and pedagogical theory, is loaded with presumed criteria that the activity should satisfy in order to pass as (good) play—for instance, a focus inward, a certain duration, a "screening off" what is going on around them, and the development of role characters and actions of role characters.[3]

From my research point of view, however, the problem is not the activity but the play concept that is largely in use in early childhood education that does not take into account the social and institutional context of the activity. I was confused over what I felt to be a lack of correspondence between the empirical data and the play concept. When children's activities are looked at from an everyday life perspective, it's obvious that children also engage in courses of action that are not strongly focused, are unclear in essence or plot, and are devoid of a clear-cut direction of development. Children act in the midst of social turbulence, and it's not unusual that, like in the episode above, the turbulence surrounding the children has the effect of pulling their attention in many directions simultaneously. The boys in the episode have a strong orientation and social curiosity toward what is going on around them; they focus on other people, other activities, and other places. In "free" activities children are on the *move*, both in a physical and a social sense. They typically do not limit their concentration only to the activity in which they are engaged at the moment; simultaneously, they look around, "absorbing" what is going on around them. Sometimes this orientation "outward" results in leaving the activity and joining in something else.

William Corsaro's study of children's interaction in a daycare center (Corsaro 1985) drew my attention to the flexibility and mobility in children's activities. He noted that activity episodes were usually short and were easily interrupted or terminated, resulting in much leaving and entering, and that much of the interaction consisted in negotiations on how to get access to activities and on protecting interactive space. In my own research, I chose to characterize children's doings as a never-ceasing *flow of activity* (see Strandell 1997, 450–51, 455–57), having no clear beginnings or endings, and going through more or less constant changes in defining the activity in social structure, in content, and often also in spatial location. Activities slip into new activities and are abandoned temporarily or definitely. One activity splits into several, or activities fuse to become one. Usually there are several activities going on at the same time, with the children commuting between them. From this perspective, children's actions can be appreciated as being *wider* than one, identifiable activity. The context includes the whole social "scene" (or parts of it), the whole group of children and adults, and all ongoing activities (or parts of them).

Encountering the Professional Discourse

When the study was published it was met with considerable curiosity and interest. Especially professionals in fields of education and childcare, mostly daycare center staff, but also school teachers, social workers, and pediatricians, wanted to hear about the findings. There was at that time a considerable openness for new perspectives on children and childhood, especially for contributions from outside the pedagogical discourse. The Finnish public daycare system had been strongly regulated, regarding both organizational matters and pedagogical instructions. The emerging deregulation started a search for alternative ways of doing things.

Against that background I was a bit astonished about how the findings I discussed were received. Whenever I have presented my findings and interpretations of what children do in the social milieu of the daycare center and how they attach meaning to actions, I have been chagrined to learn how eager my listeners have been to put phenomena and children into already dominating and fixed categories of meaning, to know what a child is and what she or he needs; to know what is good and what is bad; and to offer explanations for why things are as they are. I had a feeling that there was some sort of recontextualization or "translation" process going on: Individual findings were put into interpretive frames that stemmed from other frames of reference than those of the research. The extent of the hegemony of professional discourse and training became evident.

One of the strong contexts into which findings were put was the *social problems* discourse. There was a tendency to understand children's social openness and curiosity, as well as their moving around and looking at what's going on around them, as problems and to attribute negative rather than positive or neutral meaning to the children's actions. Typical comments were that "children cannot play anymore" and "children cannot concentrate nowadays," implying that they could do so in earlier times. Quite often I was also asked whether some children dominated over others in play situations, whether some children were marginalized from social togetherness, whether I saw lonely children, and so on. There was an implicit understanding that children run the risk of getting into trouble when staying with other children, in (big) groups of children. I think this picture is deeply rooted in our culture. Alternatively, my audience located the causes of trouble in the child's family life (about which we had gathered no information at all), apparently another conventional, knee-jerk attribution.

I do not mean to ignore the fact that children actually encounter problems in daycare centers and that for some children it can be quite tough to manage socially. What is interesting is the willingness to focus on the more problematic side, which is not at all what my study is about, and also the generalizing character of the social problems discourse: the tendency to generalize from children with special problems or from problematic situations more or less to all children and all situations. The staff's concern for the children's well-being is turned into a kind of alarming prognosis.

The social problems discourse can be understood as a way of legitimizing why attention should be paid to children and why resources should be invested in childhood. According to Barrie Thorne (1987, 89), children rarely appear on public agendas unless they are defined as a social problem. Professional child workers and research on childhood, then, have to legitimate their existence by referring to childhood problems that they can then propose to solve; they readily create "child work." Non-problematic interaction between children is a provocation against that construction, because it needs no correction.

From time to time other discursive repertoires were in use. Certain aspects of the interaction were seen as reflecting children's genuine culture or their true nature. Also some ways in which children acted could be seen as superior in comparison with adults' ways of doing things. This view stresses childhood competence. For some of the child workers the findings probably functioned as a scientific legitimation for something they wanted to do in their own working practices: to make these less adult-centric and controlling, leaving more space for the children's self-organization.

Different Needs for Knowing

The process of discussing my findings with people who work professionally with children and confronting my interpretations with theirs opened up a new phase in the research—a phase I had not anticipated, and which I had not thought of very much as belonging to the research process. Ethnographic research can be considered a chain of interpretations—including the interpretations made by the persons studied and by the researcher in different phases of the study—ending with those made by the readers of the research report and listeners to presentations of the findings. This last stage of the research, the "reception," is often ignored or thought separate from the research act itself. What happens when textual representations meet audiences, the "users" of research? In my case, the reception made me start to think about different ways of "knowing" children and of representing them. Traditionally, the relationship between the researcher and the users of research has been considered as a question of how to disseminate findings effectively. Perhaps interesting than to regard scientific knowledge as neutral is to regard it as a social practice and discourse among other social practices and discourses. Research findings are constructions that

encounter other constructions, and in these encounters new interpret-
tations are generated.

The encounters with the "users" of research findings made clear that
child professionals and sociological researchers have different
motivations *for knowing* children, and accordingly, they know children
in specific, selective ways. Professionals have knowledge interests,
which are both more pragmatic and more normative than those of the
researcher. For the professionals, concepts such as play are useful as
working tools, while researchers need concepts for analytical reasons.
Professional staff people are in a central position concerning conceptual
gatekeeping: They put concepts (such as play) into practice, and they
understand their own doings in terms of these concepts and constructions.
The necessity of putting knowledge into use is probably one of the
reasons why research on care and education of small children is very
often done from "inside," by people educated in the same educational
constructions and familiar with the same discourses as those who own or
guard the field professionally. Professional and scientific knowledge
interests become intertwined. Very often, research done from the inside
has the explicit aim of developing pedagogy and work practices, and of
interpreting findings in terms of what is good and what is bad for
children—or for child workers. There is a very close connection, then,
between professional standards and research questions.

Thus, I met not only with users of research findings but with a
construction in which knowledge is connected to the use of professional
power. In a way, the professionals "own" the field, meaning that they are
legitimated by society to tell what is going on, or what should be going
on inside it. According to Allison James and Alan Prout, the professional
view can be seen as a hegemonic concept, meaning that its "truths" are
resistant to criticism and difficult to question because they are inscribed
in the practices of teachers and social workers. "Regimes of truth"
operate like self-fulfilling prophecies: ways of thinking about childhood
fuse with institutional practices to produce self-conscious subjects who
think about themselves through the terms of those ways of thinking
(Prout and James 1990, 23–24). To come up with other views is difficult,
because there is not enough "discursive support."

There is, of course, something trivial in saying that people use
existing discourses as a means of interpreting things they hear about
children and childhood. Maybe it is not as trivial to say that child
workers "translate" findings as part of the process in which they *create
the child as the object* of their child work. The differences between the
professionals' and the sociologists' representations of childhood prob-

ably have less to do with differences in any substantial attributes or characteristics attached to the child, or in different understandings of the child's ontological status, than with different needs, on the whole, *to define* the child. A point I want to make here is that the child has to be defined in order to become a "good" object of "good" child work.

For the researcher, it is important to explicate the professionals' ways and needs of knowing, because they are used in creating the child as an object of child work—and the researcher's empirical field. However, my reflections on how children become represented in the professional field also have a mirror effect: The question of what constructions are made and used in the professional field gradually passed on to the question of what constructions I had made myself. How had I presented and represented the children, their activities, and their relations? How had I done my constructions, in the written text, and in my presentation of the study? And what was the relation between our (different) constructions?

On How Not to Define...

If child professionals need defined children, what does childhood ethnography "need"? When discussing the question of representation in childhood research, James, Jenks, and Prout distinguish between two types of processes through which knowledge production takes place: distal representation and proximal representation. *Distal* representation reflects the demand for constituting childhood through the regulation of space and time: "The 'executive summary' and the 'table of results' distill complex realities into forms which can be taken in at a glance, and ordered, and controlled. Distal knowledges present a neat and tidy outline: they can be acted on" (James, Jenks, and Prout 1998, 143). On the other hand, "proximal representations of social life as unfinished, tangled and in process have little immediate appeal as panoptical devices and therefore do not promise to function well as instruments of governance" (143).

Whether the proximal type of representation offers means of governance or not can be discussed, but it does seem to capture tendencies in the ethnographic approaches to childhood research. These are usually concerned more with exploring the social and communicative processes through which activities are organized and social relations are acted upon than with characterizing and categorizing phenomena.

Tracing social processes is a more flexible and less fixed approach than characterizing and labeling.

My picturing children's activities as an institutionally sensitive flow of activity, continuously moving and changing shape, in which children model their actions in order to deal with social turbulence and fragmentation, corresponds with the more proximal type of representation, as described above. Without exaggerating, social turbulence—obviously the overall turbulence also contains quiet, calm, concentrated, and unobtrusive activities—can be seen as a characteristic feature of the social life of the daycare centers studied.

However, I can also trace in my work an effort to define children in a certain way—as competent social actors. When I was met with others' interpretations emphasizing problems in the children's interaction, I countered with arguments underlining childhood competence. To picture children as competent actors is becoming kind of a new convention in research on childhood. "Over recent years, what can be described as a 'competence paradigm' in the sociology of childhood has emerged in a number of key publications..." (Hutchby and Moran-Ellis 1998, 8). The competence paradigm can be seen as a means of distancing analytical approaches from the premises of the developmental paradigm. "The main thrust of this research is to take issue with the perspective on children and childhood propounded by developmental psychology, and by socialization theory in mainstream sociology..." (8).

Looking at my study in retrospect, I notice that my ambivalence concerning "the competence paradigm" and how it can be used is growing. One thing is to make competence an empirical question— childhood research has contributed considerably to the understanding of how competence is construed in social practices. However, I wonder whether childhood research—in its efforts to treat children more in line with people of other ages than has been the tradition in research on children, and in order to "take children seriously as agents in their own right" (Hutchby and Moran-Ellis 1998, 8)—also runs a risk in tying itself too strongly to the competence paradigm. The doubtful side of this is that "the competence paradigm" becomes modeled as the opposite of "the developmental paradigm," reducing its theoretical scope to being more or less the opposite of that paradigm. Does "the competent child" run the risk of being trapped in a too-narrow and inflexible notion of children's agency? Already the word "paradigm" signals quite strong premises for how a phenomenon can be analytically approached.

According to Nick Lee (1998), in order to make children and childhood fit into sociological theory, the sociology of childhood has solved the ontological ambivalence between "being" and "becoming" by declaring children more or less mature and complete. By doing this, the dependencies that underlay even the most mature performance of independence have been overlooked, along with the incompleteness of social order.

In a thinking that stresses the unfinished character of social order and society, the flow of activity and the unfinished character of children's actions typical to daycare centers already make much more sociological sense. The question is not whether children are to be seen as either competent or immature. It is about *not defining* children or childhood as being of a certain kind. It is about using knowledge of children's actions and interactions for a theoretical broadening of notions of agency.

NOTES

1   "Free play" is a term used by the day care system to name certain activities of the center.
2   Hanna is a member of the staff.
3   Much of our knowledge about the activities of small children seems to stem from research settings in which "separate play" situations have been deliberately created for research purposes (e.g., by placing a restricted number of children in a separate room where "disturbing elements" have been minimized). Used in this separating way, the play concept prevents us from seeing children's actions as embedded in a social environment.

REFERENCES

Atkinson, Paul. *Understanding Ethnographic Texts*. Newbury Park: Sage, 1992.
Brannen, Julia, and Mary O'Brien, ed. *Children in Families: Research and Policy.* London and Washington: Falmer Press, 1996.
Bruner, Jerome. *Actual Minds, Possible Worlds*. Cambridge: Harvard University Press, 1986.
Bruner, Jerome. *Acts of Meaning*. Cambridge: Harvard University Press, 1990.
Clifford, James, and George E. Marcus. *Writing Culture: The Poetics and Politics of Ethnography*. Berkeley: University of California Press, 1986.
Corsaro, William. "Entering the Child's World—Research Strategies for Field Entry and Data Collection in a Preschool Setting." In *Ethnography and Language in Educational Settings*, edited by Judith L. Green and Cynthia Wallat, 117–146. Norwood, N.J.: Ablex, 1981.
Corsaro, William. *Friendship and Peer Culture in the Early Years*. Norwood N.J.: Ablex, 1985.
Deloache, Judy S., and Ann L. Brown. "The Early Emergence of Planning Skills in Children." In *Making Sense: The Child's Construction of the World,* edited by Jerome Bruner and Helen Haste, 108–130. London: Methuen, 1987.
Evaldsson, Ann-Carita. *Play, Disputes and Social Order: Everyday Life in Two Swedish After Schools Centers*. Linköping: Linköping University, 1993.
Fine, Gary A., and Kent Sandstrom. *Knowing Children: Participant Observation with Minors*. Newbury Park: Sage, 1988.
Goodwin, Marjorie. *He-Said-She-Said: Talk as Social Organization Among Black Children*. Bloomington and Indianapolis: Indiana University Press, 1990.
Gordon, Tuula, and Elina Lahelma. "'School Is like an Ant's Nest': Spatiality and Embodiment in Schools." *Gender and Education* 8 (1996): 301–310.
Hutchby, Ian, and Jo Moran-Ellis, ed. *Children and Social Competence: Arenas of Action.* London: Falmer Press, 1998.
James, Allison, Chris Jenks, and Alan Prout. *Theorizing Childhood*. Cambridge, Mass.: Polity Press, 1998.
Jenks, Chris. "The Postmodern Child." In *Children in Families: Research and Policy,* edited by Julia Brannen and Mary O'Brien, 13–25. London and Washington: Falmer Press, 1996.

Lee, Nick. "Towards an Immature Sociology." *The Sociological Review* 46 (1998): 458–482.

Mandell, Nancy. "The Least-Adult Role in Studying Children." *Journal of Contemporary Ethnography* 16 (1988): 433–467.

Marcus, George E. *Ethnography through Thick and Thin.* Princeton, N.J.: Princeton University Press, 1998.

Mayall, Berry, ed. *Children's Childhoods: Observed and Experienced.* London: Falmer Press, 1994.

———. *Children, Health and the Social Order.* Buckingham and Philadelphia: Open University Press, 1996.

Oldman, David. "Adult-Child Relations as Class Relations". In *Childhood Matters: Social Theory, Practice and Politics*, edited by Jens Qvortrup, Marjatta Bardy, Giovanni Sgritta, and Helmut Wintersberger, 43–58. Aldershot, UK: Avebury Press, 1994.

Prout, Alan, and Allison James. "A New Paradigm for the Sociology of Childhood? Provenance, Promise and Problems". In *Constructing and Reconstructing Childhood: Contemporary Issues in the Sociological Study of Childhood*, edited by Allison James and Alan Prout, 7–34. London: Falmer Press, 1990.

Rose, Nicolas. *Governing the Soul: The Shaping of the Private Self.* London: Routledge, 1990.

Strandell, Harriet. *Sociala mötesplatser för barn. Aktivitetsprofiler och förhandlingskulturer på daghem* (Meeting Places for Children: Activity Profiles and Patterns of Negotiation in Day Care Centers). Helsinki: Gaudeamus, 1994.

Strandell, Harriet. "Doing Reality with Play: Play as a Children's Resource in Organizing Everyday Life in Day Care Centres." *Childhood* 4 (1997): 445–464.

Thorne, Barrie. *Gender Play: Girls and Boys in School.* New Brunswick, N.J.: Rutgers University Press, 1993.

Thorne, Barrie. "Re-Visioning Women and Social Change: Where Are the Children?" *Gender & Society* 1 (1987): 85–109.

Tyler, Stephen A. "Post-Modern Ethnography: From Document of the Occult to Occult Document." In *Writing Culture: The Poetics and Politics of Ethnography*, edited by James Clifford and George E. Marcus, 122–140. Berkeley: University of California Press, 1986.

Chapter 2

Orators and Outcasts, Wanderers and Workers: Street Children in Brazil

Mary Lorena Kenny

"I *hate* researchers."
—Nilda, thirteen-year-old street girl

Hector Babenco's 1980 film *Pixote* dramatized, in an unsentimental way, life for street and institutionalized children in Brazil. On July 23, 1993, a massacre of eight homeless youth by police at Candelaria Church in Rio de Janeiro renewed the international attention given to street children.[1] Street children are talked about in two ways. On the one hand, they are seen as risky terrorists who put *others* at risk, and who foment fear, horror, and repulsion. They are grouped together with a homogeneous blob of "fallouts" from society that include dangerous *marginais* (deviants), gang members, drug traffickers, and thieves. On the other hand, they are represented as being *at risk* and are juxtaposed with images of ideal, home-based children who are nurtured, protected, and attend school.

What to do about these children who are *at risk* or *risky* fuels and funds political and legal campaigns, social welfare programs, and scholarly research. Women's magazines, weekly news magazines, and newspapers show stark, brutal images of street children that incite compassion, guilt, and outrage. Street children consistently arouse concern internationally and domestically, and they receive significantly more media attention than children who live in extreme poverty in Brazil but who continue to live at home. Poor children who maintain family ties and help to support their families by servicing the needs of the upper classes for inexpensive labor do not provoke the same international compassion as street children. Why? What is it about the symbolic representation of the street child that provokes so much attention?

In this article I discuss how Brazilian street children are defined as a social problem by "experts." The dual representations—*at risk* and *risky*—empower and, at the same time, render street children more vulnerable. Defined as a "special" group separate from other desperately poor in the area, street children use these representations opportunistically as tools for survival to gain social power and access to resources. On the other hand, as a metaphor for danger and criminality, exclusionary practices, violence and death are rationalized.[2]

I begin with a description of the area and then address the context that leads children to abandon and be abandoned by their families. Next, I examine the ambiguity of attitudes and treatment toward street children—why street youth are seen as a special group who are both "at risk" and "risky"—and suggest some reasons why well-intentioned programs and interventions are ineffective in eliminating street children from the urban landscape.

Setting

Although Brazil has the eighth largest economy in the world, income distribution is among the most unequal in the world. Three quarters (72 percent) of the national income is in the hands of 15 percent of the population. About half of Brazil's poor live in the northeast region of the country. Poverty is determined by household incomes that are less than that which covers the basic necessities (food, rent, transportation, hygiene, education, and insurance). The minimum amount needed to cover these basic needs is eight monthly wages (in U.S. currency, about $80/month).[3] Social welfare benefits, charity, and pensions are limited.[4] Many of those in "poverty" do not earn an income that covers the cost of birthing, feeding their children, or maintaining themselves and family members in sickness and old age (Nieuwenhuys 1994). It costs 80 percent of the monthly wage to purchase the *cesta basica* (meat, milk, beans, rice, farinha, tomatoes, bread, coffee, bananas, sugar, oil, and butter) for a family of four for one month. Rarely is a sufficient level of food available to meet the nutritional needs of all household members.[5]

Forty-eight percent of all malnourished children are from the northeast part of the country. Adults do not fare much better: An adult male sugar cane cutter in Pernambuco consumes on average fewer calories (between 1500 and 1700) than the inmates at Buchenwald (Scheper-Hughes 1996, 893). These *miseravel* (miserable) poor have been called the "undernourished arms" (de Jesus 1962, 40) of the Brazilian body.

In 1991, about 21 million persons under the age of 18 lived in the northeast (60 percent of the population), and now more than 70 percent live in the urban areas. In 1995, 65 percent of children up to age 5 in the northeast were considered poor (*Jornal do Commercio* 1995). An estimated 3.6 million youth between the ages of 11 and 17 are illiterate. Although formal education is valued as an instrument to increased prestige and material comfort, the opportunity to attend school full-time is a luxury most families cannot afford. The amount of schooling/training that is required to access jobs that lead to financial mobility is out of reach for most families.

Requirements for school attendance are often adjusted in order to optimize youths' earnings and allow them to help out at home. The number of workers between ages 10 and 14 is two times greater than any other country in Latin America. In Pernambuco, 51.3 percent of children between the age of 10 and 18 contribute to their own or their family's income by working in the informal market 5 or 6 days a week, 10 to 12 hours a day (Myers 1989). Although population data show more than 70 percent of child workers to be male, it is estimated that girls comprise 21.74 percent of those under 18 who are out of school and who work primarily as domestic servants or in services that are hidden or illegal, such as prostitution. Approximately 70 percent of these workers receive one-half the minimum salary (IBGE 1995), contributing up to half their earnings to their families (Rizzini 1994).

Approximately 63 percent of the population (2,831,750) of the Regional Metropolitan Area of Recife (RMR) is poor with about half working in the informal economy. Recife, the state capital, was cited in a 1990 *VEJA* article (a popular weekly news magazine) as the city with the fourth worst living conditions in the world, with high levels of infant mortality,[6] illiteracy,[7] and leprosy.[8] About a quarter of the population occupies 600 *favelas* (shantytowns). Tourists to the area often comment that they find the area "charming," especially the areas that receive funding targeted for historic preservation. The ornate historic district of Olinda has winding streets, sixteenth-century churches, old fountains, seminaries, and schools. This effectively masks the 60 *favelas* that fan out from the central historic district. Only 300 meters from the cobbled

streets and large homes behind high gates, barbed wire, and charred glass
are some of the most violent "housing zones" in the area that harbor the
extremely poor. A 1989 study in Olinda showed over 90 percent of the
favela population having income below one minimum-wage income,
with women he·ʼ·ling over 30 percent of the households.

These comn̲ ̲nities are bounded by what Suttles referred to as the
"shared knowledge of an underlife" (Suttles 1972, 43). "Survival"
regions such as *Ilha do Rato* (Rat Island), *Skylab*, *Vietna*, *Entra Apulso*
(Forced Entry), or *Inferninho* (Little Hell) offer overcrowding,
malnutrition, no plumbing, no garbage collection, and a prevalence of
domestic violence. The municipal health post, where ideally universal
access to health care is provided, has chronic staffing problems; on days
when staff are present, they lack medicines, water, and electricity. The
local public hospital is better; at one point in 1995 doctors were using
plastic bags during procedures because they lacked gloves. Leisure
culture, communal activity, the distribution of commodities, political
discussions, repairs, drinking, rocking babies, playing music, and
smoking marijuana take place in the *favela*'s lacunae, alongside the dogs
(pit bulls on thick chains were becoming popular), cats tied onto chair
legs by string so they would not run away, horses, and goats. Rival gangs
sporadically have *tiro-teiros* (shoot-outs). "*La onde eu moro so sai bale*
(where I live only gunshots ring out)," one resident told me.

Marx's use of the term *lumpenproletariat* to describe Paris in 1850
could also be used to describe the large number of persons in Recife with
"dubious means of subsistence…vagabonds, discharged jailbirds,
swindlers, pickpockets, gamblers, porters, rag-pickers, tinkers, beggars,
in short the whole indefinite…refuse of all classes." Pregnant women
roam from table to table in local bars with one baby in their arms and
another at their feet. Senhora Vanya, age seventy-five, laments,
"Business ain't goin' too well these days." Chris lifts his shirt to show
the scar from a bullet wound, and crippled men drag themselves across
the floor of outdoor bars. Children compete with adults for public
sympathy, unless the adult is blind or has an infant to enhance their profit.
Women "borrow" kids from neighbors because public sympathy stands
in inverse relationship to age; the younger the child, the more sympathy
and money they receive. The role of mendicant is one of the few regular
and lucrative occupations for children until they "age out" of begging.
Children parade their "blind" fathers. On the buses they ask for donations
for food or materials, or they provide unsolicited entertainment. No older
than age ten, they sing romantic *Nordestino* ballads about betrayal and
loss, about rugged life in the *sertao* (semi-arid interior), looking for

feijao (beans) to abate hunger, or begging to use *meu cellular* (my cellular telephone) to call "when you miss me." One day, an eleven-year-old girl I knew asked another, using Likert scale questioning, how the threat of physical abuse by her father affected her contributing to household income. "Do you get beaten a lot or a little if you come home with no money?" gave me answers to a question I never asked.

The police and the juvenile corrections system "police the poor" (Lewis 1986, 33) in low-income areas, although much police "activity" goes unrecorded in official statistics. *Favelas* are often viewed as "parallel states" and "occupied territories" (Pinheiro 1996), and police refuse to enter them. In November 1994, the army was authorized to enter the *favelas* of Rio in a showy attempt to snuff out drug traffickers, with televised dramatic shots of tanks and machine guns amidst the crumbling shacks of the *favela*. Public opinion polls reported general approval for the police action, although informants thought the "invasion" ineffective and comical, given the number of police involved in drug trafficking. To capture the general sentiment among the *povo*,[9] a letter from a *favelado* was published in the *Jornal do Commercio*, a local paper. It was posted on the walls of local bars and carried in the wallets of informants.

I am the beginning of a new era. Don't you understand that I am a sign? You have turned away for decades. You hate me because I am ugly, dirty, and poor. You have always removed me from your conscience, and now you will remove me with arms. Today, I am the beginning of your social conscience. The diagnosis has always been the same: migration (of unskilled workers) from the rural areas, a need for increase in the infrastructure, etc. etc. But the solution never came. No one, ever, has looked at *favelas*, because we don't exist; when the rats attack us at night, we don't exist. When we die of hunger, from the rain, we are only good photos for the papers (they sell a lot) and we provoke anguish among sensitive intellectuals...but now you are all in panic because we are armed, we are not just a moral problem. We have AR-15, AK-47, Uzis...we are united...we are the "bad" and you the "good" citizen. You don't know death; for you death is a Christian drama, for us a daily occurrence. You think we are a problem for you? You are a problem for us! Why don't the armed forces get those who sell us arms and live in Ipanema? The death of a poor person is not tragic. The armed forces are just dying to act, to justify their existence; they have something to do now besides play basketball at the headquarters. They like action (it must be hard living without a war, without a dictatorship). The solution will come after much death, after mouths are filled with ants, after you know the concrete fact of rats, instead of the sweet life of the bureaucrat and politician. Why not try a more rapid solution? A bomb, perhaps, in each *favela*...Then all the area can be urbanized and sold.[10]

Social science research has highlighted the hardworking residents, close-knit families, class and political allegiances, and the egalitarian reciprocity that exists in poor communities. In her study of a Mexican shantytown, Lomnitz (1988) notes that information (including gossip), training and job assistance, loans (money and other goods), services (errand-running, etc.), the sharing of facilities (such as a TV), and moral and emotional support in ritual situations are shared (256). Stack (1974) documented cooperating networks of nonresident kin among poor, urban African-Americans. The study of a *favela* in Rio de Janeiro by Perlman (1976) also dismantled the myth of community divisiveness and emphasized the indigenous development of cooperating networks.

In Pearse's 1961 study of a *favela* in Rio de Janeiro, however, she found that "the women insisted that they avoided intimacies with neighbors, making a point of not going into their houses and forbidding their children to do so." My informants overtly shared sentiments similar to those found in Pearse's study. Most residents and former residents I knew who lived in the local *favelas* did not express a resigned acceptance of their situation or highlight cooperation. According to Dona Bete, "Here there is no security. Babies die, even the rats die." When I asked Gloria what she would do if she found $10,000, she responded, "I would buy a house far from here, and take nothing, absolutely nothing, that would remind me I ever lived here." Tension and backstabbing between households was chronic. "I say nothing to anyone. I don't talk to anyone," one resident said. When asked whom they could depend on, residents inevitably said: "No one. When people see you are doing well, they are jealous, not happy for you."

Nonetheless, this seemed incongruous with what I observed. People joked with neighbors, exchanged food (especially stolen coconuts), childcare, clothing, watched television at the "community" TV, ran errands, helped to buy coffins ("but only for certain people"), and showed neighbors where the prime spots for begging are. Nonetheless, they continued to insist that cooperation was nonexistent, and that "everyone is out for themselves." My assessment is that residents concur more with Maria de Jesus' (1962) assessment that the *least* friendly and cooperative place is the *favela*. The solidarity, pooling, borrowing, and sharing of resources, although occurring on one level, are obliterated by suspicion and scarcity. According to Dalva, age twelve: "I am so miserable. All I do is work. Did you know that today is my twelfth birthday? What do I want? The thing I want the most is to get out of this miserable *favela*."

Leaving Home

Given the context described above, poor households must develop an array of strategies for subsistence. These strategies require constant adaptation to both internal household and external conditions (Gonzalez de la Rocha 1999). A birth brings an additional mouth to feed, an illness the loss of a primary income earner and the expense of medication. Any loss of income means adjustments in consumption. Luxury foods (meat), gas for cooking, and school supplies are forfeited in order to purchase food. The size and/or number of meals may be reduced, or children may be encouraged or even forced to consume outside the household. Redistribution of resources is often unequal. Cross-cultural studies note that "food is manipulable" (Price 1996), and it is given for good behavior and withheld as punishment. More and better food is systematically directed toward adult wage-earning males (Harris and Ross 1987; Gross and Underwood 1971; Gonzalez de la Rocha 1995, 22), resulting in differences in "well-being" among household members that are gender and age-specific (Gonzalez de la Rocha 1995, 22–23; La Fontaine 1986, 27). The data I collected on food intake, income, and expenditures for a number of households in which children contributed significantly to household earnings show that food is often the compensation for work performed. Talk about food and the acquisition of food is a constant preoccupation. The only consistent food items in their diet were rice, black coffee, and sugar. There was little that was "fixed" about their income, or their eating. One resident told me:

> Can't you see? We get some money, and buy some food. If no money, no food.
> Food is given to my father first, and then the rest divided among us.

The needs of those who appear to be the most vulnerable (young, old, sick) are not automatically given priority when triaging food (Scheper-Hughes 1992; Curtis 1986,168).

Households also triage resources by increasing members (being given a niece, stepchild, or *agregado*—an unrelated household member, usually a "helper") as a means of adding able-bodied persons for household labor or economic support. Household members might be given to repay a favor or as a response to scarcity. A move to a wealthier household, even as a maid, is seen a hypergamous move, with the potential for securing a wealthy patron in exchange for labor (Kuznesof 1998, 229).

Studies show that among low-income families, children may temporarily be "circulated" or transferred to family and fictive kin, abandoned, or "given over to the state" in an effort to reduce the number of dependents at a particular moment in the life cycle of the family. Jose's mother "let her son go" to the street and, accordingly, to the state. She said: "He is too wild, untamable. He has always been that way. I could never control him." This is seen as a response to stress and deprivation, with the intent, perhaps, of reunification at a later time (Fonseca 1986).

Many poor children are not too far afield from shifting to the street as a permanent home. A "street child" can actually eat more and better than they would at home (Hecht 1998). Children roam around the tables at bars, or wait for local merchants to give them food. On the street they could consume, for free, water (also at various houses), rice and beans, bread from the bakery, cookies, coconut water, *acaraje* (shrimp wrapped in fried beans), and *tapioca* (a cheese and coconut mixture in a tortilla-type wrap). I often witnessed kids robbing women and the elderly to get money for food. Some kids told me they could not concentrate on anything besides food and their own pain. "The hunger gets to me, Dona Mary. I am not very strong. I can't stand it. Sometimes even after I eat, the pain is still there."

Although interviewees participated in interviews with me without any contractual compensation, they consistently counted on my giving them food, and food was always given to me in return when available. Political candidates gave out free food (and sterilizations) during election time. One newspaper article highlighted how more is spent on dog and cat food than on food programs for poor children. About $350 million is spent per year on pet food, while 79 cents is spent per child/per day at one food program in São Paulo. My neighbors were often heard arguing about food (or their daughter's scandalous behavior, resulting in what becomes her predictable biweekly public expulsion from the house). In a perverse Robin Hood gesture, one local thief would treat everyone to food and alcohol after an especially "successful" day. After a sexual encounter an unmarried woman will often expect a non-coresident male to provide a *feirinha* (a little basket of food). And scavengers in the *lixao* would turn inedible food into a meal by putting an abundant amount of salt on it to "kill the germs."

One twelve-year-old boy who lived in a tree with five other kids in Boa Viagem, a wealthy neighborhood, said things were "bad at home, so I left." The tree house that he and the others had constructed was their fortress from the "bad things that happen to other kids." It also served as a strategic location for accessing resources. He was quick to point out: "We don't 'steal.' We ask for money and watch cars for people at the beach." Some kids consider themselves a burden on the family. Street children become accustomed to the freedom and resources the street provides. "How is it that I am going to return to my house?" Baixinho said to me. Their apprenticeship with homelessness includes learning to maneuver the harsh, dangerous, and exciting "street world" and identifying with the social world of the "street child."

The chronic economic insecurity, the desire for freedom from household responsibilities and obligations, the search for alternative subsistence, and the urge to use for themselves the scarce earnings they generate also "push" them from the home and "pull" them to the street in an effort to service the cravings that poverty induces. Overall, households with "cumulative handicaps" (Body-Gendrot 2000, xxiv) characterize the homes in which children have either been expulsed or have severed ties.

Children of the Street

One local NGO (nongovernmental organization) in Recife estimates the number of street children at 600,000, including children working in the street (CONDEPE 1986). According to the *Movimento National de Meninos e Meninas de Rua* (MNMMR), an advocacy group for street/working children, those who live more or less permanently on the street are estimated to be about 20,000. (Given the severe material deprivation of the area it is surprising there are not *more* street children in the area.) In studies that note skin color, almost all children are categorized as brown or black. In the RMR they are popularly referred to as *cheira cola* (glue sniffers). There are fewer girls than boys living on the street, although second-generation street children are being raised by *maes da rua* (street mothers).

"Risky" Children

The street-child identity is one that accesses resources but also forces limits. Those who are identified as street children are generally stigmatized and seen by the larger society as "abnormal" (Goffman 1963, 21) and a danger to the social order because of their criminal acts, unemployment, and lack of adult control. Despite the pronouncements of street children being *at risk*, counter images of primarily Afro-Brazilian youth—woozy and dirty, sniffing glue, toting guns, begging, thieving, and prostituting—challenge images of happy, playful, humble, *moleques* (little urchins or rascals) on the urban landscape. The representation of street children as gruesome social blemishes persuades some to utilize hostile short-term solutions by eradicating them physically from the urban landscape through extermination.

Conversations about crime, fear, and economic uncertainty are common in Brazil's large cities. Street children are blamed for much of the violence that occurs on city streets and for the decay of community and society. Contact with street children, and with the poor in general, has become the locus of fear. Other street children echoed a comment by twelve-year-old Negao: "Aren't you afraid of us? A lot of people are afraid. They think we steal and sniff glue and assault people... Some people do not want to come near us."

Caldeira (1992) notes in her study of São Paulo how the fear of random violence has enveloped the "ordinary" citizen, even though most of the victims of crime are the poor. The media reinforces the notion that one cannot rely on state means of control. The historic lack of trust in the civil police has reinforced a privatization of safety. A third of São Paulo's 35 million residents pay guards to watch over their homes (Huggins and MacTurk 2000). The wealthy hire private guards and the poor are policed by drug traffickers in the *favelas* (Pinheiro 1996).

Four-year-old Camila almost died when she approached a private home to solicit food and money. The large home is situated on the top of a hill in Olinda with a view of the sea. The family had a reputation for sitting in the front parlor with the windows open while they listened to Vivaldi. The macabre incongruity to this scene occurred when the private security guard released their dog on Camila after she knocked on the gate. The guard sensed that Camila was part of a *sacanagem*, that she was just a front for a robbery, assault, or kidnapping. So he let the dog loose on her, and the animal took a significant piece of flesh from her leg. The family apologized for the mishap, and gave her the equivalent of $10 for medication.

Douglas's (1994, 46) description of *risky* is apt for popular views of street children: menacing and polluting. They are a metaphor for what she defines as "dirt" or "matter out of place" (Douglas [1966] 1985). They are people who are out of place; dirt on the urban landscape, symbols of disorder. They are viewed as a social pathology, a symptom of broad economic and social exclusion.

A polluting person is always in the wrong. He has developed some wrong condition or simply crossed some line that should not have been crossed and this displacement unleashes danger for someone (Douglas 1970, cited in Jenks 1996, 129, 136).

Street children do not segregate themselves in the *favelas* like most of the poor, whom Bourgois has called "agents of terror confined to spaces of marginality" (1996, 253). Bounded by reputations of "social distress" (Body-Gendrot 2000, 25) and spatialized criminality, they leave the *favelas* and come to the wealthy centers, challenging the supposed exclusive public space and security claimed by the upper classes. Street children violate norms concerning use of public space by eating, sleeping, and roaming about without destination (Ward 1977), which confirms notions for some that street children are marauding youth committing vandalism and violence. One author has defined what he calls the increase in "antistreet people architecture" that includes gates, guards, electric fences, iron bars, and showerheads that prevent street children and the homeless from usurping public space (Pereira Lima 1998). Local merchants complain about the increase of street children who come from the local *favelas* and drive away the elite patrons, leaving only the *baixaria* (the unwashed, undisciplined, chaotic, idle lower classes). According to one vendor:

Things have changed. It is not like it used to be, with nice people here. Now it is very slow, because of them. Before they were just *moleques*, but now they are all thieves. They make violence. They rob and kill. *That is why you should take every one of them and kill them, one by one.*

According to my neighbor, Ramos, "People talk about class A, B, C, but the poor are class Z, like a zebra, because they came out all wrong."

Street children challenge normative categories associated with childhood (Jenks 1996, 69). They are *adults before their time*, socialized too quickly. They establish their own relationships with adults, are sexually experienced, and engage in criminal acts, justifying their expulsion from childhood (Jenks 1996, 128). They occupy a non- or deficient child status (Scheper-Hughes 1996), which "explains" their abandonment by their families. A pathological "nature" or essence is attributed to them, much the same way reformers questioned the evil disposition of "out-of-control" poor children in late 1800s industrializing

Europe (Hendrick 1990, 39; Stepan 1991), Brazil (Kuznesof 1998), and Mexico (Blum 1998, 242). Exclusionary ideologies essentialize street children as "objects" with independent origins. Their status is self-generated and their "bad" behavior intrinsic and immutable, thereby justifying containment and annihilation. When street kids resist their subaltern status they suffer retaliation: humiliation, punishment, torture, and death.

Demands are made for the increase in policing and containment of "dangerous" street children to protect the security of "ordinary" citizens. Children cannot be tried as adults for criminal acts until they reach age eighteen, but the Children's and Adolescents' Act mandates that young offenders guilty of grave crimes be kept in detainment centers for up to three years. Some argue that institutionalization protects street children from violence by vigilante groups and by the violence they inflict on one another by "keeping an eye on them" (Sheridan 1980).

The *Fundacao Estadual do Bem-Estar do Menor* (FEBEM) is a welfare and penal institution for those under the age of eighteen. It has a reputation for being an abusive and ineffectual holding tank for juvenile offenders. Being sent to FEBEM provides a measure of social control and gives the illusion that the problem of street children is being solved and that miraculously they will exit fully "rehabilitated," with the desire and skills to enter mainstream life and engage in waged labor. However, the number of interned is well beyond capacity, breakouts and riots are common, and staff salaries are delayed for months. In Pernambuco, more than 50 percent of the offenders who leave the centers are later arrested (SEJUP 1996).

Street children repeatedly told me that they know they are "difficult" to work with, that it takes years to "get any results." Eleven-year-old Negao commented:

> But you know, we don't just want to play around, games and stuff. Everyone knows we assault, rob people, and prostitute ourselves. We need to learn something useful, to have a space to work, to be useful.

He felt the only solution to the problem of street children was "to get a gun and kill everyone, then myself. Then start all over."

Some observers advocate "flushing them out" through genocide. One local resident told me: "We should have the electric chair, then people would not be so ready to kill other people." On February 20, 1997, in Belford Roxo, 15 kilometers from the city of Rio de Janeiro, three security guards of a bus company shot and killed three youth after they "made a disturbance on the bus and refused to pay their fare." Alba

Zalaur, a Brazilian anthropologist who studies urban violence, states that 70 percent of violent deaths in Brazil happen to those between the ages of 15 and 17; 50 percent of these are by death squads, 40 percent to drug traffickers, and 8.5 percent by the police. The death rate among the 15–29 age group has been increasing since the 1970s (SEJUP 1996). Assassinations have tripled during the last 15 years, with the 15-19 age group registering the highest number. More than 45,000 have been killed in 15 years (Servico Brasileiro de Justica e Paz—SEJUP 1996) almost equaling the number of soldiers killed in Vietnam during a 9-year period. Between 1989 and 1994, 784 children were assassinated in Pernambuco. From January to October 1994, there were 154 cases, 13 just in October. In Recife, "Don't kill my children" is painted on walls and printed on T-shirts.[11] In the last few years in Pernambuco, children and adolescents also *committed* 80 homicides.

Street children are highly visible and powerless targets for police violence. Begging or sniffing glue on the street increases the risk of being harassed by the police. One thirteen-year-old told me:

> You know, the police would harass me all the time, for nothing, just as a joke. The other day a cop took a friend of mine, he was sniffing glue, and just started kicking him, then took the glue and poured it on his head and body. The thing is, he could go to the *Movimento*, and make a denouncement, but he would never be safe. He would have to leave the area for fear of vengeance.

To testify, to "talk back," to make the injustice public, puts him at risk for extermination (Wiesel 1970).

Many police officers live in or near the same poor communities that the children are from. I thought that kin or community ties provided a buffer, so I asked whether the police "leave you alone" when they know you are from the area.

> No. Only if you are a relative, and even that is usually after the fact. "Oh, aren't you so-and-so's nephew? Sorry about that," meaning the kick, punch, or slap you got. It really doesn't matter, even if they are from the same barrios or *favelas*. They learn, with the uniform, that they have power. Police beat people up for the fun of it.

One thirteen-year-old girl told me that the police tend to "leave us alone because we have something to give them," meaning they perform oral sex on officers in exchange for not being sent to FEBEM. Ana Vasconcelos, the director of *Casa da Passagem*, a halfway house for street girls, said, "I am still unable to comprehend why so many policemen have this fixation with kicking pregnant girls in the stomach."

Girls would show me their cicatrized skin, visual reminders of where they had cut themselves in order to be taken to the hospital instead of the police station.

One policeman I interviewed told me that the law is a hindrance in protecting society from undesirables, that they need to "teach" criminal-bound kids about law and order. This is ironic given the poor reputation of the police as a vital link in the chain of transport for illegal goods. They threaten street children if they don't steal for them or turn over stolen goods. "It's not even worth stealing a watch because the cop would expect you to give it to him," Jose told me. He said:

> The cops know who are the thieves. So they wait for you to do a job, then take everything. Most are afraid to say it, but the civil police are thieves, *safado* (rogues). If you meet up with them at night, they will ask you for money. If you say you do not have any, wham, they hit you with the stick.

Street children view their own mortality and morbidity as a predictable misfortune, somewhat like an occupational hazard. They are killed because they are bad, not normal, "off track," as Hecht (1998) argues. They live the life of vagabonds rather than the "vida boa," the righteous life (109–12) and must pay for their sins (113–14). This reduces the lived experiences among street children, and the poor in general, to personal rather than structural terms. This also effectively works to support the attitude of people who tolerate the murder of a street child. *They were born to die that way.* The demonization of street children demands that they be treated as such: defiled, ostracized, and killed.

Children at Risk: The Problem Industry

The hypermarginal street child is the object of the gaze (Foucault 1983) of numerous studies, well-funded foreign researchers, charitable travelers, and NGOs. I first went to Recife in 1992 with a grant to study social networks among street youth, in an attempt to assess the level of resources they had for information concerning health care issues.

Soon after my arrival, street children questioned me about the source of my funding, the objectives of my research, and the ultimate use of the information. I was struck by a sense that street children were not asking these questions for the first time. Their interaction with me was profoundly influenced by a geologic layering of earlier encounters with other researchers. I was told that a few years previously a street girl from Recife filed a lawsuit against a photographer from the United States who sensationally dramatized the horrifying "lifestyle" of street children in a

U.S. weekly news magazine, and erroneously portrayed the girl as a prostitute. Over the course of fieldwork, I met a group of Italian psychologists investigating how "street socialization" affects child development; a British sociologist mapping the association between street children and crime trends; an anthropologist examining "street youth culture"; a North American law student on vacation looking for a way to defend the "rights" of street youth; and a young woman from the U.S. Midwest who was bent on "saving" street kids by putting them up in local hotels, giving them all her possessions, and paying none of the bills. The street youth actually asked me to "intervene" and talk to the woman, as they found her behavior embarrassing.

In his ethnographic study of NGOs working with street children in Recife, Hecht suggests that social welfare agencies play a "numbers game" to advance claims about the severity of the problem, citing phantom sources and research studies (1998, 101–102), in order to make the problem of street youth more significant than the needs of the masses of common poor in the area. The number of street children in an area *can* be grossly exaggerated. The source and intent of the count and the methods used to count heads can swell census numbers. Counting the actual number of children living on the street depends on the time of day surveys are conducted (day or night), and weekly and seasonal fluctuations. UNICEF estimates there are approximately 7 million, but an exact count is impossible because many children circulate in and out of homelessness. The same child may also frequent three different agencies for assistance, which can inflate institutional censuses. In addition, *meninos da rua*, or children of the street, are seen as homogeneous, ignoring the intragroup variation. *Meninos na rua*, children *in* the street, are those who work during the day and/or on weekends but return to their families and maintain family ties. Hecht also notes that at times there are more "specialists" working on behalf of street kids than there are street kids, with a staff-to-street kid ratio being about one-to-one (Hecht 1998, 23). This leaves street educators looking for "cases."

Some "gazers" are seen by street youth as potential kidnappers looking for "stray" children to service the needs of the First World, such as children for infertile couples and spare body parts for the sick. During 1992 significant media attention was given to stories of how poor children were kidnapped and sold to foreigners for their body parts (organ theft or harvesting) under the pretense of adoption (Scheper-Hughes 2000). Mothers told me long after I had first moved into the community that "I was afraid you might take my son in your suitcase for his organs." A poster was circulated in offices, clinics, and bars showing a child with its body parts priced like a cow in a butcher shop: $1,000 for eyes, $5,000 for arm bones, $5,000 for the heart, $20,000 for the kidney, $10,000 for the feet.

It did not take long to grasp that "being studied" was a significant part of their social reality, and that their sophisticated questions evolved from countless investigations by "transient information pimps," as the curious are called, who contribute little, they feel, to altering their situation. I was "positioned" when one thirteen-year-old street girl told me straight out, "I hate researchers." She had just completed a survey with a North American public health researcher from Johns Hopkins University on abortion among street girls. Although researchers may intend to "give them a voice"[12] (as if the street child were waiting patiently for them to come), the returns for these youth, according to them, are grossly unequal. Many feel their misery is used to fuel profits and advance the careers of both Brazilians and foreigners, and that there is little reciprocity or action on behalf of those whose "stories" they appropriate. For the most part, their lives go unchanged. Although a researcher can claim to have "been there," it is ultimately the researcher, not the street kid, who gives the final explanation and dominant interpretation of what is most "true" and reliable about the information that was yielded. Few, if any, are forced to submit their work to the criticism of the kids themselves. Rarely do they get to read or hear what is written about them, or to be cited as collaborators of the work. Turner (1993) suggests that between groups who do not share political, economic, and social power, there is a lingering suspicion about the motives of others in "caring for" them (1993, 3, 23). Gisele, a local resident who met many foreigners who came to conduct research, commented:

> You know, most research doesn't benefit Brazilians. To tell you the truth, I don't like gringos; most of them just want to come here to have sex with the girls, to sell drugs, and do nothing, only *Oba Oba* (have a good time).[13] I met one foreigner who said she loved Brazil because it was so "free." Free meant she could drink when she wants, throw garbage in the street, urinate in public without getting arrested, and go through lights without stopping. Some [foreigners] just want to see Brazilian *miseria* (misery), they want to take pictures, and that's about it. Why don't you just let Brazilians help Brazilians! We have seen many like you, with good intentions, who try to get to know [these kids] and end up traumatized and totally disillusioned. Look. Don't think [if they talk with you] it is because they really like you. I mean you are not a bad person, but they will hit you up for some cash. I know you want to get to know the "people," but don't kid yourself. A fishing village is the "people." This is dangerous. Don't think that because they are nice to you, they will not

show up at the door with a knife in hand. "The people" shoot each other over nothing.

Why all this attention given to street kids? According to a colleague at the local university in Pernambuco, research on street children is "sexy" and "the middle-class ideal of a good deed: It is, *they believe*, helping someone out and at the same time it is internationally relevant." The highly sensationalized accounts of meeting with the super-needy provide good copy for reports directed at potential donors. Gisele often reiterated that "without *favelas* there would be no politicians" and without *miseria* there would be no researchers like me around. What she resented was the "market for suffering" (Kleinman et al. 1997, xi) in Brazil—sightseeing around tragedy. She fears that those who see the photographs and read all those reams of paper about street kids will think there is something culturally "bad" about Brazilians that generates street kids, rather than see that there exists a terrible disparity of wealth.

Although accounts by researchers of the lives of street children can be emotionally moving for the audience, they do not always initiate action to eliminate the discrimination and inequity that lead to this condition. For example, Michael Jackson made a music video about a *favela* in Rio de Janeiro, which basically trivialized the suffering and poverty of local people by setting it to dance music for distant English-speaking foreigners. In the Sunday, May 28, 2000 edition of the *New York Times* travel section, wedged between questions and answers concerning travel tips to George Bernard Shaw's estate in England and Picasso's Paris was a question soliciting information on tours to Rio's *favelas*. For $30, one can take a three-hour tour to Rocinha, Brazil's largest *favela*. "Liberal" tourism trivializes poverty by creating a picturesque, kitschy, organized, and directed itinerary—like a perverse theme park—that is extracted, certainly, from the complexity and material reality of its residents.[14] This type of consumption contributes little to an understanding of poverty. Entertainment eclipses, for example, those who have died at the hands of violence.

Will the Real "At Risk" Kid Please Stand Up?

Being a "street child" is not a legal status but a semiotic one, an archetype for abandonment and the absence of a "home," home being an autonomous icon and primordial place of socialization. This identity becomes fixed over time, a singular attribute that displaces all other identities.

Human rights advocates begin from a perspective that every child has a "right" to be a child, and that adults have an obligation to protect children against environments and situations that are prejudicial to their healthy development. According to Ennew:

> The modern form of childhood has two major aspects. The first is a rigid age hierarchy, which permeates the whole of society and creates a distance between adults and children. The status difference is enhanced by special dress, special games, special artifacts and toys, special language and stories, which are all considered appropriate to what Aries calls the "quarantine" period of childhood. The distance is further enhanced by yet a second aspect, which is the myth of childhood as a "golden age." Happiness is now the key term associated with childhood. It must be a happy time as well as a time of separation from corrupt adult society (1986, 18).

Street kids are represented as "robbed" of the childhood they are entitled to by their parents and by society. Social welfare organizations, activists, journalists, and social scientists use these distinct markers of difference to highlight the marginal status, powerless position, murder, and sexual and psychological abuse of street children. Funding is targeted for interventions that will eliminate the harmful practices and inequities that interfere with a "protected" home-based childhood.

One kid told me about his exasperation when reporters denied him an interview because he was not a *cheira cola*—a "real" street kid, despite the fact that he had been living on the street for years. Being strung out on glue would make it more likely to extend an appeal for "a program" than it would be for an ordinary poor child eking out a living on the street.

"Real" street kids can claim access to resources, create valuable networks with researchers, journalists, psychologists, and lawyers, and speak to the larger community in a way that the more invisible poor cannot. Being a street child gives one the symbolic capital he or she needs to access benefits, especially in an area where access to scarce benefits is extremely competitive and personal connections determine eligibility for services. *Any* status that can provide an advantage is appropriated. Even when they leave the street, or are too old to be considered a street child (after age eighteen), they continue to call themselves "ex" street kids. Roberto da Silva, age thirty-nine, used material from his master's thesis at the University of São Paulo to file a court action against the state of São Paulo. As a former street child, he holds the state responsible for the conditions that led to his abandonment from his family (Servico Brasileiro de Justica e Paz—SEJUP 1996).

Street youth grow accustomed to receiving attention, free food and medicines, and other resources because they are street kids. I do not mean to suggest this is a privileged life. However, they are treated as a separate population from the desperately poor in the area, which provides them with access to resources that would not otherwise be available, at the same time locking them into an exclusive and narrow representation of poverty. Claiming the "street child" identity is really an artifact of a system that bureaucratizes poverty by splintering and classifying the poor into "target" groups to be managed by programs and experts. The fixation on the sensational aspects of extreme poverty obscures the conditions of the chronically poor in the area, leading donors to give less attention to the causes of poverty and more to its consequences—street children. There is the danger of fetishizing street children, of eclipsing the whole by focusing on the part. In general, the routine misery of the mostly invisible poor—the "ant colonies" (Hanchard 1999, 64) of persons who cut the cane, glue the shoes, pick the oranges, excavate the mines, run the errands, mind the children, sell the flowers, polish the shoes, wash the cars, scavenge, and generally provide low-cost goods and services—is rarely given attention, or it is silenced, despite the high rates of morbidity and mortality among them.

Are They "At Risk" or "Risky"?

Despite the plethora of research, attention, conferences, and political platforms addressing the issue of street children, state policy is often at odds as to what "to do" about them. Are street children *at risk* for loss of childhood? Or are they *risky*, idle, dangerous, nonproductive juvenile delinquents?

Protecting "childhood" is seen as the barometer of a civilized, modern, and progressive society (Steedman 1990, 63–64). To appear unable to do so gives Brazil a bad reputation in the international community. During a conference on street children, one of the presenters said that "in general, Brazilians do not feel guilty about this stuff." One informant assertively told me: "Oh, c'mon. You know damn well that there are plenty of people who don't give a damn, who say, 'Kill 'em all,' who do not want anything to do with the problem." Non-Brazilians frequently ask me, "What is it about those Brazilians that they murder their kids?" This naive search for a cultural or natural inclination for violence essentializes abuse and ignores the ubiquity of child abuse and exploitation (Jenks 1996, 92; Inglis 1978; Jobling 1978; Kempe and Kempe 1978).

Many projects and programs approach the problem with individual, remedial solutions, making it an issue for social workers and psychologists, rather than demanding serious social or economic restructuring that would yield improvement in the financial status of families. Lacking a "cure" for the problem of street children, they opt for social control and moral reform by "transforming" how street children live and preventing them from circulating publicly. The threat street children pose to society is grossly exaggerated, although it effectively diverts attention away from a more egregious and devastating hazard—i.e., poverty—that directly affects mortality and morbidity. Elite crimes—corruption, financial scams, tax evasion, and exploitative labor practices—are not viewed as threatening to civil society (Pinheiro 1996).

The UN Convention on the Rights of the Child (1989) states that parents and the state are expected to provide children with food, shelter, and health care in a safe environment until the age of ,eighteen that these are basic human rights. This assumes, however, that families living in extreme poverty have the same level of autonomy and control as middle- and upper-class parents in deciding which arenas are "desirable" for their children. The naturalization of a class-based prerogative renders a feeling of failure among those who are unable to meet these standards. Most programs do not provide any long-term, income-generating capacity to lift the poor out of poverty or provide parents and caretakers with the tools and material goods necessary in providing a protected and prolonged "childhood."

Some interventions are directed at reducing family size among the poor, in the hope that by controlling fertility, street kids and the poor will just eventually disappear. This assumes that by having less children, poor parents will miraculously exit poverty, have stable incomes, better-paying jobs, and more equity. It also assumes the poor have masochistic reproductive strategies, producing children they neither want nor can afford, thus leading to ineffective or incompetent socialization (part of their "culture of poverty"), and ultimately creating bad childhoods, criminals, and the abandoned. According to one of my neighbors:

> The worst violence is practiced by the federal government by allocating only $151 per month as the salary. Did you know that the government gives out free sterilizations during election time? And food? And T-shirts?[15] Politicians offer

it for free, to get votes. Women make the decision to get sterilized just because they are having a hard day.[16]

During an interview with a program officer who worked for a U.S.-based donor agency, I asked about their objectives with street children. "Family preservation," he said. Interventions are directed at containing the public street child by fostering a link to their natural family. They assume that the streets are unhealthy and that no child would choose living on the street over living at home.

Despite the cozy buzzword—"family preservation"—I wondered whether he knew that for many the streets are not any more dangerous than what they experience at home. The streets are certainly risky environments for children, exposing them to psychologically and physically threatening situations and exploitation by adults. It is naive to assume, however, that if children are not on the street, then they are at home or in school, where they are quarantined from the "depravity" of urban adult life that is seen as fostering precociousness (Nasaw 1985, 144) and interfering with a protected full-time childhood. Poor children who live in urban, northeast Brazil are not buffered or sequestered from the "violence of everyday life,"[17] or hidden in homes behind cement walls with barbed wire or shard glass on top. "Contamination" through exploitation, theft, drug trafficking and prostitution, nervous exhaustion, depression, and alcohol abuse is nothing new, nor is it something they could be shielded from.

As described above, indoor space in the *favelas* is scarce, and physical and personal privacy is negligible. Whether or not they are on the street would do little to buffer them from the *public* world of risk, pollution, and congestion. It borders on miraculous if adults are somehow able to shield their children from "growing up too fast." From a young age, their playground and workplace are the street, unlike upper-class children who remain primarily within the confines of the apartment building or house.

In addition, living with one's family can actually be one of the riskiest locations for a child (Gelles and Cornell 1985). Encouraging children to remain in households where they are unwanted or that are dangerous does little to empower them. Street children are "robbed" of childhood only if the real possibility of a pampered and privileged childhood existed. The families and former neighbors of street children live within the same ecological, economic and political spaces and are vulnerable to the same conditions—broad economic inequity, low wages, lack of access to education and health services, inadequate diets and malnutrition, disease, and crime. This is often overlooked and is certainly a major if not prime factor in "family disintegration." Compassionate programs such as "family unification" do not translate into material improvement for poor families; they eclipse political and economic structural reforms. Most parents are left struggling to provide a full-time childhood despite the limitations and constraints on achieving that captivating and very distant ideal.

One very effective and practical school scholarship program initiated by the governor of Brasilia in 1995 provides half a monthly minimum wage to families who keep their child in school. The program has been so successful that it was being piloted in fourty other areas of Brazil.

Another effective effort has been to acknowledge street children as agents, as a constituency. The feeling of sharing the same predicament, of occupying the same status within the social structure, of being stigmatized as marginal by other members of society, serves as a paradigm for consciousness-raising. "Street youth" as a political identity has gained a presence along with other special-interest groups and organizations that have become more visible since the *abertura*, the end of the military dictatorship, gradual re-democratization, and development of a new constitution in 1988. The MNMMR advocates street children's status as citizens, bonded by a political and judicial status, rather than reinforcing notions of preserving and protecting a modern middle-class "childhood" that cannot be "robbed" because it never existed for these children. Focusing on citizenship rather than distinctiveness around victimization allows street children to reinvent and manage alterative symbols and representations about themselves. It does not fetishize street children as autochthonous objects of lost childhood or youth culture standing apart from inequities of wealth, power, and status, but as citizens imbricated in a distinct economic and political system (Nugent 1999, 192).

NOTES

1   One of the children who witnessed the crime, Wagner dos Santos, moved to Switzerland with the help of Amnesty International. He returned to Rio and received approximately U.S.$ 1500 in reparations. Another survivor was killed 22 November 1996 in a *favela* in Rio. Five other adolescents who survived the massacre have died since then. In June 2000, police asphyxiated one of the survivors after he held a busload of passengers hostage for six hours in Rio.

2   Data for this paper were generated during a number of field visits between 1992 and 2000 to Recife, Pernambuco. When deciding on a research site, Recife was recommended to me as an ideal location because street children there are the focus of a significant number of social welfare projects and research. In the state of Pernambuco there are about 114 agencies that have projects addressing the issue of street and poor children (*Instituto de Estudos da Cidadania*-IDEC 1995). The data have been supplemented with municipal census data and material from other studies, workshops, in-depth interviews, and participant observation with community members. In addition, I gathered archival material from local newspapers and the Centro Luis Freire in Olinda, a research and advocacy institute that focuses on social justice issues. Discussions with faculty at the *Universidade Federal de Pernambuco* in Recife also provided valuable information. The sample of in-depth interviews with street children is small, not randomly selected, and not generalizable to all street children in the area.

    This research builds on eight years of work examining the political economy of the area and attempts by the poor to maximize or maintain their "well-being" within the confines of numerous structural constraints. It does not reduce poverty to a single issue (child abandonment), but instead attempts to analyze the composite and dynamic interaction between poverty, family, the household economy, and community (Kenny 1999).

3   *Departamento Intersindical de Estudos e Estatisticas Socio-Economicos (Dieese)*, 6 June 1996.

4   Significant scholarly attention has been given to the political economy of members of the poor, urban household (Gonzalez de la Rocha 1995; Altmann 1985; Bruschini 1986; Perlman 1976) and the various strategies they use to survive (Bolles 1981; Bossen 1981; Bromley 1982; Lewis 1961; Logan 1981; Lomnitz 1977; Motta 1983; Perlman 1976; Stack 1974; Young 1986; de Jesus 1962). For studies on low-income, urban communities in Brazil, see Fonseca 1986; Neuhouser 1989; Norris 1988; and Perlman 1976.

5   The Ministry of Health estimates that there are 1,006,400 children under the age of five who are malnourished (*Folha de Sao Paulo*, 18 November 1996).

6   IMR: 68.7/1000. *Instituto de Planejamento de Pernambuco* (Condepe) 1996. This rate is for the capital city. Higher levels are found in the rural interior—*Zona da Mata* and *Sertao*—where a lack of access to health care as well as malnutrition and drought further compromise health status.

7   According to IBGE (*Instituto Brasileiro de Geografia e Estatistica*), half of the illiterate people in Brazil live in the northeast area of the country. Thirty-three percent of the population of Pernambuco is illiterate (*Jornal do Commercio*, 9 July 1996).

8 In 1994 there were 7,404 registered cases within the 177 municipalities of Pernambuco, with 2,007 new cases in 1995. Brazil is in second place worldwide for the number of cases of leprosy.

9 Definitions of *povo* (masses) shifts depending on the historical moment (it was not used after 1964, during the military dictatorship) and who is defining. The *povo* have been romanticized as passive yet grateful proletarians (Andrade 1922), as exploited workers (Almeida 1928), and as the backbone of Brazilian nationality (Freyre 1933). The term most generally refers to the impoverished and mostly nonwhite members of the rural and urban poor, who occupy the lowest status in society.

10 *Journal do Commercio*, 2 November 1994. Translation is mine.

11 This slogan was part of a campaign by the Center for the Articulation of Marginalized People, started in 1989 to highlight the racialized oppression of Afro-Brazilians.

12 "Giving voice" suggests breaking silence, speaking truth, collaboration, and shared authority.

13 Most foreigners that descend in droves during Carnival, and throughout the year as tourists, have a reputation as intrusive and exploitative of locals, looking only for a "good time" and contributing little or nothing to the enhancement, or appreciation, of the local way of life.

14 The growing tourism of "black spots" or "death tourism" as big business is referred to in Rojek, C. *Ways of Escape: Modern Transformations in Leisure and Travel.* Houndmills, 1993, 136.

15 During the election season in 1996, candidates were notorious for handing out free food baskets, medicine, wheelchairs, and scholarships, as well as paying for tubal ligations, funerals, and light and water bills. "I am the political general clinic," one candidate said. According to the Electoral Code, article 299, "to give, offer, promise, solicit, or receive for oneself or another, to obtain…votes is not accepted" and carries a penalty of up to four years in prison.

16 "It's really impressive. In Brazil there is a culture of sterilization," said Rita Badiani, a BEMFAM employee. Sterilization increased 40 percent over the last ten years among couples, and Brazil has one of the highest rates of sterilization in all of Latin America (*Folha de Sao Paulo*, 8 October 1996). Unwanted pregnancies are often terminated by taking *Cicotec*, an ulcer medicine sold over the counter in local pharmacies which induces uterine contractions. Once contractions are induced, women and girls go to the emergency room of the hospital to "have it completed" with dilation and curettage. Young women take the medication, regardless of whether they are pregnant, as a prophylactic pregnancy prevention method.

17 Title of a book by Nancy Scheper-Hughes (1992) to describe daily life in the Zona da Mata of Pernambuco.

REFERENCES

"Assassinations Triple in Brazil During 15 Year Period. "*Servico Brasileiro de Justica e Paz (SEJEP) No. 252*, 14 November 1996.

"Avaliacao da Pobreza no Brasil." Cited from the World Bank Report. *Journal do*

Commercio, 10 May 1996.

Blum, Ann. "Public Welfare and Child Circulation, Mexico City, 1877 to 1925." *Journal of Family History* 23, no. 3 (1998): 240–271.

Body-Gendrot, Sophie. *The Social Control of Cities? A Comparative Perspective.* Oxford: Publishers, 2000.

Bourgois, Philippe. "Confronting Anthropology, Education, and Inner-City Apartheid." *American Anthropologist* 98, no. 2 (1996): 249–265.

Caldeira, Teresa. *City of Walls: Crime, Segregation, and Citizenship in Sao Paulo.* Berkeley: University of California Press, 1992.

CONDEPE. *A Situacao Socio-economica do Menor de Familia de Baixa Renda na Cidade do Recife.* Recife-PE, Brasil, 1986.

"Crianca e Adolescentes: Indicadores Sociais, Base de Dados em Formato Tabular." Cited from IBGE and UNICEF. *Jornal do Commercio,* 3 August 1995.

"Crise Nao Atinge as Escolas Particulares." *Journal do Commercio,* 23 May 1996.

Curtis, Richard F. "Household and Family in Theory on Inequality." *American Sociological Review* 51 (1986): 168–183.

de Jesus, Carolina Maria. *Child of the Dark.* New York: E. P. Dutton, 1962.

Departamento Intersindical de Estudos e Estatisticas Socio-Economicos (DIEESE). *Interunion Department of Statistics,* DIEESE, 6 June 1996.

Douglas, Mary. *Purity and Danger: An Analysis of the Concepts of Pollution and Taboo.* London: Ark Paperbacks, 1985

———. *Risk and Blame: Essays in Cultural Theory.* London: Routledge, 1994.

Ennew, Judith. *The Sexual Exploitation of Children.* Cambridge: Polity Press, 1986.

Fonseca, C. "Orphanages, Foundlings and Foster Mothers: The System of Child Circulation in a Brazilian Squatter Settlement." *Anthropological Quarterly* 59 (January 1986): 15–27.

"Former Street-Youth Plans to Sue State." *Servico Brasileiro de Justica e Paz (SEJEP) no. 251,* 6 November 1996.

Foucault, Michel. "Afterword: The Subject and Power." In *Michel Foucault: Beyond Structuralism and Hermeneutics,* 2nd ed., edited by H. C. Dreyfus and P. Rabinow. Chicago: University of Chicago Press. 1983.

Gelles, Richard J., and C. Cornell. *Intimate Violence in Families.* Beverly Hills: Sage, 1985.

Goffman, Erving. *Stigma: Notes on the Management of Spoiled Identity.* New York: Simon and Schuster, 1963.

Gonzalez de la Rocha, Mercedes. "*The Erosion of a Survival Model: Urban Household Responses to Persistent Poverty.*" Papers on Latin America #47. Columbia University: Institute of Latin American and Iberian Studies, 1999.

———. "The Urban Family and Poverty in Latin America." *Latin American Perspectives* 22 (1995): 12–31.

Griffen, Peter, and Alejandra Cox Edwards. "Rates of Return to Education in Brazil: Do Labor Market Conditions Matter?" *Economics of Education Review* 12 (1993):245–255.

Gross, Daniel R., and Barbara A. Underwood. "Technological Change and Caloric Costs." *American Anthropologist* 73, no. 3 (1971): 725–740.

Hanchard, M. ed. *Racial Politics in Contemporary Brazil.* Durham: Duke University Press, 1999.

Harris, Marvin, and Eric B. Ross. 1987. *Death, Sex and Fertility: Population Regulation in Preindustrial and Developing Societies*. New York: Columbia University Press, 1987.

Hecht, Tobias. *At Home in the Street*. Cambridge: Cambridge University Press, 1998.

Hendrick, Harry. "Constructions and Reconstructions of British Childhood: An Interpretative Survey, 1800 to the Present." In *Constructing and Reconstructing Childhood*, edited by Allison James and Alan Prout. New York: Falmer Press, 1990.

Huggins, Martha K., and Jessica Macturk. *Armed and Dangerous*. 2000. http://www.Americas.org.

Instituto de Estudos da Cidadania (IDEC). *A Producao de Informacoes sobre a Crianca e o Adolescente no Estado de Pernambuco*. Olinda-PE, Brasil: Instituto de Estudos da Cidadania (IDEC), April 1995.

Inglis, Ruth. *Sins of the Fathers: a Study of the Physical and Emotional Abuse of Children*. New York: St. Martin's Press, 1978.

Jenks, Chris. *Childhood*. New York: Routledge, 1996.

Jobling, M. "Child Abuse: The Historical and Social Context." In *Child Abuse: A Study Text*, edited by V. Carver. Milton Keynes: Open University, 1978.

Kempe, Ruth S., and C. Henry Kempe. *Child Abuse*. Cambridge, Mass.: Harvard University Press, 1978.

Kleinman, Arthur, Veena Das, and Margaret Lock. *Social Suffering*. Berkeley: University of California Press, 1997.

Kuznesof, Elizabeth. "The Puzzling Contradictions of Child Labor, Unemployment, and Education in Brazil." *Journal of Family History* 23, no.3 (1998): 225–239.

La Fontaine, Jean. "An Anthropological Perspective on Children in Social Worlds." In *Children of Social Worlds: Development in a Social Context*, edited by Martin Richards and Paul Light, 10–30. Cambridge: Polity Press, 1986.

Lewis, Jane. "Anxieties About the Family and the Relationships Between Parents, Children and the State in Twentieth Century England." In *Children of Social Worlds*, edited by Martin Richards and Paul Lights. Cambridge: Polity Press, 1986.

Lomnitz, L. "The Social and Economic organization of a Mexican Shanty Town." In *Urbanization of the Third World*, edited by Josef Gugler. New York: Oxford University Press, 1988.

Mendelievich, Elias, ed. *Children at Work*. Geneva: ILO, 1979.

Myers, W. "Urban Working Children: A Comparison of Four Surveys from South America." *International labor Review* 128, no. 3 (1989): 321–335.

Nasaw, David. *Children of the City: At Work and at Play*. New York: Doubleday, 1985.

Nieuwenhuys, Olga. *Children's Lifeworlds: Gender, Welfare and Labor in the Developing world*. New York: Routledge, 1994.

Nugent, Stephen. "Verging on the Marginal: Modern Amazonian Peasantries." In *Lilies of the Field: Marginal People Who Live for the Moment*, edited by Sophie Day, Evthymios Papataxiarchis, and Michael Stewart. University College, London: Westview Press, 1999.

Pearse, Andrew. "Some Characteristics of Urbanization in the City of Rio e Janeiro." In *Urbanization in Latin America*, edited by Philp M. Hauser. New York: Columbia University Press, 1961.

Pereira Lima, Paulo. "Sem Fronteiras." *Servico Brasileiro de Justica e Paz no. 331*, 30 December 1998.

Perlman, J. *The Myth of Marginality*. Berkeley: University of California Press, 1976.

Pinheiro, Paulo Sergio. "Democracies without Citizenship." *NACLA Report on the*

Americas, September/October, 1996.

Price, Barbara. Conversation with Author, 1996.

Rizzini, Irena, Irma Rizzini, Monica Munoz-Vegaas, and Lidia Galeano. "Brazil: A New Concept of Childhood." In *Urban Children in Distress: Global Predicament and Innovative Strategies*, edited by Cristina Saznton-Blanc. Yverdon, Switzerland: Gordon and Breach/UNICEF-ICDC, 1994.

Scheper-Hughes, Nancy. *Death Without Weeping: The Violence of Everyday Life in Brazil*. Berkeley: University of California Press, 1992.

————."Small Wars and Invisible Genocides." *Social Science and Medicine* 43, no. 5 (1996): 889–900. [Quoting Richet C. N. "Medicales sur le Campt de Buchenwalf en 1944–1945," Bulletin Acad. Med. (Paris) 129 (1945): 377–388].

————. "The Global Traffic in Human Organs." *Current Anthropology* 41, no. 2 (2000): 191–224.

SEJUP (Servico Brasileiro de Justica e Paz) No. 247, 3 October, 1996.

Sheridan, Ann. *Michel Foucault: The Will to Truth*. London: Tavistock, 1980.

Stack, Carol. *All Our Kin*. New York: Harper and Row, 1974.

Steedman, Carolyn. *Childhood, Culture and Class in Britain: Margaret Macmillan 1860–1931*. London: Virago, 1990.

Stepan, Nancy. "The Hour of Eugenics." In *Race Gender and Nation in Latin America*, 76–79. Ithaca, N.Y.: Cornell University Press, 1991.

Suttles, Gerald D. *The Social Construction of Communities*. Chicago: University of Chicago Press, 1972.

Turner, Patricia A. *I Heard It Through the Grapevine: Rumor in African-American Culture*. Berkeley: University of California Press, 1993.

Van Esterik, Peggy. Intra-Family Food Distribution: Its Relevance for Maternal and Child Nutrition. Determinants of Young Child Feeding and Their Implications for Nutritional Surveillance." In *Cornell International Nutrition Monograph No. 14*, 77–149. Ithaca: Cornell University Program in International Nutrition, 1985.

Ward, C. *The Child in the City*. London: The Architectural Press Ltd, 1977.

————."Unemployment in Sao Paulo." *News from Brazil* no. 347, 22 April 1999.

Wiesel, Elie. *One Generation After New York*. New York: Random House, 1970.

"Youth Detention Centers Totally Inadequate." *Servico Brasileiro de Justica e Paz (SEJEP)* no. 251, 6 November 1996.

Chapter 3

John, Genie, and Kaspar: Some Recent Scientific Uses of Wildness, Confinement, and Abuse

Adriana S. Benzaquén

Stories of *wild children* are stories of encounters with strange children in unusual circumstances. Since the early seventeenth century such stories have been recorded, circulated, and reproduced, mainly (but not exclusively) in Europe and North America, not simply as myths, legends, or good tabloid copy but as occurrences deserving serious scrutiny by scientists and scholars of diverse persuasions and fields of expertise. Wild children have had a privileged role as objects of knowledge in Western human science. The knowledge produced about them in different disciplines (anthropology, psychology, psychiatry, pedagogy, linguistics, sociology) has indelibly affected the social and institutional practices directed at all children and contributed to the shaping and reshaping of the modern understanding of "the child" (Benzaquén 1999).

Stories of wild children illustrate the process of production of knowledge about people as well as how this process affects the lives of both the knowers and known (Hacking 1986, 1995). The evidence on each wild child makes up a "case study" (Foucault [1973] 1975). As a discourse or set of discourses about a subject, the case study constitutes the intersection of discourse and subjectivity. Through inscription (and multiple reinscriptions) in discourse, the wild child becomes a figure for understanding and imagining "the child" and for measuring the distance between, on the one hand, normal child and extraordinary child and, on the other, child and adult. The accounts of wild children, often fragmentary and incomplete, are nevertheless a rich source of information about other lives, experiences, ideas, and knowledge. Reading the evidence requires a dialogic engagement with the many voices inscribed therein (Bakhtin 1986) and an acknowledgment of the almost complete absence from the record of the voices of the children themselves.

Since the early decades of the twentieth century, the class "wild (or feral) child" has included not only children believed to have been raised by animals or to have spent a long time alone "in the wild" (the traditional associations) but also children who suffered extreme isolation through confinement, abuse, and neglect. Scientists greeted wild children as the silent holders of answers to crucial questions about human development, heredity and environment, language acquisition, and the rehabilitation and education of "defective" or "abnormal" children. Wild children's "wildness" increasingly came to signify strangeness or extreme isolation in general.

In this chapter I examine three recent scientific uses of wild children. I first consider the efforts, achievements, and failures of the scientific teams formed around two very different "wild children" discovered in the 1970s: John of Burundi and Genie of Los Angeles. Then I consider a recent reinterpretation of the story of Kaspar Hauser (found in 1828 in Nuremberg) from the perspective of abuse and neglect. In each case, I argue, wild children became the targets of a longstanding, deep-seated will to know and the unwitting receptacles of adult anxieties and projections.[1]

John of Burundi

From 1926 (when the story made the Western headlines) until the early 1940s, two "wolf girls" of India, named Amala and Kamala by the Reverend J. A. L. Singh, the man who claimed to have rescued and reeducated them until their deaths (in 1921 and 1929, respectively), attracted the attention of a notable group of Anglo-American scientists. The case sparked heated scholarly debates, prompting investigations intended to determine whether Singh's testimony was accurate and reliable as well as studies relating Amala and Kamala to earlier cases of wild and wolf children (Singh and Zingg 1942). Why were Western scientists interested in such a case? As pointed out by William F. Ogburn (a sociologist at Florida State University, who in 1959 carried out an on-site inquiry to prove or disprove the story; Ogburn and Bose 1959), science is "greatly interested in children reared by wolves, for the light the study of them may throw on the new formulation of the old problem of heredity versus environment, which is concerned with the role of culture and of the learning process in shaping personality" (Ogburn 1959, 450). The most salient implication of the stories seemed to be the primacy of environment in human development. For most scientists, what the wolf child's brutalized condition made visible was that without a human environment human children do not become fully human (Stratton 1932).

A significant exception was the celebrated developmental psychologist and pediatrician Arnold Gesell (1941), who rendered the story of Kamala in maturational rather than environmentalist terms. Besides, Gesell did not expect Kamala to shed light on something he did not yet know. Rather, he deployed his expert knowledge of child development to explain *her*, and in so doing to confirm and extend his theory of child development (Benzaquén 2001). Other scientists, such as Wayne Dennis (1941, 1951) and Eric Lenneberg (1966), cautioned that the stories of animal-raised children should not be used as evidence for *any* social or psychological theory. Nothing certain could be learned from these cases, first, because the accumulated evidence was inadequate, and second, because even if they were authentic, the many unknown factors in the children's early history made it impossible to ascertain why some of them lived longer than others.

In a later encounter between two Western scientists—psycholinguist Harlan Lane of Northeastern University and psychiatrist Richard Pillard of Boston University—and an exotic, animal-raised, brutalized wild child, the scientists once again understood their task as a search for new (and crucial) knowledge. Lane had just published his famous book on Victor of Aveyron (Lane 1976) when his former thesis director, B. F. Skinner, forwarded him an article that appeared on April 11, 1976, in the *Johannesburg Sunday Times* informing that a wild boy had been found living with monkeys in Burundi. Like many others before him, on hearing about the discovery of a wild child, Lane was elated: "I dared not believe my good fortune if the story was true. The last time a child had been found who was unquestionably feral...was almost two centuries ago, in 1799" (Lane and Pillard 1978, 4). The wild boy of Burundi (who had been named John after John the Baptist) reminded Lane of Victor: "John had so many of Victor's traits that they were practically twins." Indeed, Lane reasoned that the similarities attested to the story's authenticity: "Surely David Barritt, the journalist who'd written the story, hadn't studied the case of the Wild Boy of Aveyron and then attributed to John the hallmarks of Victor's upbringing" (12). (Interestingly, Lane did not mention the many animal-raised children who had been in the news beginning in the 1850s.) After establishing a connection between John and Victor, Lane went on to transpose what in his view had been the consequences of the encounter between Victor and Jean-Marc-Gaspard Itard (the young physician who undertook Victor's medico-pedagogical treatment in the first years of the nineteenth century) to the potential encounter between John and contemporary researchers. Victor had been found "at the dawn of psychology and psychiatry, when no one knew how to study a deviant child, much less treat one," and yet "mankind had reaped immeasurable benefits from his capture"; "Modern methods for educating the deaf, the retarded, and the normal preschool child arose directly out of the efforts to train him" (4). If that was the case then, what could not be expected of an encounter with a wild child now?

> How much more could we now learn with the tools of modern psychology and medicine! How much more could we discover about what it means to grow up in society from this terrible experiment of nature, which chance had designed and which science could exploit? And how much more could we contribute to the education of handicapped children everywhere by undertaking the training of this latest, and perhaps last, wild child, raised in the forests utterly cut off from society (5).

Lane construed John as an accidental case of what Roger Shattuck ([1980] 1994) calls the "forbidden experiment." On his own admission, Lane knew nothing about Burundi (Lane and Pillard 1978, 4), but this did not diminish his certainty that going in search of his own wild child was the right thing to do.

In an outstanding display of energy and enthusiasm, Lane and his friend Pillard organized a trip to Burundi (1978). Lane regretted the fact that the boy's caretakers were teaching him things (to the detriment of his valuable wildness): "All this teaching the boy is well and good, but it is obliterating the traces of life in the wild and is destroying his value as a scientific discovery" (11). While planning the trip, Lane and Pillard considered what they would do "with the jungle boy once we reached him" (18). The strategy they decided on was twofold: first, they would follow Itard's model, that is, they would study John by rehabilitating him, laying emphasis on sensory training (reconceived as behavior modification); second, they would have John admitted to the Shriver Center of the Fernald School for retarded children in Boston. They would take advantage of everything that had been discovered and invented since Itard's time, in the belief that their greater knowledge and more sophisticated techniques would lead not only to a more successful training of the wild child but also to more valuable knowledge being extracted from him.

For Lane and Pillard, John, as a wild child, was also a generic child, a child who could stand for every child. His cultural context, social and geopolitical position, ethnic and linguistic background, and previous personal experiences did not have to be taken into account except as obstacles to the identification of what was important about him. The two American researchers presumed that, in the name of science, they could turn up in Burundi—a country which a few weeks earlier they did not know existed—obtain unrestricted access to the child and all the resources they needed (vehicles, assistants, translators, medical facilities), quickly ascertain what John really was, and if he proved to be a true wild child and therefore worthy of study (and expenditure), take him to the United States to give him back his language and his full humanity while making him reveal his secrets.

The new wild boy attracted the attention and interest of the North American media and the public—just as Kamala and Amala and so many others had before. But this time some people voiced the opinion that the boy was probably better off in the woods and should not have been captured in the first place. Lane received a letter from three students who were "very disturbed to hear about your rehabilitation program for a child who appears to be living in an environment suited to his needs":

> Science seems to have no place or understanding for this boy and we feel it is very inhumane to bring him back to a society based on our needs. Is it not possible to observe him in his environment? What are your motives for this "experiment"? (Lane and Pillard 1978, 42)

A university professor was concerned as well: "My concern is why you feel the child, after reportedly living in the jungle for four years, *needs* to be 'rehabilitated'. Why are 'civilized' people always trying to 'civilize' the 'uncivilized'? Why do we feel civilization is so much better?" (Lane and Pillard 1978, 42). Lane was "saddened" by these responses: "What a grim commentary on our lives! Is life in the home sweet home so punitive that we prefer life in isolation, scrabbling for food, fleeing predators, neither giving nor receiving love?" (43). Lane may be missing the point, however; some people's refusal to share his enthusiasm and hopes may not simply have sprung from a misguided idealization of the wild child's wild life. In question were precisely the scientists' quest and efforts: Their knowledge might not suffice to offer the boy a better life, and the knowledge they thought they would extract from him might not be so valuable after all.

Lane and Pillard (1978) went to great lengths to appear open, humane, enlightened, and good-humored, but their words and actions betray the overconfidence of the Western scientific researcher (and the white American male) storming into the unsuspecting Third World, which, like the wild child, functions as the underside of civilization and development. On their way to Burundi, Lane and Pillard stopped for a few days in Paris to get visas:

> I [Lane] have had a decade-old love affair with Paris and somewhat briefer affairs with a few of its inhabitants. It is the most cultured city in the world, the apogee of what society has to offer in literature, art, architecture, food, dress. The city of Hugo, Toulouse-Lautrec, Escoffier, Cardin—what better point of departure for studying a wild child utterly cut off from society? (27)

Bujumbura, Burundi's capital, seemed to them "more like a giant village than a city, and after Paris, it was hard not to find it decrepit and filthy" (84). Doctors, diplomats, and other Westerners living in Bujumbura warned Lane and Pillard that John might not be what the newspaper report suggested: "What constitutes a good account of events is not the same in Burundi as it is in America" (88). When they met John at the Gitega orphanage, they were not particularly impressed by the "strange-looking child" (99), but they dutifully proceeded to examine him and subject him to many tests, first at the orphanage, then at the Bujumbura hospital, and finally in Nairobi, Kenya.[2] In parallel, Lane and Pillard made inquiries about the boy's history and found out that John, whose real name was Balthazar Nsanzerugeze, had spent his early years in orphanages and mental institutions, not with monkeys. The testing continued anyway, and after a consultation with all the participating physicians in Nairobi, John/Balthazar was diagnosed: autism and profound retardation, for which there was no treatment.

Pillard pondered "John's future": in a large institution in the United States, like the Fernald School, "where the stress of working is so great that some wards have an almost complete turnover of personnel every few months," nobody would "know John or learn to care about him"; at the Gitega orphanage "he has Sister Nestor and Petronille, who adore him, and a stable environment." Pillard concluded: "Given that there is nothing we can offer in the way of treatment, I feel more than satisfied with the care he will get in his native land" (173). Is it too cynical to think instead that Balthazar, a poor African boy, was valueless to science and thus not worth the effort and expense? That had John's "wildness" been established, the loving care and stable environment his native land could offer him would have had to give way to the technically and scientifically superior options found in the United States, however anonymous and loveless?

Having accomplished their mission, Lane and Pillard left Burundi less than ten days after their arrival.[3] They had fun; they would do it all over again, but still the discovery that John was not a feral child was a disappointment: "The opportunity for science would have been magnificent...it would have been the find of the century" (179–80). The disappointments multiply, but the dream that science will, one day, succeed in wrenching the wild child's secrets seems to live on. As for John, he died at the orphanage in 1985 (Lane 1992, 35).

Genie of Los Angeles

Genie was about the richest source of information you can imagine...There were kinds of questions that I felt she might shed light on.
—Jay Shurley (Rymer 1993, 43)

It may be that "exotic" wild and animal-raised children are just too unwieldy. They may be too elusive, too far away from the centers of scientific knowledge-production, too radically other to be studied properly. Their wildness, taken to be the outcome of a long period spent in isolation or with animals in the wild (forest, jungle, desert, mountain), is what makes them valuable and desirable, but by its very nature cannot be controlled or observed. It is not difficult to understand the excitement of a group of scientists when they discovered a child who appeared to be the perfect surrogate for the slippery wild child. This was Genie; she was found *right here*, in our midst, and her early life held no mysteries, it seemed, since for more than a decade she had almost never left the confines of a room in her parents' home in Temple City, California. Tempted by a child who promised to reveal the secrets associated with the wild child while bearing, in her being and history, none of the wild child's uncertainty, the scientists transformed the confined child into a full-fledged wild child.

Susan Wiley, renamed Genie by the scientists, was first in the news in November 1970, when the *Los Angeles Times* reported that her parents had been accused of keeping her "a virtual prisoner since infancy" and were subsequently arrested. Although the girl was thirteen years old, she was unable to talk or walk, she wore diapers, and she did not know the most basic life skills (e.g., chewing). Her limbs and muscles were partially atrophied as a result of the physical restraint and inadequate activity. The Wileys' neighbors, who remembered having seen the girl playing in the yard now and then, thought she was mentally retarded. Genie was admitted to Childrens Hospital, Los Angeles, for malnutrition.[4] She was without question a horribly abused and extremely deprived child, but at first glance there was nothing "wild" or "savage" about her. Her case was undoubtedly a police matter, and various kinds of medical, educational, and welfare professionals would have to exert great ingenuity to find the way to rehabilitate her, heal her physical and psychological wounds, and restore her to a fuller life. But the doctors and researchers who became involved in Genie's life were not satisfied with helping her—they wanted to study her.

For people in general, Genie was an object of pity; for the scientists, she was an object of knowledge. The name the scientists gave her, Genie, indeed marked her transition from an abused child to a more extraordinary object of study. As a matter of fact, this was not the first time that scientists had related confined children and wild children. Still, while in earlier studies confined children had been *compared* to wild and animal-raised children to highlight variations in the condition produced by, and long-term effects of, different degrees and kinds of isolation (e.g., Davis 1940, 1947), none of these children was, like Genie, *identified* as a wild child from the very start. Because the scientists construed Genie as a wild child, hence singularly valuable and precious, in her case research was given primacy over all other considerations.

Genie was "rescued" from her parents' home and admitted to Childrens Hospital at the same time that François Truffaut's film *The Wild Child* (on Victor of Aveyron) opened in Los Angeles. When in May 1971 the professionals and scientists in charge of Genie's case organized a conference to make decisions concerning how she would be treated and the specific type of research that would be carried out on her, they arranged to have a private screening of *The Wild Child*. The scientists identified Genie with Victor. "It was awe-inspiring to us because here was the first case that had been documented in any scientific way," said Howard Hansen, head of the psychiatry division of Childrens Hospital (Garmon 1994). Jay Shurley, professor of psychiatry and behavioral science at the University of Oklahoma and an expert in social isolation, remarked that "[t]he impact on the whole group was stunning…All of us saw in the movie what we were prepared to see to confirm our biases" (Rymer 1993, 57). The label "wild child," borrowed from Truffaut's film, stuck permanently to Genie. She is characterized as a wild child in the scientific publications resulting from the research on her and in the more recent critical investigations of her story.

What was there in common between Victor and Genie? Both children were unable to speak and had not had the chance to learn many skills deemed essential to humanity and socialization; both had had little contact with other human beings and little exposure to human culture of any kind. But there the commonalities end. In one case isolation took place in the wild, the outdoors, nature; in the other, in a locked room in a house on the outskirts of one of the largest cities of the most developed country in the world. One child lived a rugged and dangerous but eventful existence; the other endured ongoing neglect and abuse at the hands of a small group of people. Victor experienced maximum autonomy and freedom, unrestricted mobility, and the pressing need to provide for his own subsistence; Genie suffered total physical restriction, helplessness, and dependence, in a bare human-made environment. And yet both children were considered to be epistemologically equivalent, in the sense that, for the scientists, the study of Genie and what could be learned from her were equivalent to the study of Victor. Susan Curtiss, then a doctoral student in linguistics and later a professor at the University of California at Los Angeles, also linked Genie to Victor (and, by extension, herself to Itard): "The Wild Boy of Aveyron died over a century ago, but another adolescent who affords us equally rich opportunities for study has been discovered in our own time: Genie" (1977, xii). History appeared to be repeating itself, to the scientists' great fortune. Victor had made Itard famous; what professional and personal rewards would Genie not have in store for whoever was there, ready to grab them?

Genie's newly-conferred status as a wild child had several consequences. She was portrayed as other wild children usually are: "Genie was unsocialized, primitive, hardly human" (Curtiss 1977, 9). The recent change in her life (from the locked room to the hospital) was represented using the language of discovery: "Genie was admitted into the hospital for extreme malnutrition. She had been discovered, at last" (7). Like John and other wild children, she was interpreted as a guilt-free version of the forbidden experiment. Experimental deprivation on humans "ha[s] not and cannot be carried out for obvious reasons," Curtiss maintains, but "[e]xperiments in nature" (which she defines as "tragic alterations of the normal human condition not purposefully induced by the scientific community") offer a valid alternative for scientists wishing to verify various hypotheses about human development. For Curtiss, "Genie is such an experiment in nature" (208). (A simple objection to this claim would be that even if the *scientists* did not "purposefully induce" Genie's "tragic alterations," neither did *nature*.) The more the forbidden experiment is seen as a moral evil, the more the study of the wild child finds some justification in the idea that, by forcing the child to reveal her secrets, the scientist is at least giving some meaning to her unspeakable suffering and deprivation.

In this way, the study of the wild child, however intense or intrusive, is not seen as exploitation but as a duty, even more so when none of the previous cases known in the literature had been properly and systematically studied: "The case of Genie assumes even more importance, then, because of its unique character, and because, from the time she emerged from isolation, a team of psychologists, psychiatrists, neurologists, and linguists have been working with this amazing child" (Curtiss et al. 1974, 529). What did the researchers expect to learn from Genie? Since Genie, like other isolated and wild children, was "in a retarded state of develop-ment," they wanted to know "whether a child so deprived can 'catch up' wholly or in part" (Fromkin et al. 1974, 83). The research focused on language acquisition. It was determined that Genie had not yet acquired language and "was faced with learning her first language when she was 13 years, 7 months of age" (Curtiss 1977, 11). The main question was whether language could be acquired at such a late age. Genie's learning (or not learning) would bear on Lenneberg's critical-age hypothesis (Curtiss et al. 1974, 542) and on the relation between language acquisition and brain lateralization (Curtiss 1977, xii).

Curtiss (1977) presents and analyzes the linguistic data collected between 1971 and 1975 while Genie lived with David Rigler, professor at the University of Southern California and chief psychologist in the psychiatry division of Childrens Hospital, and his wife Marilyn.[5] The account leaves no doubt that Genie was incessantly and exhaustively tested but says little about the educational or therapeutic means that may have been employed with her. Curtiss's stated purpose was to watch the emergence of Genie's innate linguistic structures; her task was not strictly to maximize Genie's learning but to ascertain whether linguistic development could resume after a prolonged period of abnormal deprivation. Since the linguistic research carried out on Genie concerned the resumption of suspended but normal development, the scientists had to defend the claim that Genie's "retardation" had been caused by isolation and deprivation only and discard two other possibilities: that she was congenitally retarded (Fromkin et al. 1974, 85) and that her early experiences left lasting psychological scars that affected her development. The scientists granted that Genie's early experiences had been distressing, but they did not view them as *traumatic*, that is, at the root of her present deficiencies.[6] After several years of work with Genie, Curtiss concluded that the girl had been acquiring language:

> We must keep in mind that Genie's speech is rule-governed behavior, and that from a finite set of arbitrary linguistic elements she can and does create novel utterances that theoretically know no upper bound. These are the aspects of human language that set it apart from all other animal communication systems. Therefore, abnormalities notwithstanding, in the most fundamental and critical respects, Genie has language (1977, 204).

Curtiss took this as demonstration that a first language could be acquired, at least to a certain degree, beyond the critical period. From the comparison between Genie's "far from normal" language and that of normal children, Curtiss drew implications pertinent to the processes of language acquisition and lateralization in general.

All in all, Curtiss's book conveyed an unwarrantedly optimistic sense of Genie's progress:

> My work with Genie continues, and Genie continues to change, becoming a fuller person, realizing more of her human potential. By the time this work is read, she may have developed far beyond what is described here. That is my hope—that I will not be able to keep up with her, that she will have the last word (42).

By the time the book was published, it was clear that Genie's life had taken a dramatic turn for the worse and that her "development" had suffered in consequence, but for some reason Curtiss chose not to refer to what happened to Genie after 1975. The National Institute of Mental Health, which had been funding the research, rejected David Rigler's application for an extension of the grant, and the Riglers gave Genie up (Rymer 1993, 140–45).

In the summer of 1975 Genie went to live with her mother (in the same house where she had been confined until the end of 1970), but the latter found life with her daughter too difficult and gave her up as well. From then on Genie lived in a succession of foster homes; she was mistreated and physically abused again; she lost the few skills she had learned at the Hospital and at the Riglers', and she stopped speaking altogether. John Miner, a lawyer and since 1972 Genie's legal guardian, saw her some time after she left the Riglers' home, noting that "[h]er regression was just overwhelming" (Rymer 1993, 154). Then, a nasty fight erupted between the scientists and Genie's mother. In October 1979 Genie's mother filed a suit against the scientists and hid Genie away.

In the end, and contrary to Curtiss's hopes, Genie did not realize more of her human potential, nor did she have the last word. The scientists involved in her life proved not only unable to rehabilitate her fully despite their advanced knowledge and techniques but also unable to provide her with a stable and loving environment in which even if she never got to be talkative or smart she might have been at least happy and safe from further abuse and neglect. Science could neither save Genie nor justify her earlier suffering: What was learned from or through her was much less, and much less certain, than what the scientists had expected (Jones 1995).

What makes Genie's story unbearably sad is not just her confined and deprived childhood but what happened to her after her purported discovery. It is, however, still too close to us, and perhaps more time has to pass before we may be able to understand it, to unravel the conflicts of interest and desire that traverse it, and to judge its protagonists. In a letter he sent Jean Butler in 1971 (responding to her accusations that the scientists were exploiting Genie), Rigler wrote:

> If this child can be assisted to develop in cognitive, linguistic and social, and other areas, this provides useful information regarding the critical role of early experience which is of potential benefit to other deprived children. The research interest inherently rests upon successful achievement of rehabilitative efforts. The research goals thus coincide with [Genie's] own welfare and happiness…This child is not for sale, but in our view and in the view of funding agencies, knowledge obtained from study of this unique child is important knowledge to be employed for humanitarian purposes (Rymer 1993, 58, 104).

The scientists may have been sincere in their belief that their study of Genie was predicated on her successful recovery. But Genie was never allowed or encouraged to form genuine and lasting relations with people who cared for her as a person. Besides, even if they had wanted to make binding decisions regarding her life and future, the scientists did not have the power to do so. For better or worse, their actions and claims were open to challenge—by other scientists, the funding agencies, Genie's mother, the welfare services. Genie was utterly helpless, but the adults around her, all of whom wanted something from her and had much to say about her, were either powerless or unwilling to give her what she most needed.[7]

Unlike Lane and Pillard, who did not see John as a particularly appealing child, the scientists who surrounded Genie emphasized how attractive and special she was. James Kent, psychologist at Childrens

Hospital and child abuse expert, declares: "I was captivated by her... she had a personal quality that seemed to elicit rescue fantasies...She was very special to me...I was very attached to her." And David Rigler: "I think everybody who came in contact with her was attracted to her. She had a quality of somehow connecting with people which developed more and more but was present really from the start" (Garmon 1994). Curtiss waxes sentimental when reminiscing about Genie:

> She was fragile, and beautiful, almost haunting, and so I was pulled, I was very drawn to her, even though I was nervous and had no idea in many respects what to expect...I could tell as all of us could just looking at her that there was a lot to Genie, and that what we had to do was to make sure we gave her opportunities to express, find a way to take what was latent and express it or somehow then, you know, acquire it, because the potential just seemed so great (Garmon 1994).

Curtiss, who wrote that Genie "has enriched my life beyond measure" (1977, xvi), stated: "I would pay a lot of money to see her" (Rymer 1993, 219). When read against the reality of Genie's life, such proclamations ring hollow. In court, Miner stated (in defense of the Riglers): "It was a matter of my not being able to understand how people not related to this child could undergo what, in fact, she was subjecting them to in terms of the strain on the household" (Rymer 1993, 181). In the attempt to justify why the Riglers gave Genie up, what Miner conjures up is no longer the beautiful, attractive, and uncannily communicative "genie" but a child so unsocialized and demanding that it is hard to see why anyone not "related" to her would want to put up with her. Miner's words at least sound sincere. Curtiss's too, when for a moment she suspends her effusiveness and simply admits, "I was really at the right place at the right time" (Garmon 1994).

Kaspar Hauser

The scientists who studied Genie turned to history to back their view that she was a "wild child" worthy of scientific attention. This being the case, it is curious that they did not relate Genie to Kaspar Hauser, the confined child whose fame matches (if not surpasses) Victor's. Kaspar mysteriously appeared in May 1828 in Nuremberg. He could barely say a few words whose meaning he did not understand, had trouble walking, and looked frightfully confused. Kaspar, like Genie, had spent most of his childhood in a kind of prison, where his basic needs were met but he could not move, had no contact with other people and almost no sensory stimulation. Yet unlike Genie, Kaspar "recovered" almost completely.

After baffling details about his childhood and rumors about his true identity began to circulate, Kaspar was attacked and wounded by a stranger. In December 1833 he was stabbed a second time in the chest at the Court Garden in Ansbach, again by a stranger, and died a few days later (Feuerbach 1833; Simon 1978). Kaspar's story brought about controversy (especially between those who believed he was the legitimate heir of Baden kidnapped to change the line of succession to the throne and those who alleged that he was a only clever liar and impostor) and lent itself to many different uses. When the class "wild child" was expanded to include cases of isolation through confinement, Kaspar began to be routinely included in lists of wild children (Singh and Zingg 1942; Benzaquén 1999).

The respected jurist Anselm von Feuerbach (1833) called the crime committed against Kaspar a crime against the life of the soul, or "partial soul murder." According to Leonard Shengold (who, like Feuerbach, discarded any connection between Kaspar and wild children), soul murder is "primarily a crime committed against children" (1978, 457). The past few decades have witnessed a sweeping reconceptualization of crimes against children, now increasingly included in the broad category of child abuse (Hacking 1991). As part of this trend, not only was Kaspar's story rendered in terms of child abuse, but, through it, the other stories of wild children were reconsidered as well. To be sure, in all accounts of wild children the underlying implication is that, if the child was not accidentally lost, some crime was committed against him or her— abandonment, neglect, physical harm, murder attempt. Still, in the many readings and uses of the stories since the seventeenth century, the central concerns were the children's wild life, strangeness, and transformation; the fact that they were victims of some sort was taken for granted but seldom placed in the foreground. In contrast, in Jeffrey Moussaieff Masson's *Lost Prince* (1996), child abuse is seen as the key factor in Kaspar's story, and by extension in the stories of wild children in general.[8]

Masson offers *Lost Prince* as a groundbreaking, up-to-the-minute scholarly work on Kaspar Hauser, "Europe's most famous wild child" (1996, 3); however, for all intents and purposes the book exists solely as a platform for the reiteration of Masson's favorite ideas. For him, Kaspar's entire story is an extended illustration of abuse: "Regardless of who he really was, here is somebody who was abused" (54). Since, as Steven Marcus (1996) holds, apart from the minority of commentators who protest that Kaspar was an impostor nobody has ever denied or glossed over the fact that he was a victim of others' crimes, why does Masson appear to be disclosing an explosive secret along the lines of his *The Assault on Truth* (1984)? And since Kaspar was the victim of many crimes, beginning with his kidnapping as a baby and ending with his murder in 1833, what specifically is Masson referring to when he claims that Kaspar was abused? Masson insinuates that the *real* (deep, momentous) abuse experienced by Kaspar was not his imprisoned childhood, his isolation and deprivation, or his murder, but some concealed (repressed) incident of sexual molestation perpetrated by an unidentified abuser. What makes Masson think Kaspar may have been sexually abused is precisely the absence of any record or memory. Although Kaspar did not remember his imprisonment as an unhappy time, especially in relation to the discomforts and pain he endured later, Masson begs to differ:

> To speak of his "happiness" in his dungeon may have only been a device that enabled Kaspar to speak of how unhappy he was made later. He suffered a different series of deprivations once he was discovered, and different kinds of trauma, and it is always difficult to compare traumas. Moreover, we do not know the full extent of what Kaspar Hauser suffered in his dungeon (60).

The implicit meaning of Masson's words is that *Kaspar* did not know the full extent of his suffering in the dungeon and his contemporaries did not *want* to know (nor do *we*), but *Masson* knows: Kaspar was sexually abused.

All the evidence he can adduce to back this supposition is indirect. First, he wields the recent data on the "reality and pervasiveness of childhood sexual abuse" (1996, 55) and findings relative to the forgetting of memories of this abuse, which "cannot be ignored if we wish to consider the possibility that Kaspar Hauser did not remember everything that had happened to him while he was in prison" (61–62). (But why would anyone else "wish" to consider that possibility?) Second, he points to Freud's "omitted" letters, which demonstrate that sexual abuse of children was rampant in his day: "the climate in German-speaking countries" in Freud's time "was no doubt the same as it had been some sixty years earlier at the time of the case of Kaspar Hauser" (58). Third, he reminds us that nobody *asked* Kaspar if he had been sexually abused, and what better indication that a giant conspiracy of silence was in place? Finally, Masson descries an unmistakable sign in the rumors that the relationship between Kaspar and his would-be protector Lord Stanhope was tinged with homosexual undertones: "Children who have been abused are often targeted later in life by older men who recognize the symptoms and take advantage of the vulnerability that is the legacy of sexual abuse" (228, n.

139). The contemporary debate on recovered/false ₁memories is, in Masson's view, "directly relevant" to Kaspar's story.

It would be pure speculation to suggest what may have happened to him in his dungeon. We have almost no clues, and Kaspar Hauser himself provided few data. He remembered almost nothing. However, he did recover some memories, and might, over the course of a normal lifetime, have recovered many more. He was never given the opportunity (63).

This is then another way in which Kaspar was "abused": uncaring people, like those who now refuse to believe the recovered memories of abuse victims, never gave him "the opportunity" to remember what had *really* happened to him. Or, perhaps, he *did* remember what he had been through but chose not to talk about it: "Is it not possible that there are no general rules, and that each person will react differently, some forgetting permanently, some repressing, some remembering permanently, and some simply unwilling to talk about it, with anyone? How can we be certain that Kaspar Hauser did not belong to this latter group, and simply elected not to talk about certain things he knew?" (64) How can we, indeed.

Masson construes the "fascination" with Kaspar's story as "a hidden acknowledgment of the reality of child abuse":

> Kaspar Hauser was abused by his parents or parent when he was abandoned as a newborn infant; abused by whoever kept him for twelve or fourteen or sixteen years locked in a dungeon; abused by Lord Stanhope for political reasons; abused by an unknown assailant who tried to murder him for reasons that could only have been obscure to Kaspar Hauser; and finally abused by the man who stabbed him to death (65).

His reasoning is two-sided. On the one hand, Masson can confidently assert that Kaspar was abused (both in the broadest sense of abuse, exemplified in the passage just cited, and in the narrower sense of sexual molestation) because he knows that a great majority of children (if not all) are abused. Thus, instead of furnishing positive evidence that Kaspar was abused, he challenges *us* (the unbelievers, the abusers) to prove otherwise. On the other hand, Masson conceives Kaspar as a figure with whom all abuse victims can identify: "The abuse to which Kaspar Hauser was subjected, while practically unique, is not really so foreign to our own experiences. Therein, I believe, lies the key to the endless fascination" (70–71). Ultimately, Masson is not drawn to Kaspar as a real person who once lived and suffered in the world; instead, he sees in Kaspar a representation of himself: "The modern reader (could it have been any different for readers in the last century), including myself, desperately wants to reconstruct Kaspar

Hauser's actual feelings, memories, and experiences while he was in his dungeon. We want to know if this story is true and, if so, what it says about human nature—that is, what does it mean for us?" (66)

Masson's appropriation of Kaspar is a consummate instance of assimilation of "the child" to the adult self (Steedman 1995): "To think about the suffering of Kaspar Hauser and the mysteriousness of it is to think about our own past suffering in an attempt to undo that mystery, recover our past, and emerge scathed but whole" (68). Masson insists: "Something about his perplexity in the face of the world touches a chord deep in everyone: *Kaspar Hauser, c'est moi!*" (71) (I am Kaspar Hauser). In Masson's hands, the confined wild child disappears, collapsed into *myself* as a child. Kaspar Hauser allows Masson to feel really sorry for himself.[9]

Other Children

In the stories of John and Genie and in Masson's reinterpretation of Kaspar's story we see how adults, scientists, and professionals in the field of childhood in particular manifest interest in wild children; how they strive to authenticate or dismiss their stories; and endeavor, directly or indirectly, to extract knowledge from them and interpret their cases in light of various theories and frameworks. Still, my contention is that from the outcome of the modern adult's engagement with the wild child we learn more about her or his dreams and aspirations than about either the individual wild child in question or "the child."

The scientists who went in search of or by chance encountered John and Genie expected to find in them "natural" or accidental (thus morally acceptable) instances of the forbidden experiment—the desire or actual attempt, recorded in legend and/or history at least as far back as ancient Egypt, to raise children in isolation with the purpose of finding out the answer to some empirical question deemed to be extremely important. Presumed to be inordinately valuable and inordinately rare, the wild child is a privileged object of knowledge that, scientists believe, or hope, may hold the key to human nature, reveal the secret of human development by solving the old question of nature and nurture once and for all, and lead to the invention of wonderful techniques and treatments to ameliorate various kinds of abnormalities and defects in *other* children who are not themselves wild but *abnormal* or in need of normalizing interventions. But the many actual children who at different times have been labeled "wild child"—temporarily (like John) or permanently (like

Genie)—have never been able to deliver on the hoped-for promise scientists identify with the fascinating and desirable "wild child." They turn out not to be *real* wild children (whatever that is taken to mean) after all, or they simply do not answer any questions.

Wild children awaken but also frustrate the desire to know, marking the insuperable limit of certain scientific aspirations. But scientists persevere. And when a "live" wild child is not available to be directly observed, examined, measured, tested, and transformed, there are still the texts that recount the stories from the past. The scientific value of wild children lies as well in the fact that the stories survive the children, and, as Masson's reinterpretation of Kaspar's essential truth shows, they are open to re-diagnosis and reinterpretation by later writers wielding newer, better theories of development, and more accurate accounts of "the child."

The irony is that the fate of most wild children—visible unhappiness, lack of recovery, early deaths—raises significant questions regarding our individual and collective capacity, and willingness, to console and restore *any* lost, abandoned, or suffering child. The meanings and uses of wild children in the twentieth century, some of which I have explored in this chapter, suggest that our excessive preoccupation with the wild child, rather than a manifestation of our putative concern with children, is in many ways a preoccupation with *ourselves*.

NOTES

1   For recent approaches to the place of childhood in the emotional and imaginative life of adults in the West, see Steedman 1995; James, Jenks, and Prout 1998; and Kincaid 1998.

2   John resisted the procedures but was overpowered by the adults: "Hold him. You two take the right. You two take his shoulders. (Harlan and I took his head.) Now, go! We quickly get six films [X-rays]. It is possible to overpower a ten-year-old boy; it's a question of numbers" (125).

3   They were sad to leave the new friends they made in Burundi, but not John/Balthazar: "At that moment he didn't enter our minds. If you think that is strange or hardhearted, you must try to understand the difference between caring for a friend and caring for a patient...Balthazar was our patient and our puzzle; we had done what we could for and with him; we felt complete" (176–77).

4   "Girl, 13, Prisoner Since Infancy, Deputies Charge; Parents Jailed" (*Los Angeles Times* [*LAT*], 17 November 1970); "Mystery Shrouds Home of Alleged Child Prisoner" (*LAT*, 18 November); and "Father Accused of Keeping His Daughter a Prisoner Ends Life" (*LAT*, 21 November). Summaries of Genie's story may be found in Curtiss et al. 1974; Fromkin et al. 1974; and Curtiss 1977. The use of the name "Genie" was meant to protect the girl's identity and privacy while "captur[ing], to a small measure, the fact that she emerged into human society past childhood, having existed previously as something other than fully human" (Curtiss 1977, xii). For more detailed and complex accounts, see Rymer 1993, and Garmon 1994.

5   In 1971, Jean Butler, a special educator at the rehabilitation center of Childrens Hospital, applied to become Genie's foster parent. Butler's application was rejected and Genie moved in with the Riglers. The scientists resented Butler's disapproval of their research, which in her view was exhausting Genie. Butler died in 1988, and thus her own version of the events could not be included in Rymer's and Garmon's accounts.

6   For Curtiss, "emotion has little to do" with language acquisition: "Certainly Genie was an emotionally disturbed child, but that wasn't relevant to my concerns" (Rymer 1993, 121).

7   The scientists most closely involved with Genie reacted strongly to what they saw as "misrepresentations" in Rymer 1993 and Angier 1993. See Fromkin's and Curtiss's messages to the Linguist e-mail list (http://linguistlist.org, April 1992 and May 1993). Also see Rigler 1993.

8   Masson relates Kaspar to the other wild children (39–41) and inserts a separate appendix on wolf children (203–209). See Money 1992 for another take on Kaspar as a victim of abuse, in which he stresses physical brutality and neglect rather than sexual molestation.

9   Kincaid's critique of the uses of the "story" of child molesting in the contemporary adult imagination is to the point, as is his injunction to replace it by a new story, in which "[t]he focus would be on the responsibilities of the present and on the grown-up. No more inner children! We are adults and need to tend to the children out-side" (1998, 292).

REFERENCES

Angier, Natalie. "'Stopit!' She Said. 'No More!'" Review of *Genie*, by Russ Rymer. *New York Times Book Review*, 25 April 1993, 12.

Bakhtin, Mikhail. *Speech Genres and Other Late Essays.* Translated by Vern W. McGee. Edited by C. Emerson and M. Holquist. Austin: University of Texas Press, 1986.

Benzaquén, Adriana S. "Encounters with Wild Children: Childhood, Knowledge, and Otherness." Ph.D. diss., York University, 1999.

———. "Kamala of Midnapore and Arnold Gesell's *Wolf Child and Human Child*: Reconciling the Extraordinary and the Normal." *History of Psychology* 4, no. 1 (2001): 59–78.

Curtiss, Susan. *Genie: A Psycholinguistic Study of a Modern-Day "Wild Child."* New York: Academic Press, 1977.

Curtiss, Susan, Victoria Fromkin, Stephen Krashen, David Rigler, and Marilyn Rigler. "The Linguistic Development of Genie." *Language* 50, no. 3 (1974): 528–554.

Davis, Kingsley. "Extreme Social Isolation of a Child." *American Journal of Sociology* 45 (1940): 554–565.

———. "Final Note on a Case of Extreme Isolation." *American Journal of Sociology* 52 (1947): 432–437.

Dennis, Wayne. "The Significance of Feral Man." *American Journal of Psychology* 54 (1941): 425–432.

———. "A Further Analysis of Reports of Wild Children." *Child Development* 22, no. 2 (1951): 153–158.

Feuerbach, Anselm von. *Caspar Hauser: An Account of an Individual Kept in a Dungeon, Separated from All Communication with the World, from Early Childhood to About the Age of Seventeen.* Translated from the German. London: Simpkin and Marshall, 1833.

Foucault, Michel, ed. *I, Pierre Rivière, Having Slaughtered My Mother, My Sister, and My Brother...: A Case of Parricide in the 19th Century.* Translated by Frank Jellinek. New York: Pantheon, [1973] 1975.

Fromkin, Victoria, Stephen Krashen, Susan Curtiss, David Rigler, and Marilyn Rigler. "The Development of Language in Genie: A Case of Language Acquisition Beyond the 'Critical Period.'" *Brain and Language* 1 (1974): 81–107.

Garmon, Linda. *Secret of the Wild Child.* Boston: WGBH-TV, 1994. *Nova* documentary.

Gesell, Arnold. *Wolf Child and Human Child: Being a Narrative Interpretation of the Life History of Kamala, the Wolf Girl.* New York: Harper and Brothers, 1941.

Hacking, Ian. "Making Up "People." In *Reconstructing Individualism: Autonomy, Individuality, and the Self in Western Thought*, edited by T. Heller et al. Stanford, Calif.: Stanford University Press, 1986.

———. "The Making and Molding of Child Abuse." *Critical Inquiry* 17 (1991): 253–288.

———. "The Looping Effects of Human Kinds." In *Causal Cognition: A Multidisciplinary Debate*, edited by D. Sperber, D. Premack, and A. James Premack. Oxford: Clarendon, 1995.

James, Allison, Chris Jenks, and Alan Prout. *Theorizing Childhood.* Cambridge: Polity, 1998.

Jones, Peter E. "Contradictions and Unanswered Questions in the Genie Case: A Fresh Look at the Linguistic Evidence." *Language and Communication* 15, no. 3 (1995): 261–280.

Kincaid, James R. *Erotic Innocence: The Culture of Child Molesting.* Durham: Duke University Press, 1998.

Lane, Harlan. *The Wild Boy of Aveyron.* Cambridge: Harvard University Press, 1976.

————. *The Mask of Benevolence: Disabling the Deaf Community.* New York: Knopf, 1992.

Lane, Harlan and Richard Pillard. *The Wild Boy of Burundi: A Study of an Outcast Child.* New York: Random House, 1978.

Lenneberg, Eric H. "The Natural History of Language." In *The Genesis of Language: A Psycholinguistic Approach*, edited by F. Smith and G. A. Miller. Cambridge: M.I.T. Press, 1966.

Marcus, Steven. "The Wild Boy of Nuremberg." Review of *Lost Prince*, by Jeffrey Moussaieff Masson. *New York Times Book Review*, 31 March 1996, 11–12.

Masson, Jeffrey Moussaieff. *The Assault on Truth: Freud's Suppression of the Seduction Theory.* New York: Farrar, Straus and Giroux, 1984.

————, ed. and trans. *Lost Prince: The Unsolved Mystery of Kaspar Hauser.* New York: Free Press, 1996.

Money, John. *The Kaspar Hauser Syndrome of "Psychosocial Dwarfism": Deficient Statural, Intellectual, and Social Growth Induced by Child Abuse.* Buffalo: Prometheus, 1992.

Ogburn, William Fielding. "The Wolf Boy of Agra." *American Journal of Sociology* 64 (1959): 449–454.

Ogburn, William Fielding, and Nirmal K. Bose. "On the Trail of the Wolf-Children." *Genetic Psychology Monographs* 60 (1959): 117–193.

Rigler, David. Letter to the Editor of the *New York Times Book Review*, 13 June 1993, 35.

Rymer, Russ. *Genie: A Scientific Tragedy.* New York: HarperPerennial, 1993.

Shattuck, Roger. *The Forbidden Experiment: The Story of the Wild Boy of Aveyron.* With a new introduction by D. K. Candland. New York: Kodansha, [1980] 1994.

Shengold, Leonard. "Kaspar Hauser and Soul Murder: A Study of Deprivation." *International Review of Psycho-Analysis* 5 (1978): 457–476.

Simon, Nicole. "Kaspar Hauser's Recovery and Autopsy: A Perspective on Neurological and Sociological Requirements for Language Development." *Journal of Autism and Childhood Schizophrenia* 8, no. 2 (1978): 209–217.

Singh, J. A. L., and Robert M. Zingg. *Wolf-Children and Feral Man.* New York: Harper, 1942.

Steedman, Carolyn. *Strange Dislocations: Childhood and the Idea of Human Interiority, 1780–1930.* Cambridge: Harvard University Press, 1995.

Stratton, G. M. "Jungle Children." *Proceedings of the Western Psychological Association.* Berkeley, Calif., June 21–23, 1932, 596–597.

PART TWO

The Child in and of History

Chapter 4

"Long Rows of Short Graves": Sentimentality, Science, and Child-Saving in the Construction of the Intellectually Precocious Child, 1870–1925

Roblyn Rawlins

In 1885, popular domestic advice writer Marion Harland concluded her chapter on "The Precocious Baby" in *Common Sense in the Nursery* with the following appeal to mothers:

> [The reader] need not tax [her] memory to invoke the vision of the long rows of short graves stretching away in mournful perspective, wherein lie the faded "flowers" of countless families. "Our best and brightest!" The phrase is not trite read through the tears of her who sets it before the ownerless name of the child for whom her hopes were highest, through whom came her sharpest grief. If by resolute self-denial of maternal vanity, right judgement of values and results, and submissive co-operation with natural laws, she can keep "best" the casket that holds the "brightest" jewel, our Precocious Baby's mother will conserve her own peace of mind and protect her darling against himself (73–74).

Some children, now generally referred to as "gifted," exhibit intellectual abilities beyond those expected for their age: They learn earlier, faster, and better than their peers. The social meaning of such early intellectual development in children shifted dramatically over the course of the nineteenth and twentieth centuries in the United States. The mid to late twentieth century white, middle-class, North American gaze sees or "makes," in Foucault's sense (1977), a gifted child who invokes optimistic visions of progress and prosperity.[1] The similarly situated gaze of the late nineteenth and early twentieth centuries saw a precocious child full of potential pathologies, one who invoked visions of long rows of short graves. This transformation is illustrated by the following pair of quotes, separated by a century, warning of the dangers of parental mistreatment of such children:

> There is also a great mistake committed by hot-bed efforts to stimulate the minds of children to precocious maturity...their bodily powers are soon exhausted; they become diseased and nervous; their brain is liable to inflammation, and a premature death often ensues! (Kirwan 1858, 34)

> By this refusal to recognize special gifts, we have wasted and dissipated, driven into apathy or schizophrenia, uncounted numbers of gifted children (Pressey 1955, 15).

For this project, I examined approximately 150 child-rearing advice manuals published in the United States between 1860 and 1930. While the pitfalls of a direct reading from prescription to practice are well-known (Mechling 1975), my focus here is not on biographical children or parents but rather on childhood as a discursive product and a sociopolitical project. Child-rearing prescriptive literatures codify, circulate, and reinforce knowledge created through the discourses of childhood and in the process offer access to those discourses. It is important to bear in mind that such texts were written by and for the middle classes and as such constitute middle-class accounts of childhood.

Whereas mid to late twentieth-century advisors urged parents to encourage the full development of the gifts of their "special child," nineteenth and early twentieth century authors of prescriptive literature urged them to severely limit the precocious child's engagement in mental activities. Over one-third of the nearly 100 child-rearing books in this study published before 1910 explicitly warned mothers[2] of the dangers of precocity: it was not unusual for an entire chapter to be devoted to this purpose (e.g., Burrell 1909; Harland 1885; Hopkinson 1863; Le Favre 1890). By contrast, in the 1910s, only 2 of the 26 manuals studied deprecated intellectual precocity and one commended it (Stoner 1914).[3] None of the 25 child-rearing manuals of the 1920s studied made any mention of intellectual precocity.

In the late nineteenth and early twentieth century prescriptive literature, the precocious child is represented as vulnerable to a range of problems or pathologies: self-consciousness with a concomitant loss of the simplicity and naturalness attributed to proper childhood; physical weakness, disease, and decline; overstimulation and eventual depletion of mental and nervous energy, sometimes to the point of insanity; and finally, the specter of death as the result of the depletion of bodily and mental strength. According to child-rearing experts, precocious children had unattractive personality traits: They were shy, peevish, and smart (Tomes 1875, 233); dreamy and peculiar (Hopkinson 1863); vain, self-conscious, and spoiled (Zenner 1912), and characterized by "intellectual hypocrisy and shallow culture" (Allen 1907, 111). These negative attitudes toward precocious children begin to appear in child-rearing advice as early as 1855. The author of *Joy and Care: A Friendly Book for Young Mothers* relates an anecdote in which a young husband, holding his three-month-old child for the first time, remarks to his wife, "I hope he is not going to be precocious; I cannot endure precocious children" (Tuthill 1855, 44).

While condemnation of precocity was the dominant nineteenth-century approach to early intellectual development in children, the discourse of precocity as pathology coexisted with tendencies among middle-class parents to valorize their children's accomplishments (Blumin 1985). Biographies and children's books held up the prodigious childhood of eminent men as exemplary (e.g., John Stuart Mill's early mastery of Latin). Nineteenth-century middle-class strategies to consolidate or improve family class position typically included encouraging the intellectual development of children, especially boys (Ryan 1981). The condemnation of intellectual precocity in child-rearing prescriptions written by and for the urban middle classes stands in opposition to these achievement-oriented tendencies. This study seeks to understand this seeming contradiction by uncovering how and why early intellectual development in children came to be constructed as pathological precocity in middle-class child-rearing prescriptions.

As the discourses of precocity or of giftedness gained dominance over opposing discourses, experts and advocates prescribed, promulgated, and ultimately produced child-rearing and educational practices that constituted precocity/giftedness and constructed the precocious or gifted child.[4] Working in a Foucauldian vein, I consider a particular construction of childhood and the child to be the consequence of the intersection of epistemology and ontology, historical context, and the interests and actions of adult social groups. I argue that romantic, sentimental views of childhood, together with scientific accounts of childhood emphasizing age-graded developmentalism and the scientific discourses of sexual and mental hygiene, form the epistemological and ontological bases for the construction of the precocious child. The great engines of social change in the Gilded and Progressive ages— industrialization, urbanization, and immigration—form the historical context within which the discourse of precocity as pathology gained dominance in the American imagination of the intellectually talented child. The interests and actions of the newly emerging middle classes are integral to this construction of the precocious child.

Intertextualities: Sentimentality and Science

The approach I take here is to examine relevant intertextualities or the ways in which concepts generated by a particular discourse depend on and reshape the meaning of concepts generated by earlier or contemporaneous discourses. A prominent discourse, such as that of pathological precocity, is naturalized and embedded within culture to such an extent that the basic propositions on which the discourse is built are assumed and therefore rarely explicitly articulated. Instead, these basic propositions are to be found by examining intertextualities, i.e., looking for their more explicit articulation within related discursive fields, such as those found in the discourses of romantic and sentimental childhood, scientific accounts of childhood emphasizing age-related developmental stages, and the scientific discourses of mental and sexual hygiene. In the mixture of sentimentality and scientism that made up nineteenth-century domestic advice literature, scientific knowledge about child development linked with romantic conceptions of the natural child to construct the pathologically precocious child.

Sentimental Culture
The concept of a natural childhood, first articulated in romantic accounts of childhood, was a key element in the development of a sentimental view of children and childhood and underlies nineteenth century middle-class disapproval of precocity. Romanticism, which idealized both childhood and nature, was arguably the dominant Western bourgeois perspective on childhood by the end of the nineteenth-century (Cox 1996; Cunningham 1995; Macleod 1998). Children were seen not only as closer to nature than adults but superior to them in important ways and

able to exert a "purifying, divine influence" on adults (Le Favre 1890, 22). Children retained qualities of freshness, innocence, simplicity, and naturalness that seemed to some adults lamentably missing in the modern, urban world of nineteenth-century America (Lears 1981). This notion was concisely expressed in a 1907 education text: "The child is the purest, truest thing in the world" (Burbank 1907, 25).

In these anti-Modernist, sentimental formulations, childhood was constructed as a space in which those qualities of nature could be preserved and protected from urbanization and industrialization. Romantic child-rearing prescriptions from Rousseau's didactic novel *Emile* (1762) onward posited that adult intervention between children and nature as well as adult subversion of the ways of nature led to poor outcomes in child-rearing. A representative quote comes from Newton Riddell's *Child Culture*: "It is unwise to crowd the education of a child beyond the natural order of growth. Thousands are injured by premature development" (1902, 95).

How were the concepts of childhood, and of children articulated in the discourses of romantic and sentimental childhood, actually employed in constructing precocity as pathology? Based on my readings of child-rearing manuals with explicit prohibitions of precocity, this is accomplished primarily through the use of the metaphor of child-rearing as horticulture and through calls for mothers to protect the simplicity and naturalness of their child's lives.

The metaphor of child-rearing as horticulture was popular among authors of late nineteenth- and early twentieth-century prescriptive literature. Luther Burbank entitled his 1907 educational text *The Training of the Human Plant*. Child-rearing as horticulture or cultivation incorporates both nurture and control/constraint. The horticultural metaphor proscribes parental efforts to stimulate, encourage, or even tolerate intellectual precocity in their children by equating such activity with the unnatural forcing of flowering plants to early bloom. "Early ripe, early rotten" was a popular aphorism of the day (Guthrie 1921). Such attempts to grow "hothouse flowers" were doomed to failure as subversions of the ways of nature, the importance of which romantic as well as scientific accounts of childhood development had firmly established. The dangers of forcing growth on children or other creatures of nature is taken as self-evident in this literature. In the words of Marion Harland: "Where is the horticulturalist so dull that he does not see to it that his rose-slips are rooted before he lets them bloom?" (1885, 70)

A simple life for children, simplicity in children, and adherence to nature's ways are all equated in this literature. As Kirwan (1858) wrote of childhood: "The more simple and natural, the better; the more artificial and complex, the worse." Simplicity was "the greatest charm of childhood" (Hopkinson 1863, 9). Mothers are warned that encouraging intellectual precocity in their children will ruin their simple nature. The display of children's precocity "spoils" the child's simplicity and leads to self-consciousness, an oft-cited vice in the nineteenth-century child-rearing prescriptive literature. As Hopkinson writes, "Anything is better than self-consciousness in a child" (1863, 144).

The discourse of pathological precocity with its image of the self-conscious, sometimes vain, always "un-natural" precocious child began with the romantic formulation of the innocent child living in a simple, natural world of childhood. This concept was then reshaped into prohibitions against allowing or encouraging children to display their intellectual abilities or "clever pranks" (Grinnell 1894, 108) to adults because such performances would lead to "the evil consequences of vanity and of a deadening self-consciousness" (Hirsch 1896, 167). If children fell under the gaze of the adult world through such performances, the simple, innocent child living in the romantic world of childhood, separated from adults and allied with nature, would become corrupt and self-conscious.

Concern with authenticity and sincerity, prevalent among urban middle-class Americans in the nineteenth-century (Haltunnen 1982; Kasson 1990), is another aspect of sentimental culture that figures in this story. These concerns arose in the context of increasing social and geographical mobility and increased contact with strangers in the urban metropolis. Genteel Americans sought means whereby they could identify and safely associate with one another without the encroachment of "confidence men" or "strivers" who represented themselves as legitimate members of the middle classes but in fact were not. Etiquette advisors elaborated codes of self-presentation for various social situations ("manners") and offered semiotic schemes promising to enable the middle-class reader to decode others' presentations and perceive their authentic social positions (Haltunnen 1982; Kasson 1990). In the child-rearing manuals analyzed here, sincerity, truthfulness, and lack of pretense are often held up as virtues to be encouraged in children. Children should never "play a part," and "genuineness" and "sincerity" are essential components of the proper child's character (Mosher 1898, 133).

The adjudication of authentic precocity in children was necessary to allay nineteenth-century middle-class concerns over sincerity and authenticity. According to one advice writer, "[p]arents are especially urged to resist the tendency of thinking all their geese are swans" (Tomes 1875). Contemporaneous scientific accounts of precocity engaged in constructing true versus false types of precocity. For example, Beard (1881) distinguishes between normal and morbid precocity: "There is in some children a petty and morbid smartness that is sometimes mistaken for precocity, but which in truth does not deserve that distinction" (262). In the absence of objective means of judging whether or not a child was truly precocious, early intellectual development in a child presented classificatory difficulties to nineteenth-century middle-class parents who were already particularly concerned with sincerity and authenticity.

Science

Ideas adopted from science were also deployed in the discourse of precocity as pathology. The authors of nineteenth- and early twentieth-century child-rearing manuals tended to cite established authorities in related discursive fields as a means of situating and asserting their own expertise. The names and reputations of American psychologist G. Stanley Hall and the German educator Friedrich Froebel were regularly invoked in this manner. Hall's Child Study movement and Froebel's educational system (implemented as the kindergarten) were the major scientific projects on children of the period,[5] so it is unsurprising that child-rearing experts would incorporate their work into the prescriptive literature. What is particularly interesting here is the extent to which Hall's and Froebel's accounts of childhood give scientific credence to concerns about pathologically precocious children.

Both Hall and Froebel sought to discover natural laws of childhood development and urged that these developmental processes be allowed to proceed without adult intervention. Hall's theory of evolutionary recapitulation, which posited that the individual child developed through stages equivalent to the evolution of the race, meant that children must be protected from the demands of modern adult life while in their "premodern" stages. Froebel's gifts and songs (simple playthings presented in an age-graded fashion) were based on the notion that children must learn and develop according to the rules of childhood, not those of the adult world (Shapiro 1983). Hall in particular was explicit about hoping to "find true norms against the tendencies to precocity in home, school, church, and civilization generally" (Hall 1904, 1:viii).

The prescriptive developmentalism of child study and of progressive educational theory in general provided a scientific rationale for the increasingly precise age grading that shaped middle-class children's lives in the late nineteenth and early twentieth centuries (Chudacoff 1989). Age grading in the schools is of particular importance in understanding perceptions of intellectual precocity. Before the 1870s, most American students did not attend formally age-graded schools: students started school at different ages and were likely to attend irregularly. As a result, age was a poor predictor of a child's level of academic skills or knowledge. By the 1870s, formally structured age-graded schools were established throughout the United States. According to an 1898 mother's book, "The basis of modern education is the unfolding of the child's powers in proportion to his age" (Mosher 1898, 67). According to Chudacoff (1989), these schools, which consisted of eight grades beginning at age six, "eliminated incidences and tolerance of precocity" (36) because their structure made it more difficult for children to enter elementary school, secondary school, or college before they had reached the institutionally stipulated ages.

For some writers on education, even delaying school entrance until age six was insufficient protection against precocity. Zenner stated, "There is a prevailing opinion that our schools burden the child's mind more than is good for it" (1912, 36). Burbank, for whom the "curse of modern child-life in America is over-education" (1907, 17), argued that children should not begin school until age ten. Sauer, a physician, concurred: "Children at the present day are too highly educated—their brains are over-taxed and thus weakened...Remember, the brain must have but very little work until the child is seven years old" (1891, 490).

Scientific accounts of childhood development thus provided another basis for concern about children whose intellectual abilities outstripped age norms. Yet far greater dangers than overeducation awaited the hapless child whose mother failed to protect him from his own precocity,[6] including the depletion of the child's mental and physical strength, the disruption of a harmonious relationship between his mental, physical, and emotional faculties; the derangement of his mind and the development of insanity; and an ultimately death. What accounts for those "long rows of short graves" (Harland 1885) filled with the bodies of precocious children? How did early intellectual development in children become linked with mental and physical pathologies?[7]

Intellectual precocity was linked with somatic consequences through the incorporation of concepts generated by the contemporaneous scientific discourses of sexual and mental hygiene. One particular thread of sexual hygiene discourse—anti-masturbation—generated concepts that shaped concepts of precocity. Child-rearing prescriptions, as well as advice literature directed to youths themselves, in the early decades of the twentieth century urgently prohibited masturbation (Kimmel 1996). Anti-masturbation texts resonate with anti-precocity texts: authors of pres-criptive literature use much the same language in discussing both vices and represent precocious children as vulnerable to much the same mental and physical dangers as masturbating children. Psychologist William Hirsch explicitly associated precocity with masturbation in 1896 when he wrote "[p]recocious children are particularly liable to a too early awakening of sexual impulses and other sexual irregularities which require the closest attention from their tutors" (153).

The similarity between the anti-masturbation and anti-precocity discourses of childhood arises from their common adoption of a model articulated in yet a third contemporaneous discourse, that known as "mental hygiene" (Warner 1906). The discourse of mental hygiene articulated a model of bodily economy that not only underpinned the "spermatic economy" formulation of anti-masturbation discourses (Barker-Benfield 1976) and the discourse of mental hygiene, but also provided a basis for explication of the dangers that early intellectual development holds for children. Unlike the sentimental cultural bases for anti-precocity beliefs, this argument against precocity was made on the basis of protecting the health of individual children rather than the maintenance of desirable qualities in childhood generally.

The bodily economy model assumes that there exists a finite amount of physical, mental, and emotional energy in a given individual and that any expenditure of one type of energy necessitates a draw-down in the other two. A harmonious relationship between the intellect, the emotions, and the body is therefore imperative. The utility of this model in organizing arguments about masturbation, the physical consequences for "brain workers" of both sexes, and the special dangers of intellectual work (including education) for women is familiar to scholars of nineteenth-century medicine, early Freudianism (i.e., Freud's use of the hydraulic metaphor), mind/body relations, and gender.

Medical authorities working in the field of mental hygiene warned of the dangers of overworked brains (e.g., S. Weir Mitchell 1874), American nervousness (e.g., George Beard 1881), and neurasthenia, synonymous disorders caused by overstimulation of the brain or nervous system at the expense of physical well-being. The bodily economy model was the predominant approach to early intellectual development in the writings of turn-of-the-century medical and psychological experts. In *Abnormal Children (Nervous, Mischievous, Precocious, and Backward)*, Dr. Bernard Hollander (1916) wrote, "Another cause of nervous disorder is the premature awakening and strain of the intellectual powers at the cost of the emotions of childish simplicity and bodily health" (28). Precocity in these formulations implies a pathologically unbalanced development of intellectual, physical, and emotional capabilities.

Child-rearing experts drew upon physicians and, to a lesser extent, psychologists as they translated the concept of bodily economy into prescriptions for the care of children. Carrica Le Favre summarized the model for the readers of *Mother's Help and Child's Friend*: "[T]he vital energies pertaining to the body, and generated in the organism, by which this growth and development are affected, are absolutely limited, says Dr. O. B. Moss. Nor can the same forces be employed at the same time for two distinct ends" (1890, 128). Early intellectual development, therefore, posed direct dangers to children's emotional and physical well-being. As Robert Tomes wrote in the popular *Bazaar Book of the Household*, "It is true of the brain, as of every other organ of the human body, that it can not be developed, especially at an early age, by a preponderating exercise without a proportionate weakening of the rest" (1875, 234).

In light of turn-of-the-century concerns about the feminization of boys (Kimmel 1996), potential enfeeblement of boys' bodies provoked much concern among child-rearing experts. Parents were urged to strive for equal development of their child's body and brain via exercise, fresh air, and avoidance of too much or too strenuous intellectual work. For ordinary, non-precocious children, it was thought that the physical problems related to overstudy were unlikely if the child took sufficient exercise (Newcomb 1872). Some child-rearing experts went so far as to suggest that if children exhibited tendencies toward precociousness, parents should delay teaching them to read or should otherwise retard their intellectual development in order to encourage their physical development. For example, Saur, a physician, advised in 1891 that "It behooves a parent, if her son is precocious, to restrain him" (500) by sending him to a quiet country place, delaying his entrance to school, and giving "directions to the teacher that he is not on any account to tax his intellect" (501).

Adult Actors and Interests in Historical Context: Class Distinction and Progressive-Era Child-Saving

The successful construction of precocity as pathology rested on the adoption and reshaping of metaphors, concepts, and models derived from the discourses of romanticism and sexual/mental hygiene and from contemporaneous scientific accounts of childhood development. What accounts for the palatability or ease of acceptance of this understanding of early intellectual development in children among the authors and readers of late nineteenth/early twentieth century prescriptive literature? The urban, native-born, rising middle classes made up the audience for the prescriptive literature in which this approach to early intellectual development was promulgated. Child-rearing advice books were explicitly addressed to the middle classes and produced by middle-class experts carving out new areas of professional jurisdiction (Abbott 1988) for themselves. Nineteenth-century middle-class strategies to consolidate or improve family class position typically included encouraging the intellectual development of children, especially boys (Ryan 1981), yet intellectual *precocity* was deprecated in these middle-class child-rearing prescriptions.

Intellectual precocity, I argue, is condemned in these middle-class formulations primarily because it was conflated with other types of precocity—economic, sexual, and social—that were the focus of late nineteenth century and Progressive-Era child-saving efforts (Boyer 1978; Cunningham 1995; Gordon 1988; Kett 1978; Platt 1969) and that figured large in middle class projects of social distinction. As the nineteenth-century progressed, the new middle classes consolidated their domestic ideology of the bourgeois home, which included clear boundaries of age and gender (Mintz and Kellogg 1988). The middle-class ideal restricted women and children to the private sphere, delimiting their public roles especially in the labor market and in the urban metropolis. The romantic, sentimental view of children—i.e., as protected by, dependent on, and separated from adults—was at odds with the precocious development of children's public roles as laboring, sexual, and social beings. The fear of precocity in children was so entrenched that charges of child neglect could be brought against parents by Progressive-Era child-protection agencies for allowing children to participate in adult conversation and social activity (Gordon 1988, 121).

Progressive-Era social reformers, many of them mothers themselves, sought to extend the white middle-class model of a protected, dependent childhood to urban children of all classes and races: These were the child-savers. [8] The entry of working-class children into urban labor markets particularly threatened the ideal of protected childhood (Zelizer 1985), as did the so-called "street Arabs," children whose public presence on urban streets violated the ideal of the domesticated, dependent child to such an extent that they seemed to middle-class observers to lack all of the accepted characteristics of proper children (Cunningham 1991). As a dependent childhood protected from the adult world became normative for the middle classes and psychological theories of child development became popular, children engaging in what were now considered exclusively adult economic, sexual, or social behaviors were seen as precocious and abnormal: These children might not really be children at all. Martha Mosher expresses this ideal in her publication *Child Culture in the Home: A Book for Mothers* (1898): "If a child's first right is to its mother, its next is that it may be a child" (51).

Many of the child-savers' reform efforts sought to impose sanctions on children engaging in adult behaviors and to disqualify youth from the benefit of adult privileges (Kett 1971; Platt 1969). The regulation of age floors for attendance at theaters, dance halls, and saloons sought to rescue children from social situations that threatened their dependency (Platt 1969). Progressive social reformers sought to enforce the middle-class construction of children and prevent precocity by legislating age rules for school leaving, restricting child labor, imposing evening curfews for youth, and legislating the age of consent for sexual relations (Chudacoff 1989; Kett 1978). Juvenile courts were developed and empowered to impose sanctions on premature independence (Platt 1969). By the early 1900s, many states had passed compulsory school-attendance laws and minimum-age labor laws, successfully prolonging the period of dependence for many children (Chudacoff 1989; Zelizer 1985).

Farm children and urban poor or working-class children, however, were unable and often unwilling (Nasaw 1985) to conform to middle-class norms of dependence: Working-class children persisted in engaging in behaviors increasingly seen as exclusively adult, especially the working adult. Middle-class observers were particularly anxious about the large numbers of working children, such as newsies and bootblacks, who could be seen at all hours in the streets of Progressive-Era American cities engaging in the kinds of social, economic, and sexual pursuits now defined as appropriate only for adults (Nasaw 1985). These forms of precocity were commonly associated with the poor, the working class, and immigrants. The precocious child, as a result, became an instrument through which the new middle classes asserted their social distinction and distinguished their children from others. Sentimental culture had infused the notion of childhood protected from adult economic, social, sexual, and intellectual pursuits with moral superiority. Middle-class families sought to assert their social distinction and moral superiority by protecting their children from the dangers posed by all forms of precocious behavior. By the end of the Progressive Era, precocious children who failed to conform to the middle-class ideal of dependent childhood were considered deviant, pathological, and sometimes criminal.

The discourse of intellectual precocity as pathology is part of the nineteenth-century middle-class projects for sheltered childhood and social distinction. The precocious child, the child who transgresses in some way the boundaries between the prolonged dependency of childhood and the independence of adult life, became the target of significant American reform efforts during the late nineteenth and early twentieth centuries. Intellectual precocity, already made suspect by sentimental views of childhood and contemporary scientific accounts of childhood and the mind/body relationship, was swept along with other forms of precocity in the rising tide of reform.

From Intellectual Precocity as Pathology to Giftedness as Virtue

As Leslie Margolin points out in his fine study, *Goodness Personified: The Emergence of Gifted Children* (1994), the social category of "gifted children" symbolizing virtue and health emerged in the first few decades of the twentieth century together with the gifted child expert. Margolin argues that these experts articulated a model of the gifted child that incorporated the values and ideals of white upper middle class, a child that embodied goodness in this particular cultural context (1994, 32).[9] I contend that the existence of the gifted child expert and hence the gifted child was predicated on the institutionalization of intelligence testing. The intelligence test, invented in 1908 by Alfred Binet in France and standardized, age-normed, and published for use in American schools by Lewis Terman by 1916 (Grinder 1985), was the means whereby precocious children were at last established by scientific authorities as objects amenable to measurement, scientific study, and authentication. By 1925 Terman was able to report the results of an initial study of 1,470 scientifically adjudicated "gifted" children, which he defined as children whose IQs tested at 135 and above (Terman 1925).

Intelligence testing offered objective, scientific assessment as a way to confer authenticity on notions of "early" and "late" intellectual development.[10] Henceforth, child-rearing experts would advise parents who suspected their child of possessing unusual intellectual abilities to obtain intelligence testing immediately and, if their child was indeed thus identified as gifted, to have recourse to gifted child experts for child-rearing prescriptions. In her 1924 advice book to mothers, Ruth Wilson begins a chapter on the use of intelligence and other psychological tests with the invitation, "Let us look into other ways by which psychologists can help a mother to recognize latent possibilities of talent in her children and so assist such hidden forces to develop" (81). She concludes by suggesting that "where the mother needs most help from the psychologist is to learn how to distinguish between the precocious child who is a budding genius and the precocious child who is only 'a small, fatigued grown-up,' who has been compared to the early-riser, 'conceited all the forenoon of life, stupid and uninteresting all the afternoon' " (Wilson 1924, 84).

Objective measurement of children's intelligence through IQ testing not only established the authenticity of early intellectual development but also helped to decouple intellectual precocity from economic, social, or sexual precocity. Intelligence testing constructs early intellectual development as a *capability* or a potential, a very different thing from the adult *behaviors* of working or having sex that economically or sexually precocious children engage in. All children possess the potential of adult behaviors: Capabilities such as intelligence quotients do not transgress the boundary between adulthood and childhood integral to the maintenance of sheltered childhood in the same way that precocious behavior does. Precocious children are now understood to include only those who engage in activities considered appropriate for adults only. Children with high intelligence quotients are no longer included in this definition of precocity.

Over the course of the twentieth century, discourse of giftedness as virtue gained dominance over the discourse of precocity as pathology. Discourses, however, rarely achieve complete dominance. The discourse of precocity as pathology lingers on, generating comic or tragic images of peculiar "eggheads," "brainiacs," and four-year-olds desperately cramming for entrance tests to elite kindergartens. Nor has the sentimental ideal of sheltered childhood gone away: Sternberg and Davidson dedicated their 1986 book *Conceptions of Giftedness* to "the parents and teachers of the world who have done their best to nurture the gifts of their children, without making these children give up their childhoods" (x).

Children continue to lack the power to represent themselves to adult publics and thus are subject to the constitutive social practices and discursive maneuverings of adults. This inquiry into the social meaning of early intellectual development in children has demonstrated how the same child has had very different social meanings. The late–nineteenth-century gaze made that child into a pathologically precocious child who symbolized loss of innocence and threatened the destruction of childhood as a haven from the adult world of urban industrial society. The late–twentieth-century gaze makes this child a virtuous gifted child who symbolizes progress and who makes childhood a repository of potentiality and hope for the future. Although their voices do not have an acknowledged place in adult discourse, both of these very different children—who are of course the same "child"—have something to say about the unarticulated longings and fears of the adults into whose world they come.

NOTES

1   An admittedly subjective indicator of the current dominance of the discourse of the gifted child is the difficulty I experienced naming such children for this project without using the term "gifted" myself, using terms that invoke the virtue/vice distinction to an unfortunate extent (e.g., "talented"), or using a term that elides an unresolved, generally unarticulated tension in giftedness discourse regarding the identification of gifted children via test scores versus high levels of achievement in school or elsewhere (e.g., "high ability" or "creative").

2   I refer to mothers rather than parents as the targets of child-rearing advice because child care is considered to be the exclusive province of women in white middle-class families by the 1860s.

3   Winifred Sackville Stoner's *Natural Education* (1914), which describes the process by which she trained her famously precocious daughter, is an early description of nonpathological precocity.   In his introduction to Stoner's book, Michael V. O'Shea, professor of education at the University of Wisconsin and author of a mental hygiene text (O'Shea 1900), notes that "[d]uring the last three or four years, the newspapers and magazines of the country have given much space to the discussion of a group of so-called precocious children" (Stoner 1914, iii).   Margolin (1994) confirms an increased incidence of stories about child prodigies in American newspapers and magazines in the early twentieth century.   Stoner presents the example of her daughter, as well as that of the precocious boy William James Sidis, in an attempt to discredit the belief of "old-fashioned folk...that all these precocious children must become physical wrecks" or insane (1914, 7). Sidis, the most famous American child prodigy of the early twentieth century, entered Harvard at age eleven and gave a celebrated lecture to the faculty on the "Fourth Dimension" (Margolin 1994; Stoner 1914).   Stoner's use of Sidis as an exemplar precocious child who "has never been a weakling" (1914, 9) was premature, because he suffered a breakdown shortly after delivering the famous lecture and was admitted to a sanitarium. Although he graduated from Harvard with honors at age sixteen, Sidis's adult career was not commensurate with expectations: He never held a job requiring mental effort. Sidis died of a cerebral hemorrhage in 1944. His case was celebrated in the American media as an example of the dangers of intellectual precocity.

4   At its most basic level, the construction of the romantic-sentimental child, who represented the ideal child for much of America from the mid-nineteenth through the early twentieth centuries, is not possible without the simultaneous construction of the precocious child, the polar opposite of the ideal romantic child. Categories of good and bad take meaning in relationship to the other. The discourse constructing the romantic-sentimental child can only exist alongside the discourse constructing the precocious child.

5   The scientific discourse about adult genius also informed the discourse of childhood precocity.   Cesare Lombroso, whose theories about criminals were popular among U.S. reformers in the late nineteenth/early twentieth centuries (Platt 1969), argued in *The Man of Genius* that "genius was a true degenerative psychosis" (1891, 333). Nineteenth-century alienists viewed genius, insanity, and idiocy as equally abnormal and as often interchangeable. "Originality of thought and quickness or preponderance of the intellectual faculties are organically much the same thing as

madness and idiocy" (1891, vi) was the thesis of John Nisbet's *The Insanity of Genius and the General Inequality of Human Faculty Physiologically Considered*, which popularized Lombroso's theories in the United States and ran to six editions.

6   I use the male pronoun here in the same sense that it is used in the prescriptive literature of the time: not as the generic "he," but rather as referring exclusively to boys. In my reading of these child-rearing manuals, girls are not included in the generic child. The imagined precocious child is a male child.

7   Other forms of precocity were also proscribed as unhealthy for children. Child-rearing experts warned against the dangers of early sitting and walking (Le Favre 1890). In the best-selling child-rearing guide of the period, Dr. L. Emmett Holt (1896) prescribed a milk-only diet for infants and young children. Milk-drinking prolongs babyhood and thus curbs precocity. Dietary prescriptions form part of the broader project to set children apart from the adult world and to shelter them from overstimulation.

8   Race and eugenics are part of the story of precocity as pathology as well. Concerns with sexual precocity and masturbation encoded racist thought insofar as nonwhite children and adults as well as certain immigrant groups were stereotyped as abnormally sexual. Eugenics, a fairly widespread system of thought concerned, in the United States, primarily with the preservation of the race through the improvement of maternal and child health (Klaus 1993), contributed to the condemnation of intellectual precocity through fears of damaging children's reproductive capability directly and, indirectly, through fears of damaging their health. The bodily economy model suggested that overstudy was particularly dangerous to reproductive capabilities for girls (e.g., Le Favre 1890) and for youths in puberty. For example, a female physician wrote in *Eutocia: Easy Favorable Child Bearing*, a book much informed by eugenics, that overstudy was particularly to be avoided between the ages of twelve and sixteen (Cook 1886, 253).

9   Furthermore, the typical gifted child—whether identified through intelligence tests, teacher recommendations, or other means—actually was (and is) white and upper middle class (Margolin 1994). Education programs for the gifted in contemporary American schools thus put race and class distinction into practice by offering these children unique educational opportunities.

10 Intelligence testing does more than authenticate intellectual capacity, however. IQ testing functions as a mechanism for normalization. The creation of normally distributed scores reconstructs deviations from the mean (precocity as well as retardation), previously understood as equally abnormal/pathological, into relations of superiority/inferiority such that precocity becomes a positive good which is better than both normal and subnormal intelligence.

REFERENCES

Abbott, Andrew. *The System of Professions: An Essay on the Division of Expert Labor.* Chicago: University of Chicago Press, 1988.

Allen, Annie Winsor. *Home, School, and Vacation: A Book of Suggestions.* Boston: Houghton Mifflin, 1907.

Barker-Benfield, G. J. *The Horrors of the Half-Known Life: Male Attitudes Toward*

Women and Sexuality in Nineteenth Century America. New York: Harper and Row, 1976.

Beard, George. *American Nervousness, Its Causes and Consequences*. New York: G. P. Putnam, 1881.

Blumin, Stuart M. "The Hypothesis of Middle-Class Formation in Nineteenth-Century America." *American Historical Review* 90 (April 1985): 299–338.

Boyer, Paul. *Urban Masses and Moral Order in America, 1820-1920*. Cambridge: Harvard University, 1978.

Burbank, Luther. *The Training of the Human Plant*. New York: Century, 1907.

Burrell, Caroline Benedict. *The Mothers' Book*. New York: University Society, 1909.

Chenery, Susan. *As the Twig Is Bent: A Story for Mothers and Teachers*. New York: Houghton Mifflin, 1901.

Chudacoff, Howard P. *How Old Are You? Age Consciousness in American Culture*. Princeton, N. J.: Princeton University Press, 1989.

Cook, Mrs. E .G. *Eutocia*. Chicago: Arcade, 1886.

Cox, Roger. *Shaping Childhood*. London: Routledge, 1996.

Cunningham, Hugh. *The Children of the Poor: Representations of Childhood Since the Seventeenth Century*. Oxford: Oxford University Press, 1991.

———. *Children and Childhood in Western Society Since 1500*. New York: Longman, 1995.

Foucault, Michel. *Discipline and Punish*. New York: Pantheon, 1977.

Friedman, Reva C. and Karen B. Rogers, ed. *Talent in Context: Historical and Social Perspectives of Giftedness*. Washington, D.C.: The American Psychological Association, 1998.

Gordon, Linda. *Heroes of Their Own Lives: The Politics and History of Family Violence*. New York: Penguin Books, 1988.

Grant, Julia. *Raising Baby by the Book: The Education of American Mothers*. New Haven: Yale University Press, 1998.

Grinder, Robert E. "The Gifted in Our Midst: By Their Divine Deeds, Neuroses, and Mental Test Scores We Have Known Them." In *The Gifted and Talented: Development Perspectives*, edited by Frances Horowitz and Marion O'Brien. Washington, D.C.: American Psychological Association, 1985.

Grinnell, Elizabeth. *How John and I Brought Up the Child*. Philadelphia: American Sunday School Union, 1894.

Guthrie, Leonard. *Contributions to the Study of Precocity in Children*. London: Eric G. Millar, 1921.

Hall, G. Stanley. *Adolescence: Its Psychology and Its Relations to Physiology, Anthropology, Sociology, Sex, Crime, Religion and Education*. 2 vols. New York: D. Appleton, 1904.

Halttunen, Karen. *Confidence Men and Painted Women: A Study of Middle-Class Culture in America, 1830–1870*. New Haven: Yale University Press, 1982.

Harland, Marion. *Common Sense in the Nursery*. New York: Charles Scribners Sons, 1885.

Hirsch, William. *Genius and Degeneration, a Psychological Study*. New York: D. Appleton, 1896.

Hollander, Bernard. *Abnormal Children (Nervous, Mischievous, Precocious, and Backward): A Book for Parents, Teachers, and Medical Officers of Schools*. London: Kegan Paul, Trench, Truebner & Co., 1916.

Hollingworth, Leta. *Gifted Children: The Nature and Nurture*. New York: Macmillan,

1926.

Holt, L. Emmett. *The Care and Feeding of Infants.* New York: D. Appleton, 1896.

Hopkinson, C. A. *Hints for the Nursery: The Young Mother's Guide.* Boston: Little, Brown & Co, 1863.

Jackson, Gabrielle. *A Series of Don'ts for Mothers Who May, or May Not, Stand in Need of Them.* Boston: Lee and Shepard, 1903.

Kasson, John F. *Rudeness and Civility: Manners in Nineteenth-Century Urban America.* New York: Hill and Wang, 1990.

Kett, Joseph. "Adolescence and Youth in Nineteenth-Century America." *Journal of Interdisciplinary History* 2, no. 2 (1971): 283–298.

———. "Curing the Disease of Precocity." In *Turning Points: Historical and Sociological Essays on the Family,* edited by John Demos and Sarane Spence Boocock. Chicago: University of Chicago Press, 1978.

Kimmel, Michael. *Manhood in America: A Cultural History.* New York: Free Press, 1996.

Kirwin, Nicholas Murray. *Happy Home.* New York: Harper and Brothers, 1858.

Klaus, Alisa. *Every Child a Lion: The Origins of Maternal and Infant Health Policy in the United States and France, 1890–1920.* Ithaca, N.Y.: Cornell University Press, 1993.

Lears, T. J. Jackson. *No Place of Grace: Antimodernism and the Transformation of American Culture, 1880–1920.* New York: Pantheon, 1981.

Le Favre, Carrica. *Mother's Help and Child's Friend.* New York: Brentano's, 1890.

Lombroso, Cesare. *The Man of Genius.* New York: C. Scribner's Sons, 1891.

Macleod, David. *The Age of the Child: Children in America, 1890–1920.* New York: Twayne, 1998.

Margolin, Leslie. *Goodness Personified: The Emergence of Gifted Children.* New York: Aldine D. Gruyter, 1994.

Mechling, J. "Advice to Historians on Advice to Mothers." *Journal of Social History* 9 (1975): 44–63.

Mintz, Stephen and Susan Kellogg. *Domestic Revolutions: A Social History of American Family Life.* New York: Free Press, 1988.

Mitchell, S. Weir. *Wear and Tear, or, Hints for the Overworked.* Philadelphia: J. B. Lippincott, 1874.

Mosher, Martha B. *Child Culture in the Home: A Book for Mothers.* New York: Sampson Low, Marston & Co, 1898.

Nasaw, David. *Children of the City: At Work and At Play.* Garden City, N.Y.: Anchor Press, 1985.

Newcomb, Dan. *When and How, or, A Collection of the More Recent Facts and Ideas upon Raising Healthy Children.* Chicago: Arthur W. Penny, 1872.

Nisbet, John. *The Insanity of Genius and the General Inequality of Human Faculty Physiologically Considered.* 6th Ed. New York: Charles Scribner, 1891.

O'Shea, Michael V. "Aspects of Mental Economy." *Bulletin of the University of Wisconsin,* no. 36, Science Series, Vol. 2, no. 2 (1900): 33–198.

Platt, Anthony M. *The Child Savers: The Invention of Delinquency.* Chicago: University of Chicago Press, 1969.

Pressey, Sidney L. "Concerning the Nature and Nurture of Genius." *Scientific Monthly* 81, no. 3 (1955).

Riddell, Newton N. *Child Culture.* Chicago: Child of Light, 1902.

Rousseau, Jean Jacques. *Emile.* Translated by Barbara Foxley, 1762. Reprinted,

London: J. M. Dent, 1957[1762].

Ryan, Mary P. Cradle of the Middle Class: The Family in Oneida County, New York, 1790–1865. New York: Cambridge University Press, 1981.

Sanborn, Katherine Abbott. *The Vanity and Insanity of Genius.* New York: G. J. Coombes, 1886.

Sauer, Mrs. P. B. *Maternity: A Book for Every Wife and Mother.* Chicago: L. P. Miller, 1891.

Shapiro, Michael Steven. *Child's Garden: The Kindergarten Movement from Froebel to Dewey.* University Park, Pa.: Pennsylvania State University Press, 1983.

Sternberg, Robert, and Janet Davidson. *Conceptions of Giftedness.* Cambridge: Cambridge University Press, 1986.

Stoner, Winifred Sackville. *Natural Education.* Indianapolis: Bobbs-Merrill, 1914.

Terman, Lewis M. *Genetic Studies of Genius: Mental and Physical Traits of a Thousand Gifted Children.* Vol. 1. Stanford, Calif.: Stanford University Press, 1925.

Tomes, Robert. *The Bazaar Book of the Household.* New York: Harper and Brothers, 1875.

Tuthill, Mrs. L. C. *Joy and Care: A Friendly Book for Young Mothers.* New York: Charles Scribner, 1855.

Warner, Francis. *The Nervous System of the Child.* New York: Macmillan, 1906.

Wilson, Ruth Danenhower. Giving Your Child the Best Chance. Chicago: A. C. McClurg, 1924.

Wood-Allen, Mary. *Making the Best of Our Children. First Series: One to Eight Years of Age.* Chicago: A. C. McClurg, 1909.

Zelizer, Viviana. *Pricing the Priceless Child: The Changing Social Value of Children.* Princeton, N.J.: Princeton University Press, 1985.

Zenner, Philip. *Mind Cure and Other Essays.* Cincinnati: Stewart and Kidd, 1912.

Zigler, Edward, and Ellen A. Farber. "Commonalities Between the Intellectual Extremes: Giftedness and Mental Retardation." In *The Gifted and Talented: Development Perspectives*, edited by Frances Horowitz and Marion O'Brien. Washington, D.C.: American Psychological Association, 1985.

Chapter 5

Realizing Modernity Through the Robust Turkish Child, 1923–1938

Kathryn Libal

The cover of the Turkish Children's Protection Society journal for June 1927 depicts a photo portrait of an unnamed Turkish girl looking contemplatively ahead (fig. 5.1). The white lace on the bodice of her dress and beads at her throat invoke notions of childlike innocence, purity, and grace, even as such dress and demeanor denote being born into an upper-class position and having obtained a proper education in manners. Beneath her picture is printed the couplet, "A nation that raises robust children will without a doubt create a healthy state" (*Gürbüz çocuk yetiştiren bir millet—hiç şüphesizki kurar sağlam bir devlet*).

When mentioning the idea of a "robust child" in Turkey today one usually elicits a smile and expressions of how quaint the phrase is. Yet, the notion of robustness and concern with child health were dominant social issues in 1920s and 1930s republican Turkey. "Robustness" was routinely cited in medical, social scientific, and popular discourses as a measure of health and a sign of the likely survival of a given child. The idea of the healthy, robust child did not belong to the realm of the family or medical practice, alone, however. As I will show, the everyday notion of the "robust child" (*gürbüz çocuk*) and attendant campaigns and practices to promote child health illustrate the interplay between emergent discourses on scientific child care, parenting, and health with broader moralistic and nationalist rhetorics of modernity, civility, and progress. In early republican Turkey, having robust children meant that individuals, families, and, by extension, the state would thrive. In its broadest sense, the figure of the robust child served as a metonym for the Turkish nation-state: By raising healthy, vital children, the state too would be strong.

Discursive preoccupation with childhood and the raising of robust children reveals the extent to which children had become an index or measure of Turkey's progress and (Western) civility.[1] Historians and social scientists of the early Turkish republic have noted the relevance of the "woman question," changing gender roles, and intersections between notions of womanhood, motherhood, modernity, and the new nation-state (e.g., Kandiyoti 1991, 1997; Arat 1997). Largely unexplored are the intersections between campaigns to create modern mothering and child-care practices, to improve the overall health of children and reduce infant and child mortality, and to shape a citizenry committed to having children, increasing the population and being loyal to the new leaders and goals of the Turkish republic. Policymakers, politicians, and a growing number of professional healthcare workers (European-trained physicians, nurses, licensed midwives, and child-care specialists) worked toward a common goal—increasing the population of the new nation-state. They advocated a two-pronged approach: encouraging women to have children and institutionalizing practices at the local and state level to ensure that fewer infants and young children died of disease, malnutrition, or neglect. A key component of campaigns to promote child health was the dissemination of the notion of the "robust child." One attained a "robust child" through fostering "çocuk sevgisi" (love of children) in mothers and the broader society. Mothers and, by extension, the nation-state could be assured of healthy children, if they learned to properly love and look after their children.

Images of "robust children" became icons of the legitimate and sovereign Turkish state, even as reformers and leaders hoped that marrying the figure of child and state would promote a stronger sense of commitment to parenting and prevent infant and child mortality. This interweaving of love for the child and love for the state was mutually constitutive—reformers sought to change the way in which people regarded their children even as they hoped to promote patriotism and nationalism. Reformers and leaders encouraged citizens to visualize the nation-state through their children, and by extension, their children's futures through supporting the nation-state.

Turkey's engagement with "the child" as both a problem and prospect of future strength points to the relevance of carefully examining the role that childhood plays in the making of modern nation-states. Sharon Stephens (1996) has recently asked researchers to consider the ways in which certain notions about children and childhood are pivotal in the structuring of modern states. Stephens asserts that "the richer and more interesting discussions of nation, gender and childhood explore complex interrelations among constructed meanings, historical circumstances and material conditions" (1996, 5–6). This chapter focuses on the nationalist rhetorics and symbol of the robust Turkish child, the meanings that were invoked by robustness, and how these meanings were constituted in a changing public sphere through radio, advertising, educational materials for mothers, and robust child contests. In doing so, I point to the importance of childhood in foundational discourses on nationhood and nation-state building in the case of Turkey. My discussion also reveals some of the complexities and anxieties of representing new nationhood to an impoverished and embattled populace.

Background

The late-nineteenth and early-twentieth centuries marked a time of great transition in the Ottoman Empire. In the first part of the century, Ottoman armies were defeated by Greek, Serbian, and Arab nationalists in various corners of the Empire. In the wake of such significant challenges to the Ottoman polity and the loss of territory, centralizing and modernizing reforms were carried out by imperial order as well as by emerging reformist elites (Zürcher 1997). Along with the increasing incorporation of the Ottoman economy into the broader capitalist economy and administrative reforms, the imperial elite encouraged changes in judicial processes, education, medicine, and public hygiene.

It was in this context that the child emerged as an object of increasing concern for both state and society.[2] The "child question" was widely addressed in professional discourses of medicine, social science, and more popular forms of journalism, even while the child came to be treated differently at the microlevel within the family. As Alan Duben and Cem Behar (1991) have illustrated in the case of nineteenth- and early-twentieth-century Istanbul, the place and meaning of childhood radically shifted. In the early twentieth century, this process was influenced by educational reforms that were based in no small part on French and German philosophies of education and child-rearing practices, brought back to Turkey by growing number of teachers and medical professionals seeking training in Europe or by visiting scholars.

The increasing integration of Western medical practices, including the emerging field of pediatrics, and the creation of a vital and relatively affordable print media to disseminate new knowledge about health, welfare, and society as a whole, were also instrumental to changing notions about children, childrearing, and the meaning of childhood.

While a detailed study of the history of Ottoman childhood has yet to be written, Duben and Behar assert that by the mid- to late nineteenth century and especially during the early twentieth century, urban elites had begun to regard children quite differently from earlier Ottoman generations. Ottoman elites had begun to make childhood "sacred" in ways similar to those mapped by Viviana Zelizer (1985) regarding American ideas about childhood. According to Şerif Mardin, "The whole Tanzimat, is suffused by [a] new interest in children as persons to whom society is going to be entrusted" (as cited in Duben and Behar 1991, 228). Duben and Behar link the "signs of a child-oriented society" in late-nineteenth and early-twentieth-century Istanbul to a trajectory of social transformation in attitudes toward the child and childhood that intensified and spread beyond this urban center by the inception of the Turkish nation-state in 1923.

By the 1920s and 1930s, state and state-supported policies, laws, and campaigns regarding child welfare were widely put into practice, monitored, and modified as a part of the art of good governance.[3] These strategies were used by state-sponsored institutions as well as by a social and political elite supporting the rapid modernization of Turkey. The emergence of the child as an object of state, scholarly, and popular discourses was not limited to abstract national realms or that of the population alone; the child's place within the household was also made more "visible" for the efforts of parents and, in particular, the Turkish mother. Normalizing discourses on the "modern family" encouraged mothers to care for their children with the helpful advice of a family doctor and with a solid education in the scientific principles of child-rearing. Rather than relying on the support of "elderly women" in the local neighborhood with their superstitious remedies, women were to trust in their own knowledge gleaned from modern books and magazines and obtained in consultation with licensed doctors and certified midwives and nurses.

The urgency of campaigns to secure child health and lower infant mortality rates must be understood within the social, economic, and political context of postwar Turkey. A succession of wars in the decade just prior to the declaration of Turkish independence, including the Balkan Wars, World War I, and the subsequent Greco-Turkish War (in

Turkish historiography, the War of Independence) devastated the Anatolian and Eastern Thracian landscape. In light of the years of political and social upheaval, nationalist reformers viewed the need to "repopulate" Anatolia, the heart of what had been the Ottoman Empire, as of paramount importance.[4] The human costs of protracted conflict were felt not only on the battlefields, but also in the homes and fields that were cared for in large part by women and children during the years leading up to the establishment of the republic in 1923. Nation-state building in the early Turkish republic meant both postwar construction of the state's infrastructure as well as renewal and recovery among those in society hardest hit by years of deprivation, epidemic disease, and dislocation—the common people (*halk*).

Indeed, state and public discourses on efforts to build a strong Turkish nation-state in the 1920s and 1930s reveal a preoccupation with Turkey's "population question" (*nüfus sorunu*).[5] Recovery of population lost during the late Ottoman Empire and strengthening of the nation-state for the future were predicated on promoting population growth. Officials from a newly established Bureau of Statistics proposed that Turkey's population would increase through promoting childbirth, decreasing mortality rates, and accepting immigrants from former Ottoman territories. The early Turkish republic deployed programs to promote all three of these aspects through pronatalist and child health and welfare campaigns and encouraging the settling of immigrants and refugees from former Ottoman territories.

At the center of the population and health campaigns was the child. As one journalist put it: "The child is the future of the nation. Nations with robust children also have strong futures" (*Vakit* 1932). Turkish nationalists sought to rectify the population problem through pronatalist and interventive child health and welfare policies largely adapted from European and American models.[6] This dual approach—encouraging more births and working to keep healthy those infants who were born— was the key to campaigns supported by both private and state-sponsored initiatives in Turkey. The state officially promoted a pronatalist platform, but proponents realized that the sheer number of births was not the key issue. Infant and child mortality rates were so high that significant work had to be done to raise children who would survive to become productive adult citizens of the modern nation-state.[7] In terms of nation-state building, this entailed a full-scale ideological campaign to transform parents' ideas about infant- and child-rearing practices and, to a lesser extent, efforts to provide more resources to the urban poor.

The Children's Protection Society (*Himaye-i Etfal Cemiyeti / Çocuk Esirgeme Kurumu*) led the movement to promote the birthing and raising of "robust Turkish children."[8] The CPS's activities were formally endorsed by the state and were supported by collaborative efforts with other philanthropic organizations such as the Red Crescent Society, the Mother's Federation, Women's Federation, various urban shelters for the poor, orphanages, people's houses,[9] and local schools. During the 1920s and 1930s, the CPS provided assistance to orphaned and poor children through distributing hot lunches at school, placing them out in homes as adoptees or in other state and private-run orphanages, and giving direct monetary assistance to a small number of needy families.

The CPS also distributed free milk to needy mothers and their infants and set up wet-nursing and clean milk stations (*süt damlası*) in larger branches throughout the republic. They organized doctors and nurses to provide prenatal and infant care in larger branches such as Ankara and Istanbul, annually giving thousands of physical checkups to children and mothers. The CPS played a key role in the transmission of knowledge through its publications and was considered instrumental in leading a campaign to heighten societal awareness of the importance of having children and raising them to survive infancy and toddlerhood. With the help of such materials, CPS employees and volunteers set about training health-care and child-care workers as well as mothers about fundamental tenets of "modern" child care (*çocuk bakımı*). A discourse on robustness and the ideal figure of the Turkish child emerged in large part because of the efforts of the CPS and other organizations with which it collaborated.

The Social Meanings of the Robust Child

The issue of "robustness" was pervasive in republican discourses on the child in the 1920s and 1930s. Writers for newspapers, journals, and serial publications often used the phrase *gürbüz çocuk* (robust child) when referring to children. They sometimes added the idea of "Turkishness" to the phrase, as in the title of the best-known publication on child welfare, *Gürbüz Türk Çocuğu*. Visual images of the *gürbüz* child were depicted in advertisements for cereal and milk products, medicinal products, and household appliances such as the refrigerator. In modern Turkish, *gürbüz* best translates into English as "robust" or "healthy." As an adjective, *gürbüz* implies health, vitality, and physical well-being. Earlier uses of the word in Ottoman Turkish implied sharpness, acuity, cleverness,

The Robust Child

Fig. 5.1. A nation that raises robust children will without a doubt create a healthy state. (Reproduced from *Gürbüz Türk Çocuðu*, June 1927).

strength, and importance (*Türk Dil Kurumu* 1967, 1880). The word appeared as early as the fifteenth century in Ottoman Turkish, when *gürbüz* meant "heroic" or "intelligent" (Devellioğlu 1970, 357).[10]

In the early republican period, other adjectives describing the ideal Turkish child were typically invoked with the notion of *gürbüz*. Words such as *sirin* (sweet), *neşeli* (joyous, merry), *güzel* (beautiful, refined), *afacan* (impish, clever), *parlak* (brilliant, wonderful), and *zeki* (bright, clever) marked the positive attributes of what every child innately should be. These notions referred to the mental capabilities, physical attributes not necessarily connected with health, and temperament of the child. At least in public discourse, this vocabulary signified more than the positive attributes of a single child. They helped to create an important imaginary type—a visualization of the ideal Turkish child of the new nation. This figure was physically robust, beautiful, and mentally capable or even exceptional. Such images of both boys and girls abound in literary, newspaper, and photographic texts.

The notion of robustness was deployed by medical personnel, educators, writers, volunteers working on child-welfare issues, social activists, and politicians in a number of ways in the early republican period. Ideas about the robust child were disseminated through the newsprint and popular magazines (in educational articles, advertising for various baby foods and products, and in photo contests for robust and beautiful children); in pamphlets about childrearing published by the Children's Protection Society (CPS); in child-care courses in urban areas; at dispensaries and clinics serving newborns and young children; and through public spectacle and exhibitions presented to "the people." The idea of the robust child was communicated through verbal and auditory forms as well, for example, in poetry, speeches, and radio broadcasts.[11] It is more difficult to reconstruct actual "speech acts" in the everyday, but the predominance of it in print media, memoirs, and transcripts of radio broadcasts suggests that the phrase was a part of everyday discourse among at least the urban middle and upper classes.

The Robust Child in Popular Culture

From the mid-1920s, the CPS began publishing an array of materials to educate healthcare workers, teachers, and mothers about childrearing. One of the Society's earliest publications, *Çocuk Haftası* (Children's Week), is replete with imagery of model robust children in photos, sketches, poetry, editorials, and articles. The idea of robustness was often invoked in materials that propagated infants and children's consumption of milk (from both the breast and the cow). In Turkish popular culture of the era, poetry was a popular mode of expression. Poetry could be recited aloud or read to oneself, thus bridging both oral and written forms of expression. Poems about children, whether didactic or more sentimental and personal, were frequently published for adults and children alike. Thought to evoke a more emotive, immediate response in the reader or listener, early republican reformers hoped poetry could more meaningfully teach parents and children health lessons. In the poem, "Milk" (*Süt*), writer and publicist Aka Gündüz linked the health of the child—and her robustness and impishness—to regular consumption of milk (1929, 121). Taking on the persona of a child, Gündüz entreated:

Milk

Mothers! If you love me
Don't feed me whatever you eat.
Whatever you give me,
I don't want anything but the freshest milk.

I am so robust, so impish,
I drink my milk cup by cup.
Those who drink ample, fresh milk,
Like me will find life.

If you want a happy home,
Raise your child to be robust.
The only solution is this:
Feed [your baby] lots and lots of fresh milk.

The real name of the water called "the water of life"
Is milk.
Give plenty of milk
To help the dear child live.

Milk means the child—
Life to your little one.
It means the children who drink milk
Will live twice as long.

Through the child's voice, Gündüz appealed to mothers to nourish their children with milk. Milk—in ample quantities, at regular intervals, and in the freshest condition—was said to be the "water of life." Through drinking this elixir, "cup by cup," the mother ensured her child's health, vitality, and spirited nature. In a common verbal convention, Gündüz closed with the assertion that, indeed, "milk means the child" (*süt çocuk demek*). Milk *was* the child. Milk came to mean the very existence of the robust and happy child, and amply providing for one's child imputed a kind of civility and modernity such as depicted in the line drawing that accompanied the poem. In the image, the contented, chubby girl reclines in a cushioned chair, grasping a bottle of milk. She was no ordinary child of the working classes, however. The cushioned leather chair, the little girl's dress, and her leather shoes signaled that the toddler belonged to a family of some means. Bottle-fed, well-dressed, chubby arms and legs assured that she would not have been wet-nursed at a local CPS "drop of milk" station (*süt damlası*).[12]

The link between milk and raising *gürbüz* children was also commonly made in newspaper and magazine advertisements and in articles that instruct mothers on modern forms of "child care" (*çocuk bakımı*).[13] Pediatricians recommended that mothers first and foremost breastfeed their children. Studies had shown that when children were breastfed, fewer died in infancy. Indeed, according to Dr. Raşid Kadri, higher rates of infant mortality in some parts of Europe than in Turkey were due to European mother's reliance on cow's milk rather than on Turkish practices of breastfeeding (Derviş 1935, 26). Pediatrician Dr. Fahriye, one of the first female physicians working for the CPS, regularly spoke on Ankara radio about child care and child health. Dr. Fahriye emphasized that breastfeeding was optimal. If for physical reasons women felt they could not breastfeed, then the next best option was to give babies fresh cow's milk that had been boiled and fed from properly sterilized glass bottles. Physicians such as Dr. Fahriye (last name unknown) warned about feeding babies powdered formulas that were increasingly available in Turkish cities, for they could cause intestinal problems and were not as nutritious as mother's or fresh cow's milk (Fahriye 1934).

Despite medical experts' encouragement of breastfeeding, they informally noted the decrease in breastfeeding, particularly among middle- and upper-class women (Derviş 1935, 26). Here, too, social class factored into options for feeding infants, for only middle- or upper-class families could have afforded the luxury of purchasing "milk powder."[14] Increasingly, formula alternatives became available to those who could afford them, and producers of local formulas were careful to depict children raised on their products as resoundingly robust. An advertisement for Besi Süt Tozu, or "Fattening Milk Powder," shows a reclining infant drinking from a glass bottle (*Cumhuriyet* 1935). The infant's hand reaches for a tub of "Besi." The text of the advertisement reads:

Fattening Milk Powder: Raise Beautiful and Robust Children. Protect your health from harmful microbes. Fattening Milk Powder is free of every kind of harmful microbe. Besi is prepared scientifically in the Kars Milk Powder factory. Look for it at pharmacies and large grocers (see fig. 5.2).

The advertisement stresses the "purity" of its product—a state obtained through scientific processes at the factory producing infant formula. The role of "science" in raising beautiful and robust children recurred thematically in such advertising and child-care literature, which emphasized the importance of "modern child-care" techniques (e.g., Belen 1935; Fahriye 1934).

While poetry and advertisements for commercial products such as milk played a role in linking notions of child health with nutrition and consumption, medical professionals and social workers strove to reeducate parents and, in particular, mothers, about the necessary skills of modern child care. For example, writers for the CPS publication *Children's Week* informed parents in one text that if they wanted to raise their children to be "robust and prosperous," they must be healthy themselves, abstain from alcohol consumption, and find a "family doctor" (*Her Ana Her Babaya*, 1929, 173). The text asserts:

1. For every step that you take, remember that you have a child who is affected by your health, your emotions, and your behavior. Therefore, every wrong step you take will send your child over the cliff before you.
2. All the alcohol you drink will poison your child's blood but not yours.
3. There are thousands of children who have gotten sick because [parents] have *neglected to find a family doctor* (emphasis added).
4. When you are expecting a child or have a child, *turn to learned and expert doctors and midwives with diplomas.* They will show you the right path (emphasis added).
5. If you want to get more information about these matters, you should go to the Children's Protection Society—the Society that does not allow even one child to get sick or die in this country. Children's Protection will give you useful advice.

Milk for the Nation's Health

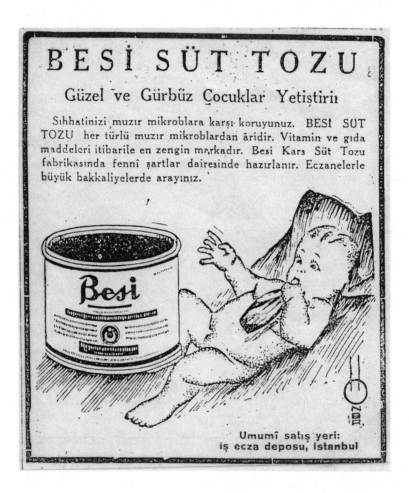

Fig. 5.2. Besi formula is for healthy infants. (Reproduced from *Cumhuriyet*, September 3, 1935).

This text illustrates doctors' efforts to lobby for the profession-alization of child-birthing and child-care practices, even as they politicized the meaning of health and the survival of children in the 1930s. Several leading doctors simultaneously served in high-ranking governmental posts or as parliamentarians. As a small but growing professional sector, such doctors made up a part of the educated cadre of republican leaders and reformers set on transforming societal values about childbirth, health, and childrearing along lines of Western biomedical practices.

Expanding and popularizing the idea of professional health care for mothers and infants in the early republic did not mean that all, or even most, women had access to such services. The few free hospitals and clinics that existed in cities were swamped with requests for assistance; patients lined the corridors and were turned away by the thousands annually in the 1920s and 1930s (Atay 1935a). The "free clinics" provided by the CPS and other philanthropic associations, despite serving thousands of mothers and children in various locations every year, could not cope with the large numbers of those who sought care. On the other hand, according to the periodic laments of doctors in their memoirs and interviews, many women resisted seeking medical attention outside the home (Derviş 1935). For some, like Dr. Kadri, reluctance to seek medical attention or hire a "licensed" midwife and instead enlisting the services of the neighborhood grandmother who helped deliver babies testified to the ignorance and fatalism of Turkish women—a barrier to be overcome for the sake of the nation-state. For working-class women, the admonitions of elite doctors to find a family physician or licensed midwife represented another reality, not one they could hope to attain or necessarily desired.

Celebrating the Robust Child

Another avenue promised more wide-reaching possibilities for Turkish citizens to envision the robust child. During the celebration of Children's Holiday, children celebrated for their chubby, contented demeanors, their cheerfulness, and apparent bodily strength-through-mass were put on display, expanding people's visions of childhood and the nation-state. Ostensibly, the purpose of Children's Week was to focus attention on children. CPS organizers intensified fund-raising efforts for child-welfare initiatives, even as they sought to promote a stronger sense of concern for children in the nation's citizenry. The first day of the week, April 23, was celebrated as a day marking the nationalist establishment of parliament in 1920. Later named "National Sovereignty and Children's Holiday," the secular commemoration became one of the most important dates on the holiday calendar and gave children and parents an opportunity to celebrate childhood and nationhood through amusements such as movies, games, parades, and various dramatic performances by and for children (Aslan 1983).

Turkish social reformers hoped that by naming and celebrating child health in "robust Turkish child" contests they would help spread the notion of *çocuk sevgisi* or "love of the child." The use of images of robust children in the print media and in the enactment of contests themselves in the late 1920s and 1930s were seen by medical experts, politicians, and social reformers as important instruments in transforming attitudes and knowledge about how to best raise children. Several types of contests were held by the early 1930s: some were based on photographs and reported heights, weights, and ages sent to local newspapers, while other contests were held during Children's Week in late April at local people's houses, orphanages, or in parks or other public gathering places. Some contests were between older children (ages five–ten), while most were devoted to competitions to name the most healthy and robust infants and toddlers. Robust child contests among older children were adjudicated by committees comprising physicians, nurses, and local newspaper professionals. Results were based on overall physical appearance and were not oriented toward exhibiting a particular talent or capability.

Contests for infants and toddlers exemplified another level of medicalized concern with robustness. Take, for example, the contest held at an Istanbul people's house in 1934. After prominent pediatrician Dr. Ali Sükrü delivered a talk on the principles of health and infant care, families entered a room set aside for the contest. The room was filled with the sound of babies crying, laughing, and yelling. Children were divided into three groups: nursing infants (*süt çocukları*), infants who ate soft foods (*mama çocukları*), and toddlers (playing children, *oyun çocukları*). Doctors conducted "checkups," carefully measuring, weighing, and examining the baby-participants. At the end of the examinations, first-, second-, and third-place winners were selected in each of the three age groups. Older children who won contests received gifts of pens, watches, or other souvenirs. Regardless of age group, prize recipients were photographed and the pictures often shown in local papers or included in CPS publications with the father's name and occupation printed along with the name of the child.[15]

The popularity of the contests grew in the late 1920s and prompted the CPS and newspapers such as *Cumhuriyet* and *Vakit* to more widely publicize the events in following years. The contests encouraged parents to demonstrate their children's robustness and, by extension, their success as parents. They provided a space for imagining the nation through the idealized bodies of Turkish children from across the country and mapping and publicizing the faces, physical features, and names of the children who embodied Turkey's future.[16] Yet this widely celebrated annual event brought to the forefront questions of the universality of childhood experience and what it meant to be a child in Turkey. The children who competed were predominately the sons and daughters of lawyers, teachers, doctors, and civil servants. In this way, robustness communicated membership in the middle or upper classes and challenged the official ideology of Turkish populism or being a class-free society.

Envisioning the Robust Child's Other

As I have argued above, the figure of the robust child was a potent image of the future citizen and offered the promise of a nationhood recognized by Europe and the rest of the world as genuinely modern and civilized. While certainly representative of some part of the Turkish populace, the image did not reflect the everyday lived realities of most children—what many looked like physically, how they were clothed and fed, and in what manner they were educated. Thus, behind the idealized visions of child health and beauty lay a much more predominant and recognizable child figure—that of the weak, impoverished, orphaned, or abandoned "little one" (*yavru*). Whether undernourished, struck by illness in infancy, left to roam the streets, or to work in factories, a large number of children in both urban and rural settings experienced lives of great hardship. Their lives challenged simple ideological statements of the strength of the Turkish nation-state and the professed achievements of its leaders. Social activists, journalists, and professionals working with children used their images as a counterpoint to the idealized "robust child," as reminder of the experiences of most children in the new republic. For some reformers, these other images—of malnourished, overworked, or begging children encountered on the streets of Istanbul, in shoddy housing at the outskirts of the cities, or in many village homes—underscored the importance of "educating" mothers and imbuing in them proper "love of the child." For other social activists, daily encounters with poor children on the streets or in workshops and factories threw into sharp relief the chasm between official ideology regarding the putative importance of children to the nation-state and the lived experience of so many children in the new republic.

On the same day as the annual competition to name the most *gürbüz* children at the people's house in Istanbul, several Turkish dignitaries, including leading female parliamentarian Nakiye (Elgün), visited the Bürhan Beyler Darülaceze, an orphanage/workhouse in Istanbul. At the orphanage Nakiye Hanım gave toddlers biscuits, chocolates, and other Turkish sweets. Dignitaries' visits to orphanages, where they handed out gifts of candies, trinkets, or clothing, highlighted an awareness of numerous social problems confronted by children in Turkey even while assuring the donors that they were giving some small amount of pleasure to children without familial support. Such visits during Children's Week raised the specter of the *gürbüz* child's more prevalent other—the *fakir*, or poor child, and the *cılız*, or weak infant. If the figure of the "robust child" had become a marker of progress and modernity in early republican Turkey, its importance was only highlighted in contrast to that of the ubiquitous poor, orphaned, or weak child. The lexicon of disenfranchisement was as developed as that of robustness or plenitude: *fakir çocuk* (poor child), *kimsesiz çocuk* (child without anyone), *yetim* (orphan), *ailesiz çocuk* (child without a family), *cılız çocuk* (weak child). The poor child, the commonplace, everyday "other" of the robust child, pointed to the realities of daily life for most peasant or working-class children and challenged social reformers and the government to do more than proclaim the child's importance to the nation-state.

Conclusion: Rhetorics of Nationhood, Modernity, and the Healthy Child

Through popular and official representations of robustness (and weakness) in childhood, Turkey exemplified the contradictions and accommodations of a nation-state struggling with the politics of population, modernization, and inclusion in the imagined community of "civilized" or modern nation-states. In this chapter I have illustrated how the figure of the child was used in the ideological work of nation-building, focusing in this instance on the emergent politics of population and child health and welfare and the representation of the idealized "robust Turkish child." Examining visual and discursive cultural productions, such as that of an imaginary or idealized robust child, complicates the politics of population, modernization, and nationhood. Such an analysis also illustrates one of the ways in which notions of childhood and the lives of children are important in the structuring of modern states.

While histories of convergence between child health and welfare initiatives and nation-state building may be familiar in other countries during this period (e.g., Cunningham 1991; Klaus 1993; van Kriekan 1991), modernization and the construction of child welfare as a social problem have yet to be fully elaborated in Turkey. The campaign to produce more and healthier children in the name of the nation-state demonstrates one way in which private or familial aspects of child care had become increasingly politicized and debated in the public sphere. Perhaps more important, signifying the robust child through popular culture, and particularly in robust child contests, highlighted modernist notions of "good mothering" practices. Doctors and other social reformers depicted mothers as agents responsible for learning and practicing modern, scientific child care, even while seeking the advice of healthcare workers.

Ultimately, being "robust" marked more than just health—children considered robust embodied the lives and practices of those more privileged than most in everyday early republican Turkey. Child-rearing practices espoused by doctors and other experts targeted a literate audience (or at the very least, an audience of those who could afford to have a radio and lived in an urban center such as Ankara or Istanbul) of women who had the time and resources to devote their attention to child-rearing. As such, the generalized campaign for robust children spoke first and foremost to an educated middle-class and upper-class elite, rather than to the whole populace. Imaging the robust child, then, conflated notions of health and social class in the building of the Turkish nation-state.

ACKNOWLEDGMENTS

A version of this chapter was presented at the annual meeting of the American Anthropological Association, December 1998, in Philadelphia. I would like to thank Ali İğmen for his assistance in answering translation questions and Ann Anagnost, Banu Gökarıksel, Clarissa Hsu, Ali İğmen, Reşat Kasaba, Irvin Schick, and Nicole Watts for their comments on earlier versions of this article. All errors in fact or interpretation are mine alone.

NOTES

1   My use of "Western" in this paper is purposeful and stems from a Turkish preoccupation with "the West" (*garp*). The construction of value-laden meanings of "West" and "East" has been importantly raised by Said (1978) and with regard to the Ottoman Empire and Turkey in the work of Göle (1996) and Schick (1999). The debate over "West" and "East" was ongoing in Turkey in the 1920s and 1930s, though reformers tended to valorize the initiatives, policies, and practices of Europe and America. In the early Turkish republican example of nation-state building and modernization, reformist efforts must be regarded in part as constitutive of notions of "West" and "East" and meanings attributed to these constructions.

2   For an outstanding source on the study of changing fertility patterns and notions about family, marriage, and reproduction in Turkey, see Duben and Behar (1991). While historical accounts of Ottoman and Turkish childhood are still largely unwritten, there is a growing interest in this subfield, particularly among Turkish scholars. See, in particular, Okay (1998, 1999) and Onur (1994).

3   Michel Foucault's (1991) work on governmentality and Jacques Donzelot's (1997 [1979]) critical discussion of family medicine have informed this inquiry. In particular, I am interested in tracing the ways in which doctors and other helping professionals, often in concert with republican leaders and civil servants, attempted to promote child and maternal health in the putative interests of creating a strong nation-state.

4   Decades of protracted conflict in the late Ottoman Empire, which culminated in the large-scale loss of life during World War I and the War of Independence with the Greeks, as well as the mandated transfer of Greek and minority populations as an outcome of the Treaty of Lausanne, had greatly diminished the numbers of people in Anatolia (Shaw 1998; Shorter 1985).

5   See, for example, Baltacıoğlu (1935) and Nabi (1939). Shorter (1985, 418) emphasizes the importance of estimating demographic statistics for the early republican period (before 1927, the first official republican census) in order to "interpret social trends and policies" in the later 1920s and 1930s.

6   See, for example, Adalan (1936), Atay (1935b, 1935c), Baltacıoğlu (1935), Çocuk Esirgeme Kurumu (1934), Nabi (1939), and Tunç (1935). Many of the articles dwell on demographic comparisons with other countries; Turkish scholars often framed such comparisons between countries considered "advanced" and those that have yet to attain full modernity. Turkey is represented as one of the latter.

7   Concern over high rates of infant mortality and child survival is more evident in historical sources than in nationalist rhetorics to procreate. Reformers were keenly aware of the high rates of infant and child mortality in Turkey, and they measured Turkey's "progress" in terms of how the state's infant morality rates compared with other nation-states (e.g., *Çocuk Esirgeme Kurumu* 1934; Nabi 1939; Zeki Nasır 1933).

8   The Children's Protection Society (CPS) was established by doctors and local philanthropists, first in major urban centers, and gradually in towns throughout Turkey. Before the foundation of the Turkish republic in 1923, the CPS was a relatively small-scale relief association that worked with orphaned or homeless children. The society was based on models of child protection societies that had formed in Europe during and after World War I. For more on the CPS, see Libal (2000).

9   "People's houses" (*halkevleri*) were a part of the Republican People's Party platform to promote populism and nationalist sentiment among youth and adults. Leaders sponsored adult literacy classes, programs to teach health and hygiene, and plays and musical programs, among other activities. The people's houses provided a community center of sorts as an alternative to mosques or other religious, traditional community practices.

10   In newsprint media of the 1920s and 1930s, I have only seen the word *gürbüz* paired with the word "child." In everyday spoken language the word may also have referred to adults, though this is difficult to assess historically.

11   The notion of robustness as an element of medical discourse could be pursued in emerging public health institutions and their curricula, which included village nursing programs and the health and social assistance section of urban and rural "people's houses" (*halkevleri*). In cities such as Istanbul and Ankara, professional midwifery and nursing programs opened the door to a new cadre of women (primarily) who would work to educate mothers about childbearing and rearing and who could provide direct services to children in need of health services. See Allen (1935) for an informative discussion of the development of the medical sciences in Turkey during the 1920s and 1930s.

12   This model for milk-feeding stations was taken from the French "gaut de lait" of the early twentieth century (Klaus 1993). Two elements of the French child welfare reforms became very popular in Turkey in the 1920s and 1930s: establishing clean milk stations where mothers could get free or subsidized milk for their babies and creating child health clinics (Libal 2000).

13   Such articles frequent the pages of newspapers, women's magazines, and gender-neutral periodicals that address educators, nurses, doctors, and other professionals. Especially good examples include local and national editions of the people's house journals and newspapers such as *Cumhuriyet* and *Tan*.

14   We know that well into the 1920s, foreign relief workers provided milk in different forms to widows and their children, to refugees, and to other indigent families in urban Istanbul, for example. When milk powder was distributed, though, it was not for purchase but was given as aid (Phillips 1922, 295–97).

15   Such visualizations of the robust child strikingly resemble similar images of the Gerber baby in American iconography of the period. The contests were most likely modeled after the "Better Baby" contests held in the United States and France beginning at the turn of the century, though I have yet to find a direct reference to those countries' practices in Turkish CPS sources. For more on the genealogy of

"Better Baby" contests in the United States and other parts of the world, see Dorey (1999).

16 The robust child and the child as a symbol of the future are constructs that are woven throughout print media, pedagogical texts, speeches, and serial publications during the early republic. The "child of the future" is also the robust child, the healthy, well-educated, hard-working child.

REFERENCES

Adalan, M. "Çocuk Düşürme: Bu Olgunun Fazlalığını Tek Başına Ekonomik Buhran Anlatamaz" (Abortion/Miscarriage: The Prevalence of This Fact Cannot Be Explained by the Economic Depression Alone). *Yeni Adam* 133 (1936): 6.

Aka Gündüz. "Süt" (Milk). *Çocuk Haftası* 1 (1929): 121.

Allen, Henry Elisha. *The Turkish Transformation—A Study in Social and Religious Development.* Chicago: University of Chicago Press, 1935.

Arat, Yeşim. "The Project of Women and Modernity in Turkey." *In Rethinking Modernity and National Identity in Turkey*, edited by Sibel Bozdoğan and Reşat Kasaba, 95-112. Seattle, Wash.: University of Washington Press, 1997.

Aslan, İffet. 1983. "Dünyanın İlk Çocuk Bayramı ve Uluslararası Çocuk Yılı" (The World's First Children's Holiday and International Year of the Child). *Belleten* 14, no.181–184 (1983): 568–593.

Atay, Neşet Halil.. "Hastahane Kapısı Değil, Baş Döndüren Derin Bir Uçurum" (It Is Not a Door to the Hospital, It Is Rather a Dizzingly Deep Pit). *Gürbüz Türk Çocuğu* 103 (1935a): 3–6.

———. "İstatistikleri Niçin ve Nasıl Okumalı?" (How and Why Is It Necessary to Read Statistics?). *Gürbüz Türk Çocuğu* 99 (1935b): 3–8.

———. "Sayıma Niçin Ulusal Bir Anlam Veriyoruz?" (Why Do We Give a National Meaning to the [Census] Count?). *Gürbüz Türk Çocuğu* 104 (1935c): 8–15.

Baltacıoğlu, İsmail Hakkı."50 Milyonluk Türkiye" (Turkey with [a population of 50 Million]). *Yeni Adam* 90 (1935): 4, 7.

Belen, Fahrettin Fehmi. "Çocuk Bakımı, Sağlık Öğütleri" (Child Care and Principles of Health). *Cumhuriyet* (5 May 1935): 8.

Cumhuriyet. Advertisement for Besi Süt Tozu. (3 September 1935): 9.

Cunningham, Hugh. The Children of the Poor: Representations of Childhood Since the Seventeenth Century. Cambridge, Mass.: Basil Blackwell, 1991.

Çocuk Esirgeme Kurumu. "Nüfus, Çocuk, Terbiye İşleri" (Population, the Child, and the Work of Education), *Gürbüz Türk Çocuğu* 97 (1934): 19–32.

Derviş, Suat. "Doktorlarımıza Göre Doğumlar ve Çocuk Ölümleri" (Births and Child Deaths According to our Doctors). *Gürbüz Türk Çocuğu* 104 (1935): 22–32.

Devellioğlu, Ferit, ed. Osmanlıca-Türkçe Ansiklopedik Lûgat (An Encyclopedic Ottoman-Turkish Glossary). Ankara: Doğuş Ltd. Şti. Matbaası, 1970.

Donzelot, Jacques. The Policing of Families. Translated by Robert Hurley. Baltimore: Johns Hopkins University Press, [1979]1997.

Dorey, Annette K. Vance. *Better Baby Contests: The Scientific Quest for Perfect Childhood Health in the Early Twentieth Century.* London: MacFarland, 1999.

Duben, Alan, and Cem Behar. *Istanbul Households: Marriage, Family and Fertility, 1880-1940.* Cambridge, Mass.: Cambridge University Press, 1991.

Fahriye, Dr. [last name unknown] "Çocuk Beslenme (1)" (Feeding Babies, Part 1). *Gürbüz Türk Çocuğu* 96 (1934): 13–15.

Foucault, Michel. "Governmentality." In *The Foucault Effect: Studies in Governmentality*, edited by Graham Burchell, Colin Gordon, and Peter Miller, 87–104. Chicago: University of Chicago Press, 1991.

Göle, Nilüfer. *The Forbidden Modern: Civilization and Veiling.* Ann Arbor, Mich.: University of Michigan Press, 1996.

Gürsöy, Akile. "Child Mortality and Changing Discourses on Childhood in Turkey." In *Children in the Muslim Middle East*, edited by Elizabeth Warnock Fernea, 199–222. Austin, Tex.: University of Texas Press, 1995.

"Her Ana Her Babaya" (To every mother and father). *Çocuk Haftası* 1 (1929): 173.

Kandiyoti, Deniz. "End of Empire: Islam, Nationalism and Women in Turkey." In *Women, Islam and the State*, edited by Deniz Kandiyoti, 22–47. Philadelphia: Temple University Press, 1991.

———. "Gendering the Modern: On Missing Dimensions in the Study of Turkish Modernity." In *Rethinking Modernity and National Identity in Turkey*, edited by Sibel Bozdoğan and Reşat Kasaba, 113–132. Seattle, Wash.: University of Washington Press, 1997.

Klaus, Alicia. *Every Child a Lion: The Origins of Maternal Health Policy in the United States and France, 1890–1920.* Ithaca, N.Y.: Cornell University Press, 1993.

Libal, Kathryn. "The Children's Protection Society: Nationalizing Child Welfare in the Early Republic." *New Perspectives on Turkey* 23 (2000): 53–78.

Nabi, Yaşar. "Nüfus Meselesi Karşısında Türkiye" (Turkey in the Face of the Population Question). *Ülkü* (September 1939): 33–39.

Okay, Cüneyd. *Osmanlı Çocuk Hayatında Yenileşmeler*, 1850–1900. (Transformations in the Ottoman Child's Life). Istanbul: Kırkambar Yayınları, 1998.

———. *Belgelerle Himayei Etfal Cemiyeti*, 1917–1923 (The Children's Protection Society in documents). Istanbul: Sule Yayınları, 1999.

Onur, Bekir, ed. *Toplumsal Tarihte Çocuk* (The Child in Social History). Istanbul: Tarih Vakfı, 1994.

Özbek, Nadir. "The Politics of Poor Relief in the Late Ottoman Empire." *New Perspectives on Turkey* 21 (1999): 1–33.

Phillips, Mabelle. "Widowhood." In *Constantinople Today, the Pathfinder Survey of Constantinople*, edited by Clarence R. Johnson, 287–321. New York: Macmillan, 1922.

Şahin, Mustafa. "23 Nisan ve Himaye-i Etfal" (April 23 and the Children's Protection Society). *Toplumsal Tarih* 40 (April 1997): 15–18.

Said, Edward. *Orientalism.* New York: Pantheon Books, 1978.

Schick, Irvin C. *The Erotic Margin: Sexuality and Spatiality in Alterist Discourse.* New York: Verso Press, 1999.

Shaw, Stanford J. "Resettlement of Refugees in Anatolia, 1918-1923." *Turkish Studies Association Bulletin* 22, no. 1 (1998): 58–90.

Shorter, Frederic C. "The Population of Turkey After the War of Independence." *International Journal of Middle East Studies* 17 (1985): 417–441.

Stephens, Sharon. "Editorial Introduction: Children and Nationalism." *Childhood* 4, no.1 (1996): 5–17.

Tunç, M. Şefik. "Nüfus Sayımı Kalkınma Çağıdır" (The Period of Preparing for the Census). *Yeni Adam* 93 (1935): 4, 11.

Türk Dil Kurumu. Tarama Sözlüğü. Vol. 3. Ankara: Türk Tarih Kurumu Basımevi, 1967.

Vakit. "Güzel ve Gürbüz Çocuk Müsabakası" (Beautiful and Robust child contest). (16 September 1932).

van Kriekan, Robert. *Children and the State: Social Control and the Formation of Australian Child Welfare*. Sydney: Allen and Unwin, 1991.

Zeki Nasır. "Halk Sıhhatı" (People's Health). *Ülkü* 1, no. 1 (1933): 70–72.

Zelizer, Viviana A. *Pricing the Priceless Child: The Changing Social Value of Children*. New York: Basic Books, 1985.

Zürcher, Erik J. *Turkey: A Modern History*. New York: I. B. Tauris, [1993] 1997.

Chapter 6

Governing Children: The Boy Scouts, the Girl Guides, and Visions of Canadian Nationhood, 1880–1921

Janice Hill

Early in the twentieth century, children everywhere donned special caps, shirts, and sashes and raced off to howl and chant with their "littermates" in weekly Boy Scout and Girl Guide meetings across Canada. While historians and sociologists recognize the sudden popularity of these organizations and others like them as significant to modern children's culture, a thorough account of the social context that contributed to their rise has yet to be produced (Strong-Boag 1988; Gillis 1974). This chapter takes a brief look at some of the historical circumstances fueling the Boy Scout and Girl Guide movements, and relates their burgeoning to the imbrication of pervasive evangelical and imperialist discourses that linked Canada's national development to the "improvement" of her children. Within these organizations, social critics and reformers alike sought to manage children's moral, mental, and physical health, and to inculcate them with qualities deemed beneficial to Canada's national development. The following analysis utilizes a governmentality framework to relate the governance of children to Canadian visions of nationhood in the earliest years of the twentieth century. In so doing, it points to various theoretical challenges in the study of childhood, particularly with respect to citizenship and nation-building.

The Rise of Children's Organizations

Despite a lack of official membership records, many historians regard the Boy Scout and Girl Guide movements as the most popular children's organizations of the twentieth century (Gillis 1974, 146; Sangster 1985, 80). Such claims are based on the international status of these organizations and their continued longevity. The Scouting movement officially emerged in England in 1909 with Sir Robert Baden-Powell's revised publication of *Scouting for Boys: A Handbook for Instruction in Good Citizenship*. This manual was widely distributed throughout the British Empire as Scouting rapidly spread to the British colonies, Europe, and North America. With no official administration or structure, ad hoc groups of Scouts and Guides found themselves meeting on street corners or in parks with Baden-Powell's manual tucked under their arms (McKee 1982, 66–68).

Fears about the disruptive potential of unsupervised groups of children spread almost as quickly as did scouting and guiding. In Canada parents, politicians, and social reformers turned to the government to legislate against unsupervised gatherings, while children looked to Baden-Powell for guidance and approval (Campbell, date unknown). Quickly, he organized an administrative structure under which Scouting flourished and in 1910 celebrated his sudden notoriety as Chief Scout of more than eleven thousand British Scouts. He directed his sister, Agnes, to initiate an independent organization of Girl Guides for the six thousand girls who unexpectedly sought membership in his "boys-only" movement. In 1912, Agnes published the *Handbook for Girl Guides or How Girls Can Help Build the Empire*, which provided a separate organizational structure under which the Girl Guide movement took shape (Rosenthal 1986; Jeal 1990).

The instant success of scouting and guiding in the early twentieth century is partly a result of the fact that club membership was already a familiar aspect of many children's lives. From the 1860s onward, membership in varied children's organizations steadily increased. Religiously-based organizations such as the Young Men's and Young Women's Christian Associations, for example, found international favor as a place where children undertook Bible study and acts of Christian citizenship (Mitchinson 1979). Similarly, membership also increased in military clubs such as the Cadet Corps. To buttress Britain's waning imperial presence, members developed physical fitness and discipline through military drill (Morton 1987). Special children's groups aimed directly at the working classes also formed within adult fraternal associations, such as the Freemasons or Oddfellows (Anstead 1992). Together, these organizations furnished an enthusiastic population from which the Boy Scouts and Girl Guides drew their members.

Unfortunately, demographics merely map migration; they do not explain why children left other popular organizations like the Woodcraft Indians and the Boy's Brigade to join scouting and guiding. A more sophisticated analysis regards their migration as part of a greater social phenomenon. I contend that the Boy Scout and Girl Guide movements developed as a manifestation of cultural expressions about Canadian nationhood as well as social fears of British imperial decline. With this in mind, our exploration of the government of children in scouting and guiding begins with a discussion of the ideology of "improvement."

The Dream That Could Be Canada

The desire to "improve" children is not new to the nineteenth century. It is evident even in early Greek and Roman societies which, like contemporary societies, believed children important to the development of the state (Wishy 1968). Specific ideas about how "improvement" is best achieved, however, are culturally distinct. Over the past two centuries, in particular, a gradual and significant shift in these ideas of "improvement" occurred. Concern for the development of virtue was replaced by promotion of character training. Whereas the development of virtue is rooted in Puritan ideas of redemption and stresses the submission of private interests for the public good, character training seeks to establish "normalized" or "proper" behaviors in children. It shapes children's identities by codifying behavior with moral meaning so that "unfit" behaviors are equated with "unfit" persons.

According to Foucault (1981), this gradual shift to character training is part of the ongoing process of modernization in which pastoral techniques of regulation are superseded by techniques of moral regulation. The rise of expert discourses such as medicine and education facilitate this shift. Subjectivities are constituted by the normalizing technology of expert knowledges, which simultaneously totalize and individualize society. Members are first categorized and then treated exclusively in terms of their membership in a set of social populations including the family, the employed, the poor, the immoral, and the undisciplined (Hacking 1991). So, modern subjectivities are the effect of constructed human taxonomies that are disseminated throughout society by pervasive discourses and regulatory practices.

Governmentality, which is the fundamental process of government in the modern liberal regime, refers to the process through which individuals come to govern themselves in accordance with these subjectivities. People adopt behaviors associated with a particular subjectivity and abandon those regarded as extraneous or inappropriate. Self-discipline makes this type of self-regulation possible as individuals learn to employ and curtail particular behaviors. A child who wishes to be a "good boy," for example, will govern himself according to the criteria that constitute this category (Foucault 1991). Moral discourses clearly order behavior that is identified as either positive and "improvement"-oriented or negative and "undesirable."

The modern discourse of "improvement" arose alongside changing attitudes to progress. Throughout the nineteenth century, modern thought had usually associated progress with positive economic and social change (Adas 1989). However, toward the end of the 1800s, Canadians became more and more alarmed by the increasingly obvious negative effects of industrialization. Pollution and disease accompanied social decay. Among other things, the dislocation of families, factory work, and political conflict pitted parents against children, class against class, and English against French (Valverde 1991; Berger 1985). Canada's welfare state and numerous philanthropic organizations emerged as governing mechanisms with agendas for "improvement" that offered a practical means to redirect society toward progress.

By the early 1900s, children actively "improved" themselves through numerous regulatory practices that pervaded their lives. More and more, discourses facilitated their moral development within an increasingly liberal family environment and an expanding public school system. Lay persons joined experts and family members in their task to teach moral self-regulation to Canada's children within a growing social arena that included their clubs and societies (Wishy 1968). The emerging Boy Scout and Girl Guide movements, with their emphasis on "improvement" and moral regulation, epitomize this implementation of character training ideals in the leisure activities of children.

The immediate popularity of these movements is partly a result of their ideological capacity to weave together two popular discourses that present different views of Canadian society and distinct visions of the country's national future. Both claim children as Canada's greatest national resource, and both advocate their "improvement" by various means. The first view is rooted in Evangelicalism. It names Canada as the preordained site of God's earthly kingdom, regarding "improvement" as the means to develop children's godly character. "Improvement" provides the measure of Canada's potential to fulfill this evangelical mission (Westfall 1989, 5–6). The second is rooted in imperialism and claims that Canada's inevitable emergence as a global leader in the twentieth century will stem the decay of Britain's Empire. The "improvement" of children secures British supremacy through the development of physical fitness, respect for colonial roots, and military training (Berger 1970, 3). In both these views, childhood emerges as a site where "improvement" is best realized, and organizations like the Boy Scouts and Girl Guides are convenient venues for the realization of these visions of Canadian nationhood.

Building God's Earthly Kingdom: The Importance of Christian Citizenship

By the early 1900s, Methodism was the largest religious denomination in Canada, constituting as much as 80 percent of her population. Many Methodists advocated ambitious social reforms and realized their philanthropic ideals within the Social Gospel movement (Westfall 1989). Their evangelical ideology found widespread support as they worked to "improve" the Christian community through acts of Christian citizenship and transform children into soldiers fit for fighting God's war against sin and vice. The Social Gospel movement initiated numerous children's clubs such as the Methodist Epworth League and the Young People's Forward Movement for Missions (McKee 1982, 27). In their view, a number of techniques, including those used by Puritans to develop Christian virtue, could be used in the "improvement" of children.

Bible study was the first of these means. Until the mid-nineteenth century, Bible study was considered essential to develop Christian virtue since it provided the intellectual context for a deeper understanding of Christian morality. The direct study of good and evil taught readers to associate particular behavior with moral constitution. Lying, stealing, or sexual promiscuity indicated degraded morality; generosity, honesty, and patience signified a finer morality (Valverde 1994). Moral education focused on the development of restraint and the prevention of behaviors associated with vice (Semple 1996, 376–82). Children displaying immoral behavior could find themselves enduring severe physical punishments, because sparing the rod often meant spoiling the child.

Evangelicals used other techniques to "improve" children as their ideas about Christian morality broadened to reflect popular perceptions of character training. Learning through example became a key focus of religious education. Congregations formed church-based literary clubs, reading circles, and debating and singing classes designed to improve the knowledge and life skills of churchgoers and encourage Christian community among like-minded people (McKee 1982, 35). As Social Gospelers undertook philanthropic and missionary work, their commitment to learning through example soon extended beyond the boundaries of church property. Christian behavior was strongly advocated by Social Gospelers who lured the working class, non-church-goers, children and others "in need of moral uplift" to weekly club meetings with the promise of fun, friendship, and free education (Semple 1996, 334–35).

The perceived need of Social Gospelers for improvement was closely tied to their collective vision of Canada's future, wherein they saw themselves and Methodism as vital to national development. In their view, only a unified Methodist spirit that manifested itself in seemingly inexhaustible philanthropic energies, along with a celebrated dedication to strenuous labor, would enable Canadians to achieve the highest moral standards on earth. When Reverend J. Edward Starr declared: "Take care of the children and the nation will take care of itself," he revealed a popular incentive behind the improvement of children. Forward-looking Christians valued children for their nation-building potential, and they focused on educating them for future Christian citizenship (Sutherland 1976, 17).

With this goal in mind, Methodists used social reform to expand the limits of pastoral care beyond Bible study to include personal and community activities. While some philanthropists and politicians focused on developing state structures and regulations that would alleviate the social conditions of those in need, others promoted the education and training of Canadian citizens through various voluntary organizations and clubs that would eventually be perceived as lying beyond the protective embrace of the church (Christie and Gauvreau 1996). Organizations such as the Girls' Friendly Society and the Little Helper's Department of the Anglican Church focused on the development of Christian citizenship, thus becoming rich sites for the training of children. Consistent with Puritan traditions, children were taught a sense of duty to God and were directed to express this duty through acts of community service. Privileging the needs of others helped children develop the moral self-discipline that enabled self-government.

Girls, in particular, flocked to organizations such as the Young People's Forward Movement for Missions, which focused on social service and missionary work and pushed them out into the world as fine examples of moral fitness and propriety. Delivering prayer books to the poor or distributing milk to impoverished mothers gave them a sense of self-worth that was tied to national development. These activities were more readily undertaken than the increasingly controversial tasks of street-corner preaching and pamphleting advocated by the Salvation Army, for example. As extensions of benevolence and charity work, they were thought consistent with Victorian notions of femininity (Marks 1996). In linking Methodism, morality, and missionary work to acts of Christian citizenship, a generation of children found personal value as agents of social change, and vehicles for ensuring Canada's future as civilization's most moral nation.

Saving the Empire: Making Right with Military Might

The Methodist vision depicting Canada as the moral center of the modern world fueled the rise of church-based children's organizations that later evolved into Christian service-oriented clubs. Other children's organizations were influenced by another vision of Canada's future, which celebrated Canada's British roots. Imperialists maintained that Canada would achieve global power during the twentieth century, leading the world "in acts of civilization...bring[ing] light to dark places... teach[ing] the true political method...[and] nourish[ing] and protect[ing] the liberal tradition." Her mission to civilize would first bolster, then renew the declining British Empire (Thorton 1963, ix). Like Methodists, imperialists were interested in the "improvement" of Canadian children who were the means to achieve political strength. Character training meant developing their children as a military resource for defense of the Canadian nation and British Empire.

As it is best known, Canadian imperialism is rooted in Loyalist sentiments of the late 1700s. It was perpetuated throughout the 1800s by popular Canadian narratives that told of the victories of British-American Loyalists against the degradation of American democracy and republicanism. Rejecting the ideals of the American Revolution, the story goes, an alienated and destitute band of "farmers and artisans, laborers and merchants...doctors, lawyers, and clergymen" abandoned their homes and families. They journeyed north, struggling through the Canadian wilderness, to live as loyal subjects of Britain's great, and white empire. These narratives celebrate Loyalist links to Britain and make heroes of those whose great moral strength privileged allegiance to Britain over family, friends, and fortune (Errington 1987, 3–5).

The importance of Canada's connection to Britain was firmly planted in her collective imagination by the early 1900s (Berger 1985). It was promoted, in part, by increasingly pervasive scientific approaches to racial development that claimed the British were the most highly evolved people on earth. This view was substantiated by the concept of recapitulation that was popularized by G. Stanley Hall, founder of the American Child Study movement in the late 1800s. His view that "ontogeny recapitulates phylogeny" meant that during their individual life span people repeated the life history of their race. Simply put, a child progressed through lower forms of cultural development such as savagery and barbarism apparent in childhood to a state of civilization in their adult years. Races developed at different paces and demonstrated different capacities for development. Blacks, he postulated, were the most limited, remaining in a childlike stage throughout their adult years. Only in rare cases could individuals develop beyond the limits of their racial heritage. Hall claimed that character training must occur during childhood when all children were naturally malleable. By the late nineteenth century, recapitulation theory had pervaded biology, anthropology, psychology, child study, and pedagogy, and influenced the development of Canada's welfare state as well as people's leisure activities (Russett 1989, 50–51).

Social programs were further influenced by Lamarckian genetics, which proposed that acquired characteristics were, in fact, hereditary. "Social vices" such as prostitution and alcoholism were thought to be transferred from generation to generation of "unfit," "improper," and "feeble-minded" people. With the fate of the Canadian race in peril, growing concerns for the miscegenation of Canada's "fit" population fueled extreme responses. For example, Helen MacMurchy, one of Canada's leading healthcare reformers, advocated sterilization of the "feeble-minded," who consisted mostly of the poor, immigrants, and the unemployed, on the grounds that the hereditary nature of these conditions endangered the quality of Canada's "normal" population (McLaren 1990, 30–45). Social reformers used scientific principles to identify and deal with populations that put Canada's future at risk.

Recapitulation theory placed British culture at the apex of civilization, thereby lending "scientific" support to the vision of Canadian imperialists who maintained that British rule was both biologically inevitable and morally desirable (Gollwitzer 1969, 160). However, prominent thinkers such as George Denison, Henry Morgan, Charles Mair, Robert Grant Haliburton, and William Foster, who in 1868 founded Canada's most influential imperialist organization, the Canada

First Movement, believed that Canadian society had the capacity to evolve beyond the limits of British civilization. These men accepted the popular myth that Canada had been formed by the hard-working hands and quick minds of British Loyalists, and they used it to champion the view that Canadians possessed the physiological, intellectual, and moral qualities required to achieve global supremacy. Canada's population was thought to be unusually strong, being constantly culled by harsh winters that left only the healthiest alive (Berger 1985, 128–30). In their view, Canada's rise to global power and her role in rejuvenating the British Empire were inevitable. Inferior peoples would soon overrun Britain because there was no similar natural select process, and the healthiest British stock had been lost in colonial wars (Pick 1989). The ongoing improvement of Canada's children would save the British Empire.

For many men and boys, in particular, militarism provided the ideological and structural framework for their "improvement." Membership in quasi-military organizations like the Cadet Corps seemed a natural extension of turn-of-the-century views of masculinity that frequently found expression in Empire Day parades, an idolatry of the monarchy, and support for the Boer War. In these organizations, character training meant "improving" morality and physique through military drill. Esprit de corps developed through fair play and civic duty, and self-discipline meant respecting authority (Millar 1998). Within these organizations, character training would transform young Canadians into superior and dependable citizen-soldiers, "improve" the health of the Canadian race, and hasten her civilizing mission (Kett 1977, 219–21).

For God and Empire:
The Imbrication of Sacred and Secular

The unprecedented success of Baden-Powell's scouting and guiding movements can be attributed, in part, to their embodiment of both evangelical and militaristic ideals, which broadened their appeal and brought their members into the mainstream of Canadian society. The imbrication of these two popular discourses meant that these organizations grew beyond the limits of the many church or military-based organizations that predate them. Children, who saw scouting and guiding as fashionable expressions of popular culture, considered their members on the cutting edge of Canadian culture (Campbell, date unknown).

The fact that historians of children's culture frequently describe scouting and guiding as secular and militaristic demonstrates the invisibility of evangelism within historical accounts of mainstream culture (McKee 1982). This problem is well-noted by theorists such as Christie and Gauvreau (1996), who challenge the presumed, marked distinction between secular and non-secular society in historical thought. They challenge theorists who downplay the influence of evangelism and construct a false distinction between the sacred and secular realms, and who relegate to the secular sphere social phenomena not overtly bounded by the church. Accounts of scouting and guiding must consider the conflation of the Methodist evangelical mission with imperial duty to the Empire, if they are to more fully understand the value of children in national development.

By the early 1900s, Canada's elite was composed primarily of Methodists who took their religious sensibilities out into the world through acts of Christian citizenship (Christie and Gauvreau 1996). This fact is reflected in the governing councils of the scouting and guiding movements, which were almost exclusively composed of influential Methodist social reformers such as Lord Strathcona, Mr. E. B. Osler, Lady Pellat, Mrs. F. H. Torrington, and Mrs. Adelaide Hoodless. Their evangelical influence is apparent as these organizations sought to produce Canadian citizens who would embody both Christian and imperial ideals. Through acts of service, Scouts and Guides would fulfill their obligations to God, the British Empire, and the Canadian nation. When Scouts helped build churches and clear snow from hospital walkways and Guides taught working-class factory girls how to pour tea or recite the Lord's Prayer, they enacted evangelical notions of morality and propriety (Dominion Council of Baden-Powell's Girl Guides, no date, unpublished).

The conflation of evangelicalism and imperialism is evidenced by the familial metaphor invoked by the scouting and guiding movements. It drew attention to the imperial obligation of Canadian boys and girls. As "dutiful sons and daughters of the empire," boys were expected to train for defense of the empire so that they would be better citizens and soldiers, while girls were encouraged to prepare themselves for their most important role as "mothers of the empire" (Jeal 1990). This metaphor was used throughout the Boy Scout and Girl Guide manuals to inspire children to find worth in the moral code and character-training agenda that these organizations espoused.

Character Training in the Boy Scouts and Girl Guides

Baden-Powell's involvement in this century's most popular children's organizations surprised even himself. Initially, he had wanted merely to produce a manual that would teach boys, through example, to govern themselves according to imperial ideals, and provide them with both the spirit and the know-how needed to defend the British Empire against moral and physical decline. However, the immense popularity of his writings fueled the need for more carefully guided administration of his ideas. Baden-Powell's desire to develop children's character through the distribution of the Boy Scout Manual demonstrates the general population's growing familiarity with expert discourses and their views on child development. His approach reflects increasingly popular educational techniques espoused by educators such as Henry Goddard, who believed that children needed only to be exposed to appropriate behaviors in order to choose them, and that most children, and especially white children, would develop self-discipline if exposed to disciplinary regimens (Margolin 1994).

Baden-Powell's manual provided boys with a strict moral structure which reflected traditional perceptions of masculinity that linked manliness to soldiering. But it delivered this morality through radical and new techniques of training that did not include the usual methods of military drill, calisthenics, or Bible study. Instead, boys built their moral and physical health and "improved" their soldiering abilities through service-oriented outings, and fantasy-oriented games and activities. Scouts were organized into patrols where they learned survival skills and the art of camp craft. He outlined games and activities that would build their moral and physical health through skills development, fantasy-oriented games, and service-oriented outings (McKee 1982). In scouting, boys were exposed to a modern, and more exciting, masculine subjectivity that stressed personal growth through challenge and adventure.

Self-discipline would make them better soldiers, and facilitate nation-building. Scouting encouraged members to exhibit manliness through militarism by developing a sense of patriotic loyalty, fair play, and boyish camaraderie. Members demonstrated their commitment to these principles by adopting special salutes and military-looking uniforms. Anxious to experience this emerging subjectivity of boy–citizen-soldier, Canadian boys raced to Scout meetings where they imagined themselves a peacetime fighting-force, ready to spring to action if called upon (Warren 1986; Bristow 1991).

Similarly, the guiding movement "improved" girls, training in the ways of womanly citizenship. The foundational belief that character training better enabled girls to fulfill their most vital role as the future mothers of the Canadian race embodied conventional Victorian ideals of femininity that associated womanliness with nurture and service to others. But under the direction of her brother, Agnes Baden-Powell embraced a more modern and highly controversial ideal of femininity that challenged the existing boundaries of appropriate female behavior and introduced girls to a new subjectivity that rejected the linking of womanliness to frailty. Guiding trained girls for self-reliance by enhancing a wide variety of their existing life skills and by introducing them to many others. The Baden-Powells justified their radical program by claiming that a well-skilled woman made a better citizen and mother (Baden-Powell 1912, 22).

Guides were to observe high standards of fitness and develop expertise in a particular sport such as sailing or cycling, receiving proficiency badges for their mastery. To earn proficiency badges, in most cases, Guides were required to meet the same criteria as were Scouts (Baden-Powell 1912). At times, their "special" status as girls exposed them to even more rigorous tests of fitness. In the early years of the organization, for example, Guides were required to swim the same distance as Scouts to earn their swimming badge. However, the girls wore a water-logged rope around their waist, which presumably made them easier to retrieve should exhaustion set in (Campbell, date unknown). Girls were also encouraged to develop skills in areas traditionally associated with masculinity, including airplane mechanics, rifle-shooting, electrical wiring, and fire brigading. Developing these skills fueled social fears that girls might become too "coarse" or "develop mustaches," and these concerns were allayed by claims that improved floral arrangement, tailoring, and cooking skills would offset masculinization   (Forbes 1984, 9; Jeal 1990, 470). Guides were also encouraged to express their "natural" feminine instincts through social service.

Both scouting and guiding codified the moral views of founder Robert Baden-Powell, who maintained that self-reliance (in both boys and girls) enabled one to lead an exemplary life of national and imperial service. His moral code, which advocated trust, loyalty, obedience, self-sacrifice, honor, and courtesy, among other things, was laid out in ten concise laws to which all scouts and guides had to adhere. Baden-Powell's commitment to the ideology of "improvement" through self-regulation was foundational, and this fueled the movements' character training agendas. This expectation is clearly encapsulated in the Scout and Guide Promise. When children promised to "do [their] best, to do [their] duty to God and the King, to help other people at all times, [and] to obey the Scout [Guide] Law," they vowed to try to become their best possible person. In Baden-Powell's mind, character training began with the realization of one's limitations and the commitment to overcome them (Rosenthal 1986, 113). The transformation of all children, the Canadian nation, and the British Empire began with this fundamental principle of improvement.

Conclusion: On the Government of Children

Over the past two decades, discourse analysis has consistently demonstrated the ways in which social processes of power constitute identity, and the reverse. This knowledge has impacted on recent approaches in the study of childhood, where researchers now understand childhood as a categorical construction that both reflects and impacts on the social world. This study of the rise of Canada's Scouting and guiding movements demonstrates the impact of discourse analysis on the categorical construction of childhood.

Analysis of evangelical and imperial discourses reveals the ways in which children are categorically constructed to embody two distinct, but compatible, visions of Canada's future. In both cases, children represent a national resource. Their management, through state and philanthropic processes, is justified by the belief that Canada's spiritual and imperial destiny rests in the hands of her children: Children are made relevant to and available for national development. When children are constructed as agents of national development, childhood is politicized. With this in mind, we are called to rethink traditional liberal and Marxist treatments of childhood that either tend to ignore children altogether, allocate their concerns to the private sphere of the family, or append them to their mothers. Further, we are encouraged to reexamine our understandings of the related concepts of citizenship and nation, which usually treat childhood as irrelevant.

Similarly, the theoretical concept of governmentality helps us re-imagine children as active agents in the constitution of their own identities and suggests a more sophisticated understanding of agency. In choosing to adopt or reject a particular subjectivity, children author themselves. The immense popularity of Scouting and Guiding in the first decades of the twentieth century, which made accessible modern constructions of masculinity and femininity, illustrates children's power of and calls into question more conventional perceptions of children as passive, or as the manifestation of genetically predetermined identities.

Our examination of scouting and guiding demonstrates the capacity of the governmentality framework to expand our understanding of the government of children to include a more thorough understanding of morality and nation-building, two areas not usually associated with the study of childhood. Moral discourses work through a variety of venues, including philanthropic children's organizations, to inculcate youngsters with qualities thought to further national goals. Conventional research has often failed to acknowledge the government of individuals through their leisure activities. Documentation of the efforts to "improve" young people through organizations such as the Boy Scouts and Girl Guides demonstrates the need to rethink the place of philanthropy and leisure in modern techniques of government.

In the early years of the twentieth century, Canadians dreamed of greatness. Hopes for realizing this dream were placed squarely on the shoulders of children, who symbolized national potential. Concerns about fulfilling this potential.pervaded a variety of discourse, and were expressed in widespread support for the "improvement" of Canadian children. Organizations such as the Boy Scouts and Girl Guides evolved alongside of this increasing desire for national progress. Clearly, children joined these organizations for a variety of reasons. Perhaps they simply wanted friendship, fun, and adventure. Or they wished to explore the alternate and more modern forms of masculinity and femininity that these organizations encouraged. Also, possibly, perhaps children were called by a sense of commitment to fulfill Canada's national dream. Regardless of their motivations, the Boy Scout and Girl Guide movements were the most popular sites for achieving all three of these possibilities.[1]

ACKNOWLEDGMENT

I would like to thank Dan Cook for his editorial assistance and patience as I worked to produce this Chapter. I thank Gordon Darroch and Steven Longstaff for their contributions to earlier treatments of this topic. I assume responsibility for any errors and omissions found within.

REFERENCES

Adas, Michael. *Machines as the Measure of Men: Science, Technology, and Ideologies of Western Dominance*. Ithaca: Cornell University Press, 1989.

Anstead, Christopher. *Fraternalism in Victorian Ontario: Secret Societies and Cultural Hegemony*. Unpublished Ph.D. diss. London: University of Western Ontario, 1992.

Baden-Powell, Agnes. *The Handbook for Girl Guides or How Girls Can Help Build the Empire*. London: Thomas Nelson and Sons, 1912.

Baden-Powell, Robert. *Scouting for Boys: A Handbook for Instruction in Good Citizenship*. London: Thomas Nelson and Sons, 1909.

Berger, Carl. *The Sense of Power: Studies in the Ideas of Canadian Imperialism, 1867–1914*. Toronto: University of Toronto, 1985.

Bristow, Joseph. *Empire Boys: Adventures in a Man's World*. London: Harper Collins Academic Press, 1991.

Campbell, Mrs. Colin. *Oral History: Interview Collection*. Toronto: National Girl Guide Archives, [date unknown].

Christie, Nancy, and Michael Gauvreau. *A Full-Orbed Christianity: The Protestant Churches and Social Welfare in Canada 1900–1940*. Montreal and Kingston: McGill-Queen's University Press, 1996.

Commachio, Cynthia. *Nations Are Built of Babies: Saving Ontario's Mothers and Children, 1900–1914*. Montreal : McGill-Queen's University Press, 1993.

Dominion Council of Baden-Powell's Girl Guides. Unpublished *Minutes of Meetings: 1909-1921*. Toronto: National Girl Guide Archives, no date.

Errington, Jane. *The Lion, the Eagle, and Upper Canada: A Developing Colonial Ideology*. Montreal and Kingston: McGill-Queen's University Press, 1987.

Forbes, Cynthia. *Girl Guide Album*. London: Girl Guide Association, 1984.

Foucault, Michel. "Omnes et Singulatim: Towards a Criticism of 'Political Reason.'" In *The Tanner Lectures*, edited by Sterling M. McMurrin. Salt Lake City: University of Utah Press, 1981.

Gillis, John. *Youth and History*. New York: Academic Press, 1974

Gollwitzer, Heinz. *Europe in the Age of Imperialism 1880–1914*. London: Thames and Hudson, 1969.

Hacking, Ian. "How Should We Do the History of Statistics?" In *The Foucault Effects: Studies in Governmentality*, edited by Graham Burchell, Colin Gordon, and Peter Miller. Chicago: University of Chicago Press, 1991.

Hall, G. Stanley. *Adolescence: Its Psychology and its Relations to Physiology, Anthropology, Sociology, Sex, Crime, Religion and Education*, vols. 1 and 2. New York: D. Appleton, 1901.

Jeal, Tim. *Baden-Powell*. London: Hutchinson, 1990.

Kett, Joseph. *Rites of Passage: Adolescence in America 1790 to the Present*. New York: Basic Books Inc., 1977.

Margolin, Leslie. *Goodness Personified: The Emergence of Gifted Children*. New York: Aldine de Gruyter, 1994.

Marks, Lynne. *Revivals and Roller Rinks: Religion, Leisure, and Identity in Late-Nineteenth-Century Small-Town Ontario*. Toronto: University of Toronto Press, 1996.

McKee, Leila Gay Mitchell. *Voluntary Youth Organizations in Toronto, 1880–1930*. Unpublished Ph.D diss., North York: York University, 1982.

McLaren, Angus. *Our Own Master Race: Eugenics in Canada, 1885–1945*. Toronto McClelland and Stewart, 1990.

Millar, Carman. *Painting the Map Red: Canada and the South African War, 1899–1902*. Montreal and Kingston: McGill-Queen's University Press, 1998.

Mitchinson, Wendy. "The YWCA and Reform in the Nineteenth Century." *Histoire Sociale/Social History* 24 (1979): 368–84.

Morton, Desmond. "The Cadet Movement in the Moment of Canadian Militarism, 1909-1914." *Journal of Canadian Studies* 13, no. 2 (1978): 56–68

Pick, Daniel. *Faces of Degeneration: A European Disorder, c. 1848–c.1918*, Cambridge, Mass.: Cambridge University Press, 1989.

Rosenthal, Michael. *The Character Factory: Baden-Powell and the Origins of the Boy Scout Movement*. New York: Pantheon Books, 1986.

Rules, Policy and Organization. London: Girl Guide Association of Canada, 1919.

Russett, Cynthia Eagle. *Sexual science: The Victorian Construction of Womanhood*. Cambridge: Harvard University Press, 1989.

Sangster, Dorothy. "Girl Guides: 75 Glorious Years." *Chatelaine*, June (1985): 80-86.

Semple, Neil. *The Lord's Dominion: The History of Canadian Methodism*. Montreal and Kingston: McGill-Queen's University Press, 1996.

Strong-Boag, Veronica. *The New Day Recalled: Lives of Girls and Women in English Canada, 1919–1939*. Toronto: Copp Clark Pitman, 1988.

Sutherland, Neil. *Children in English-Canadian Society*. Toronto: University of Toronto Press, 1976.

Thorton, Archibald P. *The Imperial Dream and its Enemies: A Study in British Power*. London: MacMillan, 1963.

Valverde, Mariana. *The Age of Light, Soap, and Water: Moral Reform in English Canada, 1885–1925*, Toronto: McClelland and Stewart, 1991.

Valverde, Mariana. "Moral Capital." *Canadian Journal of Law and Society* 9, no. 1 (1994): 1–19.

Warren, Allen. "Baden-Powell, Scouts and Guides, and an Imperial Ideal." In *Imperialism and Popular Culture*, edited by John MacKenzie. Manchester: Manchester University Press, 1986.

Westfall, William. *Two Worlds: The Protestant Culture of 19th Century Ontario*. Montreal and Kingston: McGill-Queen's University Press, 1989.

Wishy, Bernard. *The Child and the Republic: The Dawn of Modern American Child Nurture*. Philadelphia: University of Pennsylvania Press, 1968.

PART THREE

The Social Value of Children

Chapter 7

"China 'R' Us"?:
Care, Consumption, and Transnationally Adopted Children

Sara K. Dorow

Lynn Besky, the director of Adoption Links, was clearly torn, aware that she worked in a business rife with the contradictions and overlaps of care and consumption. It didn't help that at the heart of the business lay children, constructed as both needy and valuable and often held up as a measure of the social moral pulse. As I questioned Lynn about these tensions, she gave a wry laugh. "Well, as we say, we *always* say, 'The client is the child.' But our clients in this case don't pay the bills! So you do serve somewhat at the mercy of your families, who are paying your bills." Adoption Links[1] is an international adoption agency whose continued service relies heavily on the payments of adoptive parents and whose statement of philosophy is: "We believe in meeting both the child's needs and the adoptive family's needs throughout the adoption process." As Lynn's statement suggests, however, those perceived needs do not always neatly coincide, in part because the commitment to care coexists with the exigencies of competition and consumption. That "the child" is not only client but also object of desire and exchange in the process of international adoption brings into further relief these uneven and sometimes uncomfortable relationships among care, consumption, and the construction of need.

It is the relationship between care and consumption—how they conflict, overlap, and construct each other—that is my main concern in this essay. While cultures of care and rationalities of the market are often pitted against each other as opposing or even incompatible forces (Tronto 1993; Kuttner 1996), I want to explore how market and nonmarket sensibilities interrelate. Central to this approach is an understanding of needs, interests, and desires as produced through and in complex social relations—relations between parents and children, states and families, caregivers and care receivers, and discourses[2] of care and consumption. How is it that practices can refer to care and consumption, familism and the market, without contradiction? How are needs produced at the intersections of these different discourses as actors enter into relationships with each other? And what does it mean that the value and needs of children figure so centrally? I respond to these questions through the specific case of the international adoption of Chinese children into U.S. families.

The Case of Transnational Adoption of Chinese Children

Chinese adoption is a rich and provocative site for investigating the construction of needs within the operations of care and consumption. Although U.S. adoption of Chinese children appeared on the formal adoption scene in a significant way only about eight years ago, it has quickly grown to become one of the two largest international programs in the United States[3] and has gained quite a bit of public attention. This attention was focused in 1995 and 1996 on controversial reports of human rights abuses in Chinese orphanages but has also included media coverage of adoption travel narratives, individual children's stories, and even the alleged fashionability of adopting a Chinese girl.

The growing popularity of the China program, in general, is due in large part to a relatively straightforward and predictable process, the availability of healthy infant girls, generous age requirements, and openness to nonmarried adoptive parents. This package appeals, in part, to the desires and needs of a population of well-educated, professional, well-to-do, and mostly white families in the United States who for a variety of reasons are entering the international adoption arena. Many have experienced infertility, some express charitable humanitarian and/or religious motivations, and some have simply chosen adoption as a preferred way of family-building. For many parents, the imagery of China's ancient history and culture (however vague or clear this notion might be), and in some cases the vision of a beautiful "China doll," also contributes to the appeal of the program.[4] Indeed, around the U.S.

Consulate in Guangzhou (where all U.S. families apply for their adopted children's visas) this imaginary is packaged by tourist shops that urge adoptive parents to take home everything from silk baby outfits to Chinese/English calligraphy name cards as a memento for their children; one shop is even called "China Doll."

Transnational adoption is broadly useful for examining care and consumption because it brings into the field of analysis a variety of cultural practices, social actors, and institutional arrangements, both local and global. It therefore nudges exploration of the multilayered social relations in which care and consumption are understood and practiced. At the same time, the centrality of children to the adoption process provides an analytical focal point for the complex web of desires and needs that cohere around them. To unpack that complex web means looking at the variety of social relations that surround the child in adoptions from China. While I cannot deal sufficiently with all or even most of those actors in this chapter, I concentrate on the Adoption Links agency and on adoptive families in a *parent-run* support organization that I call Red Threads; both are in a metropolitan area in the western part of the United States. I conducted more than a dozen in-depth interviews, participated in and/or observed at numerous events, and examined video and written materials produced by both organizations. In addition, I refer to data gathered over three years of research on this topic in both the United States and China, of which this particular essay is a part.

Since children are at the center of the process I am analyzing, I should say a word about the subjectivity of children and why it is that they may seem absent as actors in this project. While I did not directly interview or extensively observe children adopted from China for this particular project—in part because most of them were still quite young— children always figure into my analysis via the social relations of which they are a part, through both everyday practices and cultural representations. I take seriously the need to take *children* seriously as active subjects in social relations, not merely as objects of care, consumption, or exchange. Anne Solberg (1997) and Barrie Thorne et al. (1998), for example, demonstrate that childhood is variously understood and negotiated both by children and adults. I also heed Sharon Stephens' (1996) warning: "The child—as a crucial modern symbol of nature and the object of protection and enculturation—is at risk of being written off as yet another postmodern discursive fiction" (10). I want to avoid making children into either static nonactors upon which the world acts or merely abstract texts off of which to read the social.

Nevertheless, it is precisely because the child is "a crucial modern symbol of nature and the object of protection and enculturation" that children are simultaneously a much-contemplated site of care and increasingly the target or even the product of commodification and consumption (Suransky 1982; Glenn 1992; Anagnost 1997). Danae Clark (1998) demonstrates, for example, that depictions of adoption on television capitalize (quite literally) on the discomfort and fascination evoked by images of the exchange of children adopted and then reclaimed—images that simultaneously upset and tap into a "pure" model of family care. While transnationally adopted children are not bought and sold, as they "change hands" and cross borders, the people and institutions around them enter into social relations of exchange, meaning, and value that are both caring and consumptive. Lynn's reference to the child as "client" is one example of these interlocking discourses of care and consumption in the transnational adoption of Chinese children. As Anagnost (1999) points out: "The anxiety that the child might be a commodity is aroused by the incontrovertible fact that as the child moves from one site of nurture to another, money has to change hands; agencies are established; 'baby flights' are chartered; tour packages are assembled" (8). In spite of this anxiety, or perhaps in part because of it, funds are raised for "unadoptable" orphans; training services are enhanced; strategies are devised for confronting the deplorable question, "How much did she cost?" Thus, care and consumption are found impossible to disentangle, even more so as we examine the construction of needs in transnational adoption.

Conceptualizing Care, Consumption, and Needs

The starting point for my theoretical understanding of the relationships among care, consumption, and needs is Joan Tronto's (1993) *Moral Boundaries*. In this provocative book, Tronto argues for reinserting an ethic of care into public discourses of citizenship and the social good. In doing so, she usefully pulls morality from the grasp of a bounded Kantian framework based on abstract, formal, and universal principles and places it instead on the grounds of political and social practice, emphasizing the interdependence of caring practices. Despite these important steps, I am uncomfortable with the way Tronto's argument seems to reinscribe an individualized and autonomous subject. The identities of caregivers and care recipients are not fully intersubjective;

rather, they are characterized as possessing individually identifiable needs, as well as certain amounts and types of power, that are dangerously close to being essentialized.[5] Thus, caring practices become discrete acts between individualized giver and receiver, rather than activities embedded in complex social relations of power.[6]

This is not to say that Tronto ignores power and politics. She asserts that moral situations are complicated by power imbalances (3, 13) and asks, "How can political contexts affect the acceptability of moral arguments?" (5). But Tronto's approach to power could be thicker; I want to add that one must also ask, "How do political—including economic—contexts create arguments that are taken to be moral?" The first question makes it possible to separate moral arguments from power relations and sociohistorical processes; the second makes it impossible. This may seem an unnecessarily subtle point, but it is important to the task of rethinking power as productive of caring relations and to understanding the needs, interests, and desires within which one is disposed to care. Needs and interests are thus seen to be constructed within social relations of exchange that are as much about processes of market and consumption as they are about a morality (or even a politics) of caring.

Finally, while Tronto acknowledges the false dichotomy of private and public, she uses metaphors of invasion—"capitalism has continued to spread to all corners of the globe, and to infiltrate the lives of people everywhere" (150)—that pit market and care against each other and also reify the market as a unified force.[7] Kuttner (1996) creates a similar picture when he asserts that "more aspects of human life are on the auction block" (39) or concludes: "Consumers have wants. Citizens have values" (47). I find problematic the characterization of the market as a unified invader, let alone a recent one. Of interest is not how capitalist relations of power are necessarily antithetical to caring practices but possibly intertwined, and how consumers and citizens have been and are created together, if sometimes disjunctively.

Haskell's (1985) work on the historical relationship between capitalism and humanitarianism is useful on several counts for reframing Tronto's argument. Haskell is interested in establishing a connection between the growth of humanitarian sensibility and market rationality "without reducing humane values and acts to epiphenomena in the process" (341). He does so by arguing that sympathy follows certain "recipes" of perceived causation and intervention, facilitated by market practices and technological changes. The link Haskell posits between capitalism and humanitarianism may thus be summarized as follows: The market teaches the "lessons" of promise-keeping and of attention to remote consequences, and it opens up the possibility of new techniques for efficacy in human affairs.

Haskell's genealogy highlights several issues absent or lacking in Tronto's framework. First, he takes on the burden of demonstrating how the market, "an institution that explicitly foreshortens or confines within narrow, formal limits the responsibility of each person for his fellow man, [can] be said to have extended anyone's sense of moral responsibility" (548). The market is not just the evil opposite of care and sympathy, but even possibly helps to explain the disciplines that allowed for the (limited) extension of them. Second, his framework intimately ties sentiment to social practices that are economic, political, and ideological. While Haskell may be seen to unnecessarily recreate an economic determinism, his concept of the market accommodates both material and cultural processes. In such a framework, needs and interests are not *a priori* extant but are constructed within social relations of exchange that are both facilitated and constrained by a particular discourse, or cognitive style.[8]

Haskell says he does not want to be an apologist for capitalism; neither do I. Rather, I want to say that capitalism, like care, is a discourse (see Mitchell 1998) that operates in different places and times in different ways. I think it is unhelpful and possibly even dangerous to frame the market as a monolithic threat, or care as a uniform good, for then certain relations of power get erased.

It is unfortunate that Haskell falls short of explicitly theorizing power on more than the level of individual action and that he inadequately acknowledges cultural practices of sentiment and market across locality, particularly within global capitalism.[9] In trying to better understand care within relations of power, I find the work of Selma Sevenhuisen (1998) helpful. Like Tronto, Sevenhuisen is looking for a way to bring care into political life and citizenship, arguing that a focus on practice is the most useful starting point. But in doing so, she adopts a theory of power *à la* Foucault that is more nuanced than that of either Tronto or Haskell. In her framework, conflicting notions of care become elements in power strategies, and it is in the analysis of how human agents engaged in caring practices perceive and interpret them that power relations are understood. Care is both a discourse and a practice:

> Practices and discourses exist independently of particular social subjects, yet they are also constituted by constellations of human action and behav-ior...Against this background, care can be seen as a mode of acting in which participants perceive and interpret care needs and act upon these needs. How

their interpretations and acting proceeds varies according to the situation and
social and institutional contexts... (21–22)

This framing of care allows me to look at it in conjunction with the
market, and not just in opposition to it. In short, care and consumption
are both discourses that are made in and through each other. Needs and
interests may be seen as produced through the relationships of differently
positioned actors within this process.

Care and Consumption in Transnational Adoption

The comments from Lynn with which I opened this chapter demonstrate
anxieties over the variety of competing and overlapping needs that are
produced as different actors enter into adoption relations. Lynn
recognized that Adoption Links creates and promotes itself within the
sometimes competing discourses of need, care, and consumption, a
position made all the more uncomfortable by the centrality of children,
whose sentimental value is held up as antithetical to and ideally protected
from the market (see Zelizer 1994).

The Adoption Links agency and its staff are one "actor" in this
complex story. Parents, birth families, adoption and orphanage officials,
and adopted children are other actors. In the following pages I draw on
evidence from interviews and participant observation that shows several
ways in which discourses of care and consumption meet in the process of
adoption. Sometimes images and practices of care are quite consciously
counterposed to commercialized and commodified processes, while at
other times they are overtly marketed or even created through consumptive practices. So while care and market may discursively and
practically set limits on each other, relationships between actors in the
adoption process also draw on the interaction of these discourses. Needs,
desires, and interests are produced and interpreted at the heart of this
process.

Discourses of care, particularly around reference to family and
familism, abound in adoptive relationships. While this may seem an
obvious point for a process in which family-building is the focus, images
of sisterhood, extended family, and reproduction reach beyond the
adoptive or birth family *per se*. Adoption Links demonstrates its care for
parents by billing itself as an extended family—what Lynn called "a
community of families." Jan, a facilitator at Adoption Links' orientation,

held up a photo of her daughter and six or seven other little Chinese girls lined up on a couch. All adopted by parents in the same travel group and from the same province, Jan said that they are now all "little Anhui sisters." And Zhuli Pan, a facilitator of Adoption Links' own China Program, described her role as follows:

> I just feel as a Chinese woman myself—I feel very good about my role as a coordinator because I see myself as a bridge, in a way. A lot of my adoptive families regard me as the midwife, or they ask their children to call me 'Auntie Zhuli,' you know, *ayi*.[10]

Zhuli, Lynn, and the leaders at Adoption Links' orientation often referred to "my" and "our" families, further solidifying the idea of *famil*-iarity and belonging.

This model of care presented itself in contradistinction to other more conspicuously commercial adoption agencies, yet ironically, it was packaged and marketed. Care and familism were not just a way of doing things, but a selling point. As Lynn put it,

> There's a finite number of agencies and the market share, if you want to call it that, keeps getting smaller and smaller. You really need to push those things that distinguish you from others. So we do try to be real accessible to clients, I mean, anybody can call up and talk to anybody in the office—me, our program director, Zhuli.

Indeed, Zhuli was very accessible, indicating that this was what distinguished her from other facilitators at larger agencies.

Adoption Links markets itself as family-like, caring, and accessible. Is this care packaged for the market, or are market expediencies couched as caring? It seems nearly impossible, at least from a distance, to tease these apart. The discourse of familism and care not only helps to resolve anxieties about the consumptive and competitive side of adoption, but at the same time, it becomes a tool of consumption and competition for agencies that feel they "need to push those things that distinguish you from others." Further examples of this sometimes ironic relationship may be found on the Chinese end of the adoption process. An adoption facilitator in China discussed with me the competitive and sometimes lucrative nature of this business in the same breath as he insisted it's about love, saying, "we have experienced facilitators to *care* for these parents"—parents who have paid for caring adoption services, but who, in turn, are taking on the care of needy children. One Western hotel manager in China spoke of adoptive families as a "cash cow" for his hotel, and yet he lamented that the management had stubbornly refused to provide free congee (rice gruel) for the adopted babies in the morning. This was recognition of a delicate balance: Care is a good marketing tool, and the market can be a tool for caring.

Indeed, care and consumption bleed into each other in a variety of ways, including in the language of "choice." Providing choice and leeway in decision-making is seen as an act of caring, a way of affording autonomy and respect. On the other hand, it feeds right into the logic of market processes (Kuttner 1997). So, when facilitators at the Adoption Links recruitment orientation emphasized that parents had choices, this was an appeal to both consumption and care. It sent the message, "We care enough to give you choices, and choices are of course what you should have." My fieldnotes provide details:

> Susan tells the group she has a "funny story" about how she worked herself into a tizzy, convinced there was something wrong with her daughter's hearing when she was in Peru. "Your mind goes nuts," she explains. She says she called Adoption Links and they were very supportive, telling her to do what "felt right." It turned out nothing was wrong. Then Jan launches us into the next part of the program by saying that parents should feel free to ask any questions tonight, from "Can I ask for a particular gender or shade of skin?" to "Can I reject a child?" I feel a tension in the room, broken just a bit when one of the men takes the opportunity to ask Susan—if her son had indeed had a serious problem, then what? Are there stories of rejections? Susan says she doesn't know, but certainly you do have a choice.

Here the language of choice is a way of saying that we trust you to make choices *and* you can trust us to give them to you. One might even call it a caring contract. But it is fraught with difficulty, as "choice" may suddenly bring the tangled web of care and consumption to the foreground in unforeseen ways. A number of families have traveled to China only to be faced with the impossible decision of whether to proceed with the adoption of a child who was severely ill, or who clearly was not the same child whose photo and materials they had received weeks or months before. In some cases, especially several years ago, adoptive parents reported that facilitators or orphanage directors had urged them to go ahead and "pick another one."[11] For most people this is a horrifying prospect, this seemingly direct commodification of the child that destroys the *magic* of a child and her parent(s) being "chosen" for each other, even as parents and adoption workers make choices about which children should be adopted, or what adoption costs should be.

The giving and granting of choices as both caring and consumptive is not unrelated to the production of needs in this process. Adoption Links bills adoption through its agency as the mutual meeting of needs and desires, and relying on those needs as central to its package of caring. The agency promotional video (which I saw at the orientation) is called "Needing You, Needing Me," the song "Somewhere Out There" suggesting that mutual needs can be fulfilled through this process of bringing disparate people together. Similarly, the agency brochure opens with two vignettes, one about a "tiny little soul" in an orphanage who doesn't even have a name, the second about a woman named Carol "who doesn't know that her baby girl is already waiting for her new mommy...Carol and her husband really like the name Cristina." Together, these narratives suggest the simple idea that a child needs and desires parents, parents need and desire a child, and adoption is a matter of getting them together so that the child who needs a name can be given one by those who need and desire to give one. Again, this sense of a magical and mutual meeting of needs occurs both through and in contrast to market forces. In a *Good Housekeeping* story, one mother of a Chinese adopted child explains why she and her husband chose to avoid domestic adoption, in which parents seemed to be jostling for children: "Competition seemed the wrong way to start a family. My deepest sense of adopting a baby was that somewhere out there was a child who needed me, really needed me, as much as I needed her" (Laskas 2000, 118).

The mutual construction of need translates into a mutual construction of fortune. My interviews, as well as in videos made by both Adoption Links and adoptive parents, indicate that two different framings of fortune coexist. One mantra is that these children are so lucky. Parents often report people on the streets of China seeing them with their Chinese babies, giving them the thumbs up and saying "lucky girl." Indeed, many people in China told me how "xingfu" (happy, lucky) or "xiangfu" (enjoying a life of comfort and ease) these children were to be going to the United States, some joking that *they* would like to be adopted. Zhuli, the coordinator of Adoption Links' China Program, explained it this way:

> First of all they feel this child found a family. She has a mommy and daddy, parents now. That's very lucky, and her fate has transformed so much—that's one level. Another one, for ordinary Chinese going abroad to America or European countries, that's such a dream, like you go to paradise. So these children now not only have a family, they have a family in America.

Some parents echo this opinion, but others are wary of the unequal relations of power it suggests; "like my daughter should be eternally grateful or something," as one parent put it. So a second mantra emerges, in opposition to the first one and emphasizing the fulfillment of parents' needs over the child's: It is the parents who are the lucky ones. As many parents told me, their children have brought them joy and have fulfilled a need, and so it is they as parents who should be grateful. Again, a delicate kind of balancing act emerges in the midst of discourses of care and consumption, and this is haunted by unequal relations of power and choice.

There is little question that many parentless children need families and that many childless parents need children.[12] But in the midst of a competitive adoption business, it is not as simple as that. It should neither be nor seem that parents go out and acquire a child, yet parents request particular countries or types of children through a program that promises choices, services, or sometimes guarantees—and they have certain expectations of the kind of child that will fulfill their needs and desires. Lynn told me: "Some of the countries in which we don't really work, there are many children in need, but the *process* doesn't work. It's gotta be someplace where the process works. Because otherwise you're just taking people's money and it's not going to work out." But defining where the process "works" is in part a function of a competitive market that promises to fulfill parents' desire for a short waiting time, healthy infant girls, [13] and a predictable process with a "guaranteed" outcome. Facilitators at Adoption Links' orientation, for instance, told the audience of anxious parents not to worry, there was a child out there for them and they would come out the other end of this process with a child. This is particularly reassuring for parents who have been through the emotional roller coaster of infertility or have heard one too many stories about birth mothers in the United States reclaiming children.

The China program has become popular in part because it is relatively straightforward and predictable, and because healthy infant girls are available. The *Good Housekeeping* story celebrates these desirable characteristics of the China program (even as it declares discomfort with competition), simultaneously constructing a needy child and a process that works. This makes for a heady package, so that adopting from China sometimes has been characterized as trendy, the perfect market for demanding American parents (see, for example, *the Economist*, 3 February 1996). In short, the China adoption program embodies tensions within and between discourses of care and consumption. This made Lynn uneasy:

> It's a constant juggling of what's the best needs of the family, and the best needs of the child. We *do* want to find homes for children. I mean, that is our goal. But you do find yourself sometimes feeling like you're following the market as opposed to being the trailblazers out there. One parent was always on

my case about so many families going to China. She said, "We're becoming China 'R' Us." And I said, it's not like we steer people toward China. Oftentimes they come in because they've been on the Internet, and they know people who know people. And there's so much media attention given. And they want to be on the fast track. Everybody wants to be home with a baby in six months. And there aren't a lot of programs out there that work as quickly and as smoothly as China does…oh, and then there's the preference for girls… In some senses, China has gotten really easy. You submit your paperwork, you travel with a group, you go through, and you get your baby, and it's all very simple.[14]

Lynn found herself and her agency torn between care and the market. The China Program is their bread and butter, meets the perceived market demands of parents, and helps them do what they promise: meeting parents' and children's needs. But it feels *too* easy, too convenient. Lynn seemed to imply that "caring work" neither feels like or appears to be caring unless there is some kind of sacrifice. It isn't as if children in Chinese orphanages have an easy life; what could explain Lynn's uneasiness? The dilemma seemed to be: How does one both adequately fulfill the caring work of placing "children in need" but also limit the sacrifice to a level that is palatable to "parents in need?"

It is true enough that parents in the adoption process want to have and exercise choices about the kind of child they parent, and there are legendary stories of extreme cases of consumerist parenting. Lynn angrily told me the story of a family that "rejected" a school-age child after placement because she didn't "measure up" academically and socially. Zhuli contrasted demanding parents to those with a more caring attitude, that is with the proper emotion and openness:

I think the majority of families are very reasonable and they do it with their heart. Just sometimes with a few families I find it is kind of difficult when they say they want a child really really young, and it's not possible. You know, if I have a client who is really demanding, that makes me uncomfortable when they tell me, "Well, I want my child to have this shape face, or that shape eyes." Or "Oh, I don't want my child to have very dark skin." You know, that kind of talk. That's not very common, but it does exist.

This experience with overly demanding adoptive parents suggests that the agency might find itself at the mercy of parents, their caring work potentially stunted by the consumer.[15]

Yet, it is too easy (and false) to paint a simplistic picture of adoption as a market in which parents are the demanding consumers, children the commodified objects, and agencies and facilitators the brokers. I want to show here instead that all of these actors are situated in discourses of both care and consumption that variously position them across social relations and situations. Standing in parents' shoes, for example, might show how their decisions about parenting and family-building are also embedded in larger social discourses of care and consumption. Some parents have complained to me that the competition between agencies for their business makes them reluctant consumers. And the anxieties and desires they bring to the adoption process are, at least in part, a product of what social representations and practices hold up as normal or correct parenting and family life. Parents are surrounded by expertise about caring parenting, packaged and produced for their consumption by adoption agencies, psychologists, state organizations, and the like.

Indeed, expert knowledge is an important conduit for the construction of needs within both caring and market discourses, and it also becomes a conduit for meeting perceived needs in China. I asked Lynn how she thought the China adoption process might be made more caring, and she replied:

> If we had big batches of money, there are so many wonderful things we could do. We could send a group of social worker trainers over to China to work in the orphanages, to talk about things orphanage workers can do, just to make the situation better for kids. We could publish a lot of the information we have, we could print it in Chinese, we could distribute it.

Care thus becomes defined in terms of sharing expert knowledge— knowledge on child development and on caring practices that assumes a particular set of needs that I would argue should get constructed and disseminated along with the expertise. Children's needs are being taken care of, but those needs are subtly tied up with the needs and expectations of adoptive parents and adoption administrators. A Chinese social worker providing services for special needs children in China worried that donations of goods and expertise were being funneled back into the nurturing of healthy adoptable children, under the assumption that if there wasn't enough to meet all children's needs then it made sense to help those who would most benefit by having a family (or more cynically, those who would most benefit the orphanage by bringing in more adoption money). And in two cities I visited in China, the staff of Western organizations sometimes found themselves at loggerheads with local leadership over the cares and needs of children in the orphanages. At the heart of these tensions lay differing claims on expertise for identifying and responding to the needs of children, claims on a sense of efficacy and good, and sometimes claims on the children themselves.

Nowhere was this tension around the construction of needs more clear than in the way Zhuli described her role as a bridge between Chinese orphanages and officials on the one hand, and American parents and agencies on the other. Her job as cultural interpreter in both directions becomes one of needs interpretation as well:

> I tell families a lot of cultural issues they should be aware of when they go to China. What they should expect, what they should not expect, and those kinds of things. And then with the Chinese, you know, the orphanage itself—I talk to the orphanage directors a lot, and I let them know the expectations of families here and what's better for the children and for the families, what they need, those kinds of things.

I asked Zhuli for examples of the kinds of expectations and needs about which she was informing each side. She named a number of specific child-care practices, including the example of explaining to the orphanage that they needed to make the process more personal; they needed to give the children meaningful names that would seem beautiful and unique to adoptive parents; and they should show signs that their children were cared for as valuable individuals. Parents' "need" to know their children are being cared for as unique individuals, as signified in naming, is translated as children's "need" to be treated as such. But what about needs and wants translated in the other direction? Zhuli related that she had to explain to parents why their eight month-old might not be crawling (children are bundled up tight in winter, and floors are cement), or why their baby's head might be shaved (to help keep them cool in hot summers). Notions of proper caring flow in both directions but are translated into needs for the future of the child on one side and into curiosities of the child's past on the other.

Some parents' stories also indicated expectations of proper care that were embedded in commodified definitions of need and then mediated by facilitators like Zhuli. Consider this excerpt from an interview with parent Patty Lou:

> We found out later that John [the facilitator] had sent American formula over there before we came, to get the babies used to it. And he sent diapers. 'Cause she had on Pampers, or Huggies, or something when we got her, which surprised me. I thought she would just have cloth diapers. But then we found out he had sent everything for them. So they were in excellent shape.

Care and consumption are in dialog here in the judgment of needs and their fulfillment, as signified by Huggies. Furthermore, it seems an instance of the invasion of care by the market, where consumption overwhelms the defining of needs. Indeed, other parents were quite sensitive to this possibility.

Mark and Candace White, parents quite active in Red Threads, said they thought some parents were sick of the commercialization associated with adoption. Once they had their child, some parents "drew the line" even at giving money to orphanages, especially if the request came from agencies whose competitive motives were sometimes suspect. Mark and Candace were upset that a local agency had used the Red Threads address list to send greetings to all the adoptive families in the directory. They saw this as a market move—a way to recruit families for second adoptions from China—while the agency director, when confronted, asserted that this was just their gift to those they considered to be part of their adoption community.

While from the perspective of some Red Threads families this action represented an excess of consumption and competition, from the agency's perspective it might have been a way of indicating care via the market. Might market practices be seen as not only a vehicle but a catalyst for care? As Haskell (1985) reminds us, it is via the market that certain relationships are made possible, and these relationships might translate into a heightened awareness and even practice of care. The following conversation with Zhuli addresses this possibility:

> Sara: Do you think the orphanages you're working with have undergone any changes since they started placing children in Western homes, and if so, how?
>
> Zhuli: I think so. I think they are probably more aware, just by interacting with adoptive families for that short time, they are more aware that children need a lot of love and holding and those kinds of things.
>
> S: You don't think they know that already?
>
> Z: They know that, they know that. But [sigh], how should I put it? [pause] You know, I think in China, the orphanages have so many children, and I don't think a lot of orphanages have enough staff members. Just for practical purposes, they want to make sure these children are healthy when they are adopted. You know, that will serve the purpose of the children receiving good care. For the orphanage, they don't want the families to go there and find that this child is so sick she can't even travel.

I read Zhuli as saying that the actual practice of caring occurs within a complex set of needs, interests, and relationships. Surely, orphanage workers know children need love and care, but they are pushed into practicing that care in part because they know that families are going to show up expecting healthy children. That there are people who want and need abandoned children gives them *value* in a number of senses—as objects of exchange, desire, and sentiment, and as human beings. Zhuli further indicated that facilities at orphanages have improved because of the money coming in, and that care has improved because orphanage officials have seen how happy adopted children are in their families. This has been confirmed in numerous orphanages I have visited in China, although the problem remains in some institutions of separate and often better facilities for children who are considered adoptable.

The market not only makes possible relationships that potentially lead to improved care (although as I have indicated above that what defines that improved care is complex), but care may in a sense exceed the market, spurred by the symbolic and sentimental value of the child. I give two examples here of how care might be seen to not just counteract but to go beyond consumption. Mark and Candace helped start a project through Red Threads that raises money for foster care and equipment in Chinese orphanages—not just for children who will be adopted but also for those who will not. As conversations and presentations at Red Threads events indicated, relationships forged with orphanage officials through the adoption market make this project possible, and familial relationships with adopted children spur a sense of responsibility for other children in Chinese orphanages. The project is quite consciously formulated outside of the rubric of adoption agencies because, as Mark said, it seemed parents were more willing to give money if it was not tied to the business of adoption.[16]

A second example of care being catalyzed by, but then exceeding, the market comes from Zhuli. She told me she had no idea there were so many children in Chinese orphanages until she got involved as a facilitator. As a Chinese person she feels responsible not only for children in orphanages but for the children who do get placed in families. And the extent to which she meets needs and practices care exceeds what a competitive market in adoption services might require; her practice continues long after her "job" is done.

> Well, the immediate need I have to satisfy is the adoptive families'. Because they are the ones I need to serve in the first place—I need to translate their papers, coordinate the referral, answer questions, prepare them for the trip, and all that. But for the children, after they come home, I do have a lot of connections with the families afterward. Like there is this girl who comes to my house every Tuesday—I try to teach her Chinese, writing and all that. Or like with this single adoptive father, they come here a lot. The child was three years old when she was adopted, so I was able to assist with language a little bit, and just a mother figure, you know, because she doesn't have one...

Concluding Remarks

Zhuli's remarks demonstrate the breadth of care and show that just as the market can "invade" care, so can care "invade" the market. But her words also point to the complex construction of needs. Zhuli must take care of families' needs "in the first place" because she is paid to meet demands within a business built around care. But then when the business is done, she attends to the perceived continuing needs of children. These are constructed as needs of identity construction—exposing children to Chinese heritage and providing them with a mother figure. Important here is that Zhuli seems to distinguish parents' needs, constructed under more marketized relations, from children's needs, constructed under more sentimentalized notions of care. Once again, needs are constructed within a variety of practices and meanings built around the value and identity of the child.

As I have tried to show here, care and consumption are not diametrically opposed but interwoven practices. At times they work through and in conjunction with each other; at other times they set limits on each other or exceed those very limits. Transnational adoption is a useful case for understanding these relationships because it is suggests that "kinship and consumption are simply each other's context, with no clear direction for reductionist analysis...kinship and commodity have become inextricably linked" (Miller 1995, 155). In other words, care is neither equal to familism nor antithetical to consumption. I have tried to demonstrate how relations of power work through discourses of both care and consumption, especially in the construction of needs and desires. By attending to the social practices and representations within a process such as transnational adoption, we can begin to understand the complex web of needs, consumption, and care. The powerful intricacies of this web are highlighted by the centrality of children—in need of protection, imbued with symbolic and sentimental value, and changing hands and crossing borders.

ACKNOWLEDGMENTS

Research in both the United States and China was made possible by two fellowships from the Social Science Research Council—the Advanced Disciplinary Training Fellowship and the International Migration Fellowship—as well as a Grant for Research Abroad from the Graduate School at the University of Minnesota and a Bright Research Award from the Sociology Department at the University of Minnesota.

NOTES

1   All personal, place, and organizational names have been changed.
2   By "discourses" I refer to both practices and representations, materiality and culture. Employing discursive terminology does not imply that something is not "real" but rather that it is understood and given meaning through cultural practices.
3   The number of children adopted from Russia by U.S. families has stayed close to the number from China in the last couple of years.
4   Many families I interviewed refer to the appeal of China's ancient culture, and most say how beautiful these Chinese children are; some explicitly use "China doll" as a term of endearment (while just as many find this offensive).
5   See, for example, Tronto's (1993) discussion of the need for activities that "share power" with those who have less (p. 20), as well as her discussion of whites not recognizing the needs of blacks because of privilege (p. 121). I am not dismissing this approach, but I am suggesting that it might be useful to think in different terms. For example, I would argue that caring practice is not just a matter of whites recognizing the needs of blacks but of recognizing that the needs assigned to them and the reparations devised to take care of those needs within public discourse are products of racialized relations of power. In other words, it is not necessarily the case that "true" needs are being masked, but it may be that certain needs are taken to be real in specific historical and political moments.
6   To be fair, Tronto is attending to what care ought to be, but I would like to argue that one can also reach normative formulations by teasing out the relations of power that inform care. And those relations of power are not just "political"; they are also economic. That is why I insist on examining care and consumption together and in relation to each other.
7   One solution to the impersonal and even violent rationalities of the market is making an ethic of care a part of public life; and for Tronto, this requires democratic, liberal institutions (158). Kuttner (1997) puts a twist on this argument when he points out that the market thrives in democracy because they both work through ideologies of choice and individual liberty.
8   One useful example of the construction of needs at the historical juncture of ideologies and practices of both care and consumption is Marjorie DeVault's (1991) book *Feeding the Family*.
9   I do find implicit in Haskell's framework a likeness to Gramscian hegemony and theoretical elbow room for the construction of diverse local practices. Haskell says he avoids the word "hegemony" because it makes action and domination too

"purposeful," but I would argue that lack of conscious intention—indeed, a kind of ordinariness—is, in part, what makes hegemony such a powerful term.

10 While unpacking the meaning of this familism is beyond the scope of this paper, it is noteworthy that Adoption Links taps into family metaphors in a business where a certain anxiety about kinship haunts the heart of the process.

11 In almost every one of these difficult cases I have heard about, parents have chosen to keep the child physically presented to them.

12 A Chinese reporter who has written about China-U.S. adoptions told me he used to wonder why Americans adopted Chinese children but now realizes they *need* these children because they are unable to have children by birth and/or because of an emotional void.

13 My own experiences working in the adoption field and my communications with other adoption administrators indicate that for a variety of reasons, adoptive parents request girls more than boys.

14 The China program is still relatively predictable, although waiting times have increased since this research was first conducted. The process is, at the time of this writing, closer to a year, and children are rarely younger than eight or nine months old at time of placement.

15 How race plays into care, consumption, and choice is too important a subject to try to address here in a few words. I address these intersections in other forthcoming work.

16 It is noteworthy, however, that there are now several such organizations in the United States, with indications of a sense of "competition" among them over the best ways to meet the needs of waiting children.

REFERENCES

Anagnost, Ann. *National Past-Times: Narrative, Representation, and Power in Modern China*. Durham, N.C.: Duke University Press, 1997.

——. "Scenes of Misrecognition: Maternal Citizenship in the Age of Transnational Adoption." Unpublished manuscript, 1999.

Clark, Danae. Mediadoption: Children, Commodification, and the Spectacle of Disruption. *American Studies* 39, no. 2 (1998): 65–86.

DeVault, Marjorie. *Feeding the Family: The Social Construction of Caring as Gendered Work*. Chicago: University of Chicago Press, 1991.

Dizard, Jan E., and Howard Gadlin. *The Minimal Family*. Cambridge: University of Massachusetts Press, 1990.

Fraser, Nancy, and Linda Gordon. "A Genealogy of 'Dependency': Tracing a Keyword of the U.S. Welfare System." *Signs* 19 (1994): 309–336.

Glenn, Evelyn Nakano. "From Servitude to Service Work: Historical Continuities in the Racial Division of Paid Reproductive Labor." *Signs* 18 (1992): 64–80.

Haskell, Thomas. "Capitalism and the Origins of the Humanitarian Sensibility (part 1)." *American Historical Review* 90, no. 2 (1985): 339–361.

——. "Capitalism and the Origins of the Humanitarian Sensibility (part 2)." *American Historical Review* 90, no. 3 (1985): 547–566.

Kuttner, Robert. *Everything for Sale*. New York: Alfred A. Knopf, 1996.

Laskas, Jeanne Marie. "Giving My Heart to Anna." *Good Housekeeping*. December
     2000: 116–122.
Miller, D. "Consumption and Commodities." *Annual Review of Anthropology* 24 (1995):
     141–161.
Mitchell, Tim. "Fixing the Economy." *Cultural Studies* 12, no. 1 (1998): 82–101.
Sevenhuisen, Selma. *Citizenship and the Ethics of Care*. New York: Routledge, 1998.
Solberg, Anne. "Negotiating Childhood: Changing Constructions of Age for Norwegian
     Children." In *Constructing and Reconstructing Childhood*, edited by A. James and
     A. Prout. Washington, D.C.: Falmer Press, 1997.
Stephens, Sharon. "Children and the Politics of Culture in Late Capitalism." In *Children
     and the Politics of Culture*, edited by S. Stephens. Princeton: Princeton University
     Press, 1996.
Suransky, Valerie Polakow. *The Erosion of Childhood*. Chicago: University of Chicago
     Press, 1982.
Thorne, Barrie et al. "Transnational Childhoods: The Participation of Children in
     Processes of Family Migration." Unpublished paper, 1998.
Tronto, Joan. *Moral Boundaries: A Political Argument for an Ethic of Care*. New York:
     Routledge, 1993.
Zelizer, Viviana A. *Pricing the Priceless Child: The Changing Social Value of Children*.
     Princeton: Princeton University Press, 1994.

Chapter 8

The School Shooting as a Ritual of Sacrifice

Mark D. Jacobs

Child sacrifice is the most sacred act imaginable. All sacrifice is a means of speaking to the gods, and children are the most sacred objects of sacrifice. The act of childbirth conjures awe for the *mysterium* of the cosmos; deliberately negating that act conjures perhaps even greater awe. The moment of sacrificing a child is time out of time. The God of the Old Testament could have devised no greater test of Abraham's faith than to demand the sacrifice of Isaac; for that very reason, Abraham had the most sacred obligation to meet that test.

The mass shooting on April 20, 1999, at Columbine High School in Littleton, Colorado—resulting in the death of the two gunmen, a dozen other students, and one teacher—can only be understood as an act of child sacrifice. The extent and intensity of the societal reaction to that shooting indicates that it touched a sacral chord. The mundane reasons popularly given for that and other school shootings—the breakdown of community and parental controls, vengeance visited by members of an out-group against an abusive in-group, unbearable frustration turned to murderous aggression—simply do not fit many facts of the case, including the actual profiles of the shooters, their parents, and their community. Nor do those reasons adequately explain all of the shooters' actions: Why, for example, did they target their victims so indiscriminately? Social psychological explanations can only be partial. A series of acts that touch the sacred so directly can only be explained by their *cultural* logic. They must be seen as a response to a *sacrificial crisis*, arising not from enduring conditions but from fundamental societal *changes*. Why the sacrificial crisis persists despite those repeated sacrificial rituals is yet another question that demands a cultural explanation.

What Social Psychology Can't Explain

Both psychologically and phenomenologically, the Columbine killers played out sacrificial scripts. The code of masculinity may require the performance of sacrifice as a rite of passage (Pollack 1998). According to the diaries and videotapes the shooters left behind, they saw in their act an opportunity for moral self-transcendence. Their accounts fit the profile discovered by Jack Katz of persons who commit "righteous slaughter": "For the impassioned killer, the challenge is to escape a situation that has come to be seen otherwise as inexorably humiliating" (1988, 9). The very profanity and offensive epithets on the videotape and on one shooter's Web site represent—as in Katz's study—"an eminently sensible way of making a subsequent attack into a service honoring the sacred. Now the attack will be against some morally lower, polluted, corrupted, profanized form of life, and hence in honor of a morally higher, more sacred, and—this bears special emphasis—an eternally respectable realm of being" (37–38). In Katz's analysis, this kind of slaughter is experienced by the criminal as "an impassioned attempt to perform a sacrifice to embody one or another version of the 'Good'" (1988, 13). It is revealing that in his diary, Eric Harris referred to the planned day of the shooting as "Judgment Day."

Columbine was unsettling not only because the level of carnage was unprecedented in a school setting—and because the victims were suburban youth, all but one, white—but also because the event seemed so inexplicable. Based on entries from the diary of one of the shooters, newspaper headlines described the shooting as an act of revenge by social outcasts against students (especially "jocks") who had ridiculed them for being different. Eric Harris and Dylan Klebold, the shooters, tended to wear dark clothes and trench coats and were said to be members of their school's "Trenchcoat Mafia." But members of Columbine's small Trenchcoat Mafia did not regard the shooters as part of their group. And the shooters—despite playing violent Internet fantasy games and listening to German techno-rock—were not clearly outcasts. Nor were they loners. Klebold drove a black BMW, participated in a baseball fantasy league, and had just gone to the senior prom with a girl who belonged to the National Honor Society. Harris had played soccer until 1998. The shooters did not specifically target students who had teased them.

Even the most up-to-date available scientific knowledge did not contemplate a Columbine. Although the 1998 volume of *Crime and Justice: A Review of Research* (Tonry and Moore)—perhaps the most authoritative criminological annual—was entirely devoted to "Youth Violence," none of the collected essays pertained to a Klebold or Harris. The risk profile presented by David Farrington, for example, included "individual factors (high impulsiveness and low intelligence), family factors (poor supervision, harsh discipline, a violent parent, large family size, a young mother, a broken family), peer delinquency, low socioeconomic status, urban residence, and a high-crime neighborhood" (421).

Yet both Harris and Klebold were good students. Both came from intact families, with "good enough" parents and beautiful homes. Klebold's father, a former geophysicist, ran a small mortgage business from his home; Klebold's mother was an employment counselor at the local community college. She had forbidden him as a child to play with toy guns; he had forbidden any guns in the house. Harris's father, a retired Air Force Major and decorated pilot, worked for a defense contractor. He had been a scout leader and a youth athletic coach and had attended every one of Eric's Little League baseball games. Harris's fifth-grade teacher recalls that his parents attended every parent-teacher conference together. Harris's father had just spent five days with Eric visiting the University of Arizona, to which Eric had gained admission. Littleton is an affluent suburb, with relatively little crime. Columbine High School sends virtually all of its graduates to college.

Harris and Klebold had no official record of trouble at school. They had minor involvement with the juvenile court: A year before the school shooting, they had broken into a van to steal some electrical equipment. After successfully completing a year-long diversion program ordered by the court, their records were cleared. Harris had been in private therapy for the year before the shooting. Based on this record of minor trouble and seemingly timely intervention, they presented low risks of violence.

A sociocultural analysis can explain what a social-psychological one cannot. Quickening demographic, technological, and cultural changes in the broader society are transforming the moral ecology of the high school. The clique structure of the high school is becoming more differentiated, and the symbolic boundaries demarcating school cliques are becoming more permeable. With the status hierarchy of cliques loosening, cliques are not necessarily oppositional. These transformations are unsettling cultural distinctions, producing a "sacrificial crisis" that evokes sacrificial rituals. Although the psychological and phenomenological states of the shooters serve the ritual logic of sacrifice, it is as if the ritual works through the shooters in ways that transcend their personal motivations. Ironically, however, modern social conditions prevent these rituals from producing *communitas*. Moral panic in the no-fault society leaves the sacrificial crisis unresolved.

The Moral Ecology of the School

In the videotape they made before their rampage, the Columbine shooters identify their motivation as vengeance against the "jocks" and "stuck-up" kids who teased and harassed them. It therefore makes sense to start the search for a sociocultural explanation by examining the social tensions that define the moral ecology of the school.

High schools have always been cliquish. Although the labels change from time to time, there have always been jocks and preppies, geeks and freaks. "Goths" and "trenchies" (the latter originating as a term of derogation but defiantly adopted by its subjects) are newer forms. Jon explains,

> Goth is a style—of music, dress, state of mind. In general, Goths wear black; hang out on the Net; experiment with androgynous styles; are sometimes drawn to piercings, tattoos and white makeup; and love Bauhaus, Sisters of Mercy, and the Cure. Among their cherished authors are Sartre, Burroughs, Shelley, and Poe. Fascinated with death (a taboo in the media and certainly in schools, along with sex and the open discussion of religion), Goths see it as a part of life (www.slashdot.com 1999).

Trenchies are more intellectual, Goths more dramatic or performative. Trenchies are more likely to play fantasy games and to be hackers. Goths are closer to freaks, trenchies to geeks. Some measure of antagonism has always existed among cliques; in particular, kids asserting their difference have always had reason to hate jocks. The Columbine shooting spree reportedly began with the words, "All jocks stand up!"

Cliques overlay structural bases of social differentiation. The social life of the high school is ordered segmentally, with tendencies toward segregation by grade, sex, race, and place of residence. It is impossible to deny the racial dimension of school shootings, almost all of which (including that at Columbine) have been committed by white students. Harris's diary proclaims his admiration for Hitler; the Columbine shooting was planned for Hitler's birthday. At the end of the summer, when students first returned to the Columbine School after the shooting, they found swastikas spray-painted on the building. The shooters' videotape was filled with tirades against "niggers, spics, Jews, gays, f...ing whites." The parents of the one black victim, an athlete, claimed that their son was singled out because of his race; an eyewitness reported that one of the gunmen said, "Look, there's that little nigger," before firing the fatal bullet. Their son had reported receiving racist taunts by members of the Trenchcoat Mafia; three days before the shooting, he had asked them what their reaction would be to racist killings. The shooting, in other words, could be coded as a white supremacist act— notwithstanding evidence that Eric Harris was personally opposed to racism. Before his move to Columbine, Harris's closest friends had been black and Asian. Harris's Web site listed "racism" among the things he hated. The Web site also proclaimed that people biased against "blacks, Asians, Mexicans, or people from any other country or race besides white-American" should "have their arms ripped off" and be burned. He wrote: "Don't let me catch you making fun of someone just because they are a different color." Ten days after Columbine, a mixed-race classmate of Harris and Klebold asserted to the *New York Times*: "When the media is coming up with this thing that Dylan and Eric were racist, they weren't. They were my friends. They were very nice to me, both of them."

The Columbine shooting (as with all other school shootings) could also be coded "masculine." Statistically, of course, men are far more likely than women to commit violence. Indeed, the shooting expresses what William Pollack calls the "Boy Code"—a gender straightjacket, "a set of behaviors, rules of conduct, cultural shibboleths, and even a lexicon, that is inculcated into boys by our society" (1998, xxv). It is a "distorted and outmoded image of the ideal boy" (xxv), transmitted in part by parents and teachers, that prevents boys from expressing needs, vulnerabilities, or a full range of emotions. It teaches them, too, a "mythic view of manhood...that boys must go through some solitary hardening ritual, some heroic mission, to prove their courage and solidify their masculinity" (96). Klebold was rejected by the Marines just days before the shooting; on the videotape left by the shooters, Harris began listing every girl who had refused to date him.

A Sacrificial Crisis

Although gender, racial, and interclique hostilities contribute to the etiology of school shootings, however, these are not sufficient causes. The cruelty of school life, after all, is hardly new: the work of George Orwell ("Such, Such Were the Joys") and William Golding (*Lord of the Flies)*, for example, suggests that cruelty was as extreme at mid-century, and those pioneering black students who integrated American schools in the 1960s and 1970s experienced abuse as insufferable as any encountered today. Moreover, the layered divisions of age, sex, race, and clique are not as rigid and menacing as they are often portrayed. Although cliques may form around a few stable core members, most clique affiliations are provisional and labile. (Harris and Klebold, for example, were only "trenchies" to the extent that they were personal friends of someone who was a recognized member of that group.) Like the urban street gangs described by Gerald Suttles, the structure of cliques provides young people "a way of gaining associates, avoiding enemies, and establishing each others' intentions" (1968, 234) in settings otherwise too large and too indeterminate to generate a sense of personal security. Cliques are primarily defensive, rather than oppositional, social formations. Interclique variation in styles of dress, language, and pop-cultural consumption is more symbolic than meaningful. Clique structures establish rough cognitive maps of social relations that enable individuals to leverage their limited sets of face-to-face relations into more inclusive networks of acquaintance and minimal trust. The truly "popular" students are those who can form personal relations that bridge different groups.

The explanation for school shootings is more likely to be found among the *changes* taking place in the moral ecology of the school, deriving from demographic, technological, and popular cultural changes in the broader society. Demographic changes—primarily as a result of great waves of immigration—have produced increases in both the size and diversity of school populations. Those increases, along with a proliferation of styles in popular culture, have led to increased differentiation of the clique structure of the school. The Internet constitutes a virtual community affording geeks and nerds vastly expanded webs of group affiliation; the exponential growth of chat rooms, discussion boards, and instant messaging implies corresponding increases in Durkheimian moral density as well as Simmelian group expansion. And the importance of information technology to the new economy has unsettled the social hierarchy of cliques. In particular, it is becoming more difficult to marginalize hackers and computer "geeks" when they are the ones equipped to inherit the future. The broader cultural currents of feminism and antiracism have similarly unsettled the local culture of the high school, forcing previously dominant social cliques on the defensive. The cumulative result of all these changes is to produce what Rene Girard calls the "sacrificial crisis":

> The sacrificial crisis can be defined…as a crisis of distinctions—that is, a crisis affecting the cultural order. This cultural order is nothing more than a regulated system of distinctions in which the differences among individuals are used to establish their 'identity' and their mutual relationships…Order, peace…depend on cultural distinctions; it is not these distinctions but the loss of them that gives birth to fierce rivalries and sets members of the same… social group at one another's throats (1977, 49).

A Modern Ritual of Sacrifice

Sacrifice is necessary to restore the basis of social order in situations of "sacrificial crisis." Summarizing ethnographic evidence (drawn primarily from the work of Victor Turner), Rene Girard conceives sacrifice "as a deliberate act of collective substitution performed at the expense of the victim and absorbing all the internal tensions, feuds, and rivalries pent up within the community…The purpose of the sacrifice is to restore harmony to the community, to reinforce the social fabric" (1977, 7–8). The social disunity Turner reported among the Ndembu of Zambia existed as well at Columbine High School in Littleton, Colorado. In Turner's own words, "We see a field of social relations, in process of irreversible change, which viewed microscopically in terms of its day-to-day crises of living, exhibits a series of persistent, even desperate, attempts to retain its traditional regularities of structure" (1981, 24). Rituals bring out into the open illicit hidden drives, in order to exorcise and purge them. "The typical development of a ritual sequence is from the public expression of a wish to…redress breaches in the social structure, through exposure of hidden animosities, to the renewal of social bonds" (272).

The scope and depth of the societal reaction to Columbine demonstrates that the event assumed ritual proportions in its reception as well as in its execution. The memorial service for the victims drew 70,000 people—many times larger than the networks of bereaved intimates, and indeed double the entire population of the town. Pilgrims from all over the nation came to erect and visit public shrines in Littleton; after protests by some victims' parents, Christian crosses representing the pair of shooters were removed. Several of the victims became seen as martyrs, inspiring crusades. Eyewitnesses among the survivors spread a story that Cassie Bernall, a seventeen-year-old born-again Christian, asked by one of the shooters during the rampage whether she believed in God, answered "yes" just before being shot to death. That the story was probably apocryphal only strengthens the claim that the shooting had ritual properties. Nonetheless, Bernall's parents wrote a best-selling book about her, and she became the focus of a worldwide revival movement. The parents of another victim, Rachel Scott, formed a popular ministry, the Columbine Redemption. Tom Mauser, father of yet another victim, started a national campaign for gun control in honor of his son, Daniel.

The nature and magnitude of this societal reaction to Columbine appears all the more remarkable given the normalization of juvenile homicide in the United States. In 1997, for example, 2,100 persons under the age of 18 were murdered in the United States—3 murders for every 100,000 juveniles. Homicides of juveniles between the ages of 15 and 17 were more likely than homicides of adults to involve firearms. The rate of homicides involving firearms of children under the age of 15 was 16 times greater in the United States than in other industrialized nations. And for every 2 youth under the age of 19 murdered in the United States, 1 other committed suicide (Snyder and Sickmund 1999, 15–25). Columbine victims instantly became candidates for martyrdom, while thousands of "normal" child homicides and suicides have gone largely unnoticed year after year.

Viewing Columbine as a sacrificial ritual explains some aspects of the story that remain puzzling from a social-psychological view. The shooting was inevitably a racialist act, given racial tensions in the school, even though personally the shooters may not have been especially racist. And even though the shooters experienced a psychological and phenomenological compulsion for vengeance against certain types of students, they seemed to shoot at random. In so doing, they served a cultural logic, acting out the sacrificial crisis by effacing cultural distinctions. In ritual, the sacrificial victims are always surrogates or substitutes. Indeed, it makes ritual sense for the shooters and their victims to be *monstrous doubles*. Girard's exegesis of sacrifice in *The Bacchae* applies equally well to Columbine: "Surely it is the similarity of doubles that is being suggested; that of the surrogate victim and the community that expels it, of the sacrificed and the sacrificer. All differences are abolished" (1977, 163). It is worth remembering that the shooting was a murder-suicide; all the more reason for those killed to resemble the killers, because the latter were sacrificial victims as well. The very same children are often at once the bullies and the bullied—as indeed, according to the sheriff's report, Klebold and Harris were, even before the shooting.

A Moral Panic

Rituals of sacrifice are supposed to produce *communitas*, a form of communal solidarity based on the leveling of symbolic distinctions. Instead, Columbine produced a moral panic. As defined by Goode and Ben-Yehuda (1994, 156–58), what characterizes a moral panic is a heightened, disproportionate, and volatile level of concern over the actual or alleged behavior of persons in a certain category; an increased level of hostility toward those persons; and some degree of consensus about the reality and seriousness of the threat. Those categorized as the stock villains at the center of the moral panic turn into "folk devils" (Cohen 1972).

In the week after Columbine, bomb threats, menacing email messages, and rumors of terrorist attack swept schools throughout the nation. Similarly vague and unfounded rumors recurred for no apparent reason on May 10; across the continent from Littleton, in Montgomery County, Maryland, 36 percent of all students (six times the normal absentee rate) stayed home from school on that day. Absenteeism at Columbine High School reached three times its normal rate on the six-month anniversary of the shooting, amidst one student's threats to "finish the job" there.

School security measures instituted throughout the nation as a result of Columbine also indicate the level of fear generated by the event. Many schools installed metal detectors, video cameras, and panic alarms and also stationed security guards at doors; required identity passes for students; and conducted drills for SWAT teams. The National Institute of Justice issued a research report outlining "appropriate selection criteria, techniques for use, maintenance, and expected lifespan, costs, and performance testing standards for closed-circuit television and walk-through and handheld metal detectors." Also highlighted in the report: "X-ray baggage scanners; entry-control technologies, including magnetic security cards, personal identification numbers, and retinal and fingerprint scanning; and duress alarm devices" (Green 1999).

Moreover, schools instituted rigid "zero-tolerance" discipline policies that renewed and indeed redoubled the harassment and abuse a particular "type" of student had traditionally endured at the hands of other students. A series of articles about Columbine on *slashdot.com* by Jon Katz, an Internet journalist sympathetic to the "geeks, nerds, and gamers" of his virtual audience, elicited tens of thousands of responses—many similar to the following, posted by "Dan from Maryland" half a year after Columbine:

> Jon, for the past six months I've been the target of the most vicious and most violent gang in the school—the football team. They've locked me in my locker, spray-painted my face, taken my laptop—yes, I am most definitely a proud geek, gamer and raver—and gone through my personal stuff. I sort of lost it yesterday when one of them snapped a towel in the locker room that caught me in the eye and called me "geek-boy."
>
> I said I was going to get a gun and kill him, just like Columbine. I don't have a gun, and have never seen one or touched one, but they reported me to the principal, and I was sent home. He said there was no choice, he had to protect the school from people like me. My mom says I might have to go to an alternative school for two years, as the principal says I'm possibly dangerous, and I can't be ignored. Is there anything I can do? My dad says I've ruined my life, that this will be in every government computer forever, and in my college file. I can't understand what's happened to me. Do words count so much more than actions? All my teachers know me, I'm not dangerous. But they won't talk to me now. And yes, I play Doom. That won't help either, I guess. How can you prove that you won't kill somebody?

The Federal Bureau of Alcohol, Tobacco, and Firearms developed a computer profile (based on actuarial risk factors, which are of course invalid bases for clinical prediction) for evaluating and rating the violence potential of individual students, in a pilot program initially involving twenty schools. School systems from Denver, Colorado to Prince William County, Virginia formally banned the wearing of trench coats.

The news media doubtlessly contributed to the climate of fear that led to this overreaction by government officials, school administrators, parents, teachers, and students. As David Altheide has demonstrated (1997), news reports filter events through a "problem frame" that—in giving the news the flavor of entertainment—produces public fears. This problem frame, among other things, strips events of their ambiguities and their larger structural contexts. To pander to an increasingly fearful public, the press places ever-increasing emphasis on stories that inspire fear. From 1990 to 1998, for example, according to a survey conducted by the U.S. Department of Justice, televised newscasts about homicides increased 473 percent, although actual homicides decreased 32 percent during that period. Yet, as other analysts note, the power of the press to sustain public concern about particular issues is limited. Joel Best, for example, while critiquing the melodrama of the current public preoccupation with "random" violence, notes that journalists require help from politicians, activists, and experts to institutionalize such concern (1999).

Whatever the role of the media in creating undue fear, however, it is striking that the media paid disproportionate attention to Columbine even relative to other school shootings and murderous rampages. The major network news programs initially devoted a total of 144 minutes to Columbine over five days, compared with 25 minutes that the networks devoted over two days to a shooting of four people in the Springfield, Oregon high school the year before. The network news shows devoted only 12 minutes to the killing of twelve people in a rampage in Atlanta two months after Columbine, and discontinued significant coverage after a single day. (In part, of course, this differential in the amount of coverage reflected levels of public interest: Over 3 million households tuned into CNN in the first five hours after Columbine, twice as many as those who tuned into CNN after the Atlanta shootings.)

Columbine seems to have crystallized a decade of growing public fear about youth violence. In that period, almost every state toughened its juvenile justice laws by lengthening sentences, encouraging (and in same cases requiring) the waiver of juveniles for trial in adult courts for more serious offenses, and eliminating or reducing the confidentiality of juvenile court proceedings. These state-level changes culminated in the passage of California's "Proposition 21" in March 2000. What is paradoxical about this legislative trend, however, is the decline in youth violence and other pathological behaviors during this period. According to the FBI, the juvenile arrest rate for violent crime fell 36 percent from 1993 to 1999; during that same period, the juvenile arrest rate for murder fell 68 percent, its lowest rate since the 1960s. The Center for Disease Control and Prevention found that the rate of teenagers carrying weapons within the previous month declined from 26 percent in 1991 to 18 percent in 1997. The Department of Education reported that in the 1997–1998 school year, 31 percent fewer students than in the previous year were expelled for carrying a firearm in school.

The No-Fault Society

In addition to the effects of moral panic, a chronic weakness of modern society inhibited the development of *communitas* as a consequence of Columbine. Tellingly, it proved impossible to apportion individual and corporate accountability for allowing the shooting to happen. It proved similarly impossible to agree on the larger structural forces at play. This dissensus is characteristic of what I have called the "no-fault society": the inability even to conceive the bases of accountability in a society characterized by constrictive individualism, the blurring of public and private action spheres, and laxity of the rule of law. As I have applied that concept to the system of juvenile justice and child welfare in the United States, it explains the pattern of contentious evasion that prevents related agencies from working together toward fulfilling their common goals (1990).

Thus, at Columbine, "jocks" blamed the "Trenchcoat Mafia," and vice-versa. The victims' parents blamed the sheriff for failing to respond more quickly to the reports of the shooting. The sheriff in turn blamed the shooters' parents for not knowing what their children were planning. Neighbors of Eric Harris blamed the sheriff for ignoring a fifteen-page complaint they had filed months before the shooting, detailing the death threats against their son that Harris had posted on his Web site. Those neighbors had earlier complained to the same sheriff's deputy who was investigating Klebold and Harris's van break-in that they had exploded pipe bombs. Although that complaint came in only a week before the juvenile court hearing, the deputy never reported it to the prosecutor or the juvenile magistrate. Nor did he report either complaint to the pair's unknowing probation officer, who closed the cases two months early— two months, that is, before they shot up the school. School officials were similarly not notified about those complaints, although an English teacher had communicated to them her concerns about the boys' potential for violence.

The national policy debate ensuing from Columbine exhibited the same pattern of reciprocally disavowed accountability. The White House organized the Forum on Guns, Youth, and Popular Culture, but the key actors from the National Rifle Association (NRA) and from the entertainment industry didn't show up, even though the President had promised (invoking a mantra of the no-fault society) that "we should not be fighting about who takes the blame." Congress, which before Columbine had seemed ready to pass the "Consequences for Juvenile Offenders Act"—combining, in characteristic log-rolling fashion, provisions both for increased prevention and tougher punishment—argued over a plethora of opposing approaches until abandoning the legislation to stalemate. Democrats largely followed their Hollywood supporters by pushing gun control, while Republicans largely followed NRA supporters in deploring media violence and pushing for the restoration of religious and family "values." The NRA went so far as to break with those gun manufacturers who agreed to install safety-locks on handguns.

Tomorrow, and Tomorrow, and Tomorrow

Although the deadliest, Columbine was of course only one in a series of school shootings. Pearl, Mississippi; West Paducah, Kentucky; Jonesboro, Arkansas; and Springfield, Oregon came before.   Conyers, Georgia; Fort Gibson, Oklahoma; Flint, Michigan; and Santee, California came after. Like Macbeth, we might wonder, "What, will the line stretch out to th' crack of doom?" In Victor Turner's analysis, the atavistic fury of Columbine—by evoking a response that assumed the dimensions of a national ritual—should have provided the communal catharsis strong enough to resolve the sacrificial crisis. "An event…that falls outside the orthodox classification of society is, paradoxically, made the ritual occasion for an exhibition of values that relate to the community as a whole, as a homogeneous, unstructured unity that transcends its differentiations and contradictions" (1969, 92). Yet moral panic and the no-fault society act in concert to impede that ritual reunification. The scapegoating of "folk devils" reinscribes cultural distinctions that no longer necessarily apply; the diffusion of accountability prevents ritual closure and recreates the sacrificial crisis by blurring those obsolete distinctions. Moral panic also heightens the phenomenological attraction of "righteous slaughter." The rationalization of modern society only heightens children's symbolic nature as most sacred objects, and these children will therefore continue to be targets of ritual sacrifice for those seeking moral self-transcendence.

REFERENCES

Altheide, David L. "The News Media, the Problem Frame, and the Production of Fear." *Sociological Quarterly* 38 (1997): 647–688.

Best, Joel. *Random Violence: How We Talk About New Crimes and New Victims.* Berkeley: University of California Press, 1999.

Cohen, Stanley. *Folk Devils and Moral Panics: The Creation of the Mods and Rockers.* London: MacGibbon and Kee, 1972.

Farrington, David P. "Predictors, Causes, and Correlates of Male Youth Violence." In *Crime and Justice: An Annual Review of Research*, vol. 24, edited by Michael Tonry and Mark H. Moore. Chicago: University of Chicago Press, 1998.

Girard, Rene. *Violence and the Sacred.* Translated by Patrick Gregory. Baltimore, Md.: Johns Hopkins University Press, [1972] 1977.

Golding, William. *Lord of the Flies.* New York: Perigree, 1954.

Goode, Erich, and Nachman Ben-Yehuda. "Moral Panics: Culture, Politics, and Social Construction." *Annual Review of Sociology* 20 (1994): 149–171.

Green, Mary W. *The Appropriate and Effective Use of Security Technologies in U.S. Schools: A Guide for Schools and Law Enforcement Agencies.* Washington, D.C.: National Institute of Justice, 1999.

Jacobs, Mark D. *Screwing the System and Making It Work: Juvenile Justice in the No-Fault Society.* Chicago: University of Chicago Press, 1990.

Katz, Jack. *Seductions of Crime: Moral and Sensual Attractions in Doing Evil.* New York: Basic Books, 1988.

Katz, Jon. "The Price of Being Different." *Slashdot.com*, 29 April 1999.

Orwell, George. "Such, Such Were the Joys." In *Selective Essays.* New York: Doubleday Anchor, 1954.

Pollack, William. *Real Boys.* New York: Henry Holt, 1998.

Snyder, Howard N., and Melissa Sickmund. *Juvenile Offenders and Victims: 1999 National Report.* Washington, D.C.: Office of Juvenile Justice and Delinquency Prevention, 1999.

Suttles, Gerald D. *The Social Order of the Slum: Ethnicity and Territory in the Inner City.* Chicago: University of Chicago Press, 1968.

Tonry, Michael, and Mark H. Moore, ed. *Youth Violence. Crime and Justice: An Annual Review of Research*, vol. 24. Chicago: University of Chicago Press, 1998.

———. *The Drums of Affliction: A Study of Religious Processes Among the Ndembu of Zambia.* Ithaca, N.Y.: Cornell University Press, [1968] 1981.

Turner, Victor. *The Ritual Process.* Ithaca, N.Y.: Cornell University Press, 1969.

Chapter 9

Fashioning Innocence and Anxiety: Clothing, Gender, and Symbolic Childhood

Susan B. Kaiser and Kathleen Huun

> Our children are sacrosanct. We do not think of them as sexual beings, yet we do think of them very distinctly as boys and girls. Their gender is important to us. We believe strongly that all children are innocent and must be kept that way for as long as possible (Spencer 1995, 404).

> This is the profound secret of innocence, that it is at the same time anxiety... The anxiety that is posited in innocence is in the first place no guilt... In all cultures where the childlike is preserved as the dreaming of the spirit, this anxiety is found. The more profound the anxiety, the more profound the culture (Kierkegaard [1844] 1980, 41–42).

Is it possible to understand childhood both as highly gendered and as sexually innocent? This paper suggests a cultural-historical framework for interpreting the anxieties surrounding this implicit question in the United States. We explore the ways in which clothed children's bodies have been used to represent—indeed, to *constitute*[1]—dominant cultural anxieties located in a number of contradictions associated with modern parenting, consumer capitalism, and sexual identity. Modern, white, middle-class anxieties about gender and sexuality, we suggest, can be best understood in the context of complex and often contradictory cultural impulses that have played out, and continue to play out, on the bodies of young children. For example, the desire to preserve childhood innocence coincides with an anxious goal of fostering development toward adulthood. Whereas innocence is often framed toward the past, anxiety has a future orientation. Both innocence and anxiety, however, can be linked to what Kierkegaard ([1844] 1980) called the "ambiguity of subjectivity" (197). That is, both innocence and anxiety entail an array of mixed emotions: bittersweet, nostalgic recollections of times gone by that coexist with symbolic detachments from the past in the name of progress and modernity; and a sense of anticipation or even hope that coexists with uncertainties and fears about the future, respectively. In many ways, contemporary childhood constitutes a kind of momentum that simultaneously constructs visions of the past and of the future.

Fashioning Childhood History:
Gender Ambivalence and Anxiety

The emergence of childhood as a concept can be traced, in part, to its visual articulation in the painted portraits of the late sixteenth and seventeenth centuries. Aries (1962) indicates that a new sensibility—one acknowledging that the child, too, has a soul and hence a personality—emerged in the context of the growing influence of Christianity on everyday life between the thirteenth and seventeenth centuries (43).[2] During this period, there was little change in mortality rates; families had a number of children because of the notion that only a few would survive. Although, demographically speaking, the concept of childhood should have emerged much later when emotional attachments to infants could be more easily forged, the idea of childhood as a distinct life stage was evident by the end of the sixteenth century and throughout the seventeenth century (Aries 1962, 43). The acceptance of childhood as a concept largely paralleled the emergence of innocence as a construct. By the 1740s, a change in social attitudes toward children had occurred in the middle and upper classes; children, like nature, were viewed as inherently good and were becoming seen as naturally innocent (Plumb 1982, 291).

For a number of reasons, the topic of symbolic childhood is especially compelling in the context of clothing and representations of innocence and anxiety. First, culture seems to entrust clothing with messages it cannot otherwise articulate. The cultural studies concept of articulation (Slack 1996) is especially helpful in thinking through how contradictory concepts can be expressed and joined together visually; clothing and appearance styles are adept at making the nonlinear kinds of connections that articulation requires. Second, as Foucault (1980) argued, sex was "put into discourse" in the late nineteenth century as modern societies were having to work through a number of anxieties about power, knowledge, and pleasure (11). This discourse on sexuality required a cultural surveillance of childhood pedagogies and, indeed, of children's very bodies. Third, capitalism seems to thrive on the various and profound contradictions that underlie social thinking about childhood, gender, and sexuality. Giroux (2000) suggests that capitalism has "proven powerful enough both to renegotiate what it means to be a child and to make innocence a commercial and sexual category" (14). As the children's apparel industry developed in the first half of the twentieth century (Cook 1995), a process of visual negotiation was also underway in terms of gender-coding. The *idea* of gender-coding at an increasingly younger age took hold, although there was considerable flux throughout this period in terms of exactly which symbols (e.g., pink versus blue) should represent which gender.[3] Fourth, for adults there is enormous potential for vicarious display and consumption regarding children. Adults can, in various ways, use children as "vehicles of social emulation," projecting their own social attitudes as moral imperatives of childhood (Plumb 1982, 292).

The nature of anxieties regarding gender, sexuality, and innocence can be understood through a larger cultural-historical analysis of the visually negotiated relationship between childhood and adulthood. Davis (1992) has argued that ambivalences and ambiguities related to identities such as gender and social class fuel fashion change, and similarly, we submit that age-related ambivalences, ambiguities, and (we would add) anxieties foster and articulate the shifting visual boundaries between childhood and adulthood.

Prior to the seventeenth century, children in the West dressed like miniature adults. As soon as they abandoned the swaddling bands that were wrapped around their bodies during infancy, they adopted the clothes of men and women of their class. In the early seventeenth century, young children of privileged families in Europe wore long dresses similar to those that adults had worn one hundred years earlier (Aries 1962, 50). The idea of children dressing differently from their parents was beginning to emerge, albeit in an archaized version of adulthood. There was a general trend in the seventeenth century toward the "effeminization of the little boy" (Aries 1962, 58); it was virtually impossible to distinguish a boy from a girl before the age of four or five. The long white dress was to become an androgynous fixture in the child's wardrobe for more than two hundred years. Only after the First

World War in the twentieth century did boys drop "this effeminate habit" (Aries 1962, 58). Contributing to the staying power of this garment was the representation of the "naturally innocent child body" or the "romantic child" that was visually articulated by British portrait painters in the latter half of the eighteenth century (Higgonet and Albinson 1997). The dramatic increase in the number of individual children's portraits during this period suggests a greater emotional investment on the part of parents with the economic means to represent their children in this way (Plumb 1982, 289).

The French philosopher Jean-Jacques Rousseau's ([1762] 1974) influential book on childhood pedagogy, *Emile*, offered a philosophical rationale for the new image of childhood. He argued that innocence should be preserved until adolescence, in part by de-emphasizing gender difference until the age of puberty, when changes in the body occurred (172). His ideas about childhood innocence resonated well in the United States in the nineteenth century (Kaplan 1992, 21). By the end of the nineteenth century, however, the idea of (relatively genderless) sexual innocence was beginning to coexist somewhat uneasily with the quest for "normal" child development and the institutionalization of homophobia. Contributing to this obsession were fashion,[4] capitalism (Spencer 1995, 407), and middle-class culture (Rotundo 1993, 7). By the 1950s, infants were becoming systematically gender-coded (i.e., pink versus blue, frills versus plain styling; Paoletti and Kregloh 1989; Huun and Kaiser 2001).

The nature of contemporary cultural anxieties regarding childhood has shifted somewhat. There has been little if any debate in contemporary popular discourse about gendering infants and young children, except for a brief period following the second wave of feminism in the 1970s (Paoletti and Kregloh 1989). However, concerns regarding the loss of innocence (sexual and otherwise) have intensified. Media panics surrounding violence and teen pregnancy abound, often centering on their respective associations with gang-banging–inspired male appearance styles and the premature sexualization of girls' bodies. These concerns implicate dominant middle-class anxieties about race and social class as well as gender and sexuality.

For example, Elijah Anderson (1999) describes the complex bind that inner-city, African-American boys experience with respect to visual identities. They need to elicit respect from their peers both by possessing status symbols and by marking their resistance to "conventional white society" (Anderson 1999, 112). To the extent that resources allow, some use stylish objects such as jackets, sneakers, and gold jewelry to show their "willingness to possess things that may require defending"

(Anderson 1999, 73). In addition, they mark their resistance to dominant culture through the *way* in which they wear their clothes and accessories (e.g., pants worn below the waist, baggy shirts, caps turned backward) (Hethorn and Kaiser 1998). The same looks that garner local respect from their peers are the source of stereotyping and demonizing by white and black middle-class cultures. Moreover, the white, suburban middle-class males who emulate black urban images of hipness or fashionable "badness" have the advantages of greater resources to buy the status symbols, the luxury of being able to abandon these fashionably "bad" styles when necessary, and a reduced likelihood of being stereotyped as violent.[5]

Anxieties surrounding girls' appearance styles tend to revolve around premature sexualization. At a young age, girls learn that they are rewarded for being pretty according to a white beauty canon (i.e., blond, thin, dressed in fashionable clothing). Yet, dominant culture sends mixed messages regarding the boundaries between pretty and sexy. The cultural obsession with the murder of the young beauty queen, JonBenet Ramsey, points to "a paradoxical fascination in our society with precocity" (Medved and Medved 1998, 7). An article in the *New York Times Magazine* describes how one mother first enrolled her shy three-year-old daughter in a beauty pageant to help her become more outgoing, and it worked. Four years later, Dotti-Dawn indicates: "I like playing dress up. I do lots of attitude and smiles" (Saint Louis 2000).

Meanwhile, a trend toward provocative clothing for girls at a younger and younger age parallels concerns about premature sexual activity. A recent report indicates that one in twelve children are no longer virgins by the age of thirteen, and "even those kids who remain virgins are not necessarily innocent" (Cool 2001, 156).[6] *Teen Vogue* advises girls to mediate carefully between "sassiness" and "sluttiness":

> We're not suggesting that you limit your wardrobe to twinsets and school kilts (although plaid is in this year), but getting it right is all about striking a balance… Go ahead and embrace this season's miniskirt trend, but wear your micro with preppy loafers, a funky jacket, or even knee-high boots (a la Samantha Mumba), not a pair of stiletto sandals and a cropped halter. Likewise, a tiny sliver of tummy (and *tiny* is the operative word here) can appear alluring, especially when you're going for a relaxed, low-key vibe like Cameron Diaz's, but when major cleavage is involved, the look goes from flirty to downright flashy… When it comes to sassy style, clothes, or the lack of them, don't tell the whole story. Makeup and jewelry have the power to tip the scales in either direction ("Not That Innocent" 2001, 108).

Might there be at least some connection between fifty years or so of heavily gendered clothing symbolism at birth and the current anxieties regarding clothing as a hyperbolic signifier of youthful male violence and female sexuality? In the cases of both masculine and feminine development, there may be reason to examine the social and semiotic consequences of systematic gender and heterosexual coding from an early age.[7]

Amid contemporary images of lipstick-laden girls and tough-looking boys as young as four years, questions are emerging about just what innocence means and how early it should be "lost." The trend within the apparel industry toward the "downsizing" of teen styles into children's styles exacerbates these concerns in everyday representations and choices. A good example of "downsizing" is Abercrombie and Fitch's opening of forty-five stores for children's sizes 7 to 14 in the year 2000. Despite the controversial, racy pictures of teenagers (including males in provocative poses), their sales have fallen with teens and college students, and now they are hoping to capture the emerging "tween" market (Williams 2000). This market, which a special edition of *Children's Business* (e.g., *Tween Business*, 1999) highlights periodically to project roughly six months in advance, hopes to capture the younger portion of the 70 million children born in the United States to baby boomers since 1979.

Dubbed "Generation Y" or the "Echo Boom," this larger market follows a trend established more than twenty years ago with Brooke Shields's endorsement of Calvin Klein jeans: the idea of bringing name brands to young consumers (Connelly 1999, 26). The apparel industry has never looked back but rather continues to look forward as successful marketing concepts trickle down to younger consumers who are anxious to become teens. The "tween market," positioned ambiguously between childhood and the teenage years (i.e., sizes 7 to 14, approximately), is one whose tastes change rapidly, but their spending power is enormous and roughly one third of it is devoted to clothing (King 1999, B1, 4). "Tweens" comprise a generation that is "stuck on fast forward, in a fearsome hurry to grow up…The girls wear sexy lingerie and provocative makeup created just for tweens in order to complete what some parents call the Lolita look. The boys affect a tough-guy swagger— while fretting about when their voices will change" (Kantrowitz and Wingert 1999, 64).

The emerging tween market contributes fuel to a cultural discourse that expresses alarm regarding the loss of childhood innocence. Over the last twenty years, books such as Winn's (1983) *Children Without*

Childhood, Elkind's (1988) *The Hurried Child: Growing Up Too Fast Too Soon*, Medved and Medved's (1998) *Saving Childhood: Protecting Our Children from the National Assault on Innocence*, and Giroux's (2000) *Stealing Innocence: Corporate Culture's War on Children* have expressed concerns about what is happening to childhood, from a wide range of theoretical and political positionalities.

The commodification of both boys' and girls' bodies contributes to what is often perceived as fashionable images of premature development. Given the hegemony of dominant masculine coding at birth (i.e., not pink, no skirts, no frills), the appearance associated with heterosexual masculinity has become almost a foregone conclusion in the socialization of young boys. The image of heterosexual femininity produces more anxiety; for one thing, the loss of sexual innocence can result in early pregnancy. Girls' bodies are especially "marked" when it comes to the issue of losing sexual innocence. For example, Maury Povich's talk shows focus primarily on girls, engaging a redemptive, makeover narrative for girls who dress too provocatively in short skirts and tight tank tops with visible bra straps: "Stop Staring at My Teen Daughter's Body!" and "My Teen Needs Sex to Survive!" (MacGregor 2000).

As Phelan (1993) notes, the politics of cultural visibility are exceedingly complex. If visibility means power, then "almost naked" young, thin, white girls—made up to look older—should be running the country, and this is clearly not the case (10). The imagery of a "knowing" girl marks a shift in the history of representations of "ideal childhood." Higgonet (1998) maps out such a history and suggests that a shift from the "romantic child" to the "knowing child" indicates that "an ideal of childhood innocence has entered a crisis out of which a new definition of childhood is emerging" (7). Is a renegotiation of the visual boundaries between childhood and adulthood underway? And if so, to what extent and how is this renegotiation being gendered and sexualized? Are we witnessing a return to the idea of children as miniature adults, albeit this time in downsized ready-to-wear labels such as Abercrombie & Fitch, Tommy Hilfiger, and Donna Karan?

Understanding the current possibility of a newly constructed childhood requires the lens of a cultural-historical framework that engages issues of innocence and anxiety. The cultural history of representing children's clothed bodies can be seen as a process of negotiating and renegotiating these issues, as well as those of gender and sexuality, and childhood and adulthood. The collective identity work that brings age, gender, and sexuality into visual discourse also inevitably generates a range of cultural emotions about the past, present, and future.

Inasmuch as fashion enables the collective imagination and delineation of the past, present, and future (Blumer 1969), changes in clothing styles can be expected to symbolize shifts in social thinking about childhood, along with other interrelated topics such as an ethos of "quality" preparation; modern mothering, teaching, and consumer capitalism; and "normal" sexual development. The following sections pursue these topics in turn.

"Quality" Preparation

> Wherever are gathered together an exceedingly fine race of people, the flower of the race, individuals of the highest mental and moral distinction, there the birth-rate falls steadily...[W]ith high civilization fertility inevitably diminishes. Under these circumstances it was to be expected that a new ideal should begin to flash before men's eyes. If the ideal of *quantity* is lost to us, why not seek the ideal of *quality*?...Are we not left free to seek that our children, though few, should be at all events fit, the finest, alike in physical and psychical constitution, that the world has seen? (Ellis 1912, 194–95)

We get the distinct impression that the term "quality" becomes a significant code word in the history of childhood. For example, in addition to Ellis's use of the term, Aries (1962) refers to the "child of quality" (50)—presumably a boy—who ceased to be dressed like an adult in the seventeenth century. He suggests that boys were the "first specialized children" (59). The idea of distinguishing children from adults was confined to boys in the school life of the late sixteenth and early seventeenth centuries. Ironically (from a contemporary lens), in the process this specialized young male dressed like a girl who was indistinguishable from a woman. The civilization of modern Western times was essentially masculine (Ariès 1962, 61), however, and toward the end of the eighteenth century the idea of a (male) child as a "beacon for the man" was becoming an important concept (Kincaid 1998, 53).

What is the relationship between "quality preparation" and the experience of parenting? Although the cultural creation of childhood as a construct preceded the demographic revolution (Ariès 1962), it is evident that by the end of the nineteenth century the white middle-class view of the model family had changed to one with fewer children. Between 1800 and 1900, the total fertility rate dropped by about half (Historical Statistics of the United States 1975; Schwartz and Scott 1997, 222).[8] Increased education of middle-class women and improved health conditions contributed to this decline in birth rate. Although infant mortality was still a concern in major eastern cities and among low-income minority populations, by the beginning of the twentieth century, most white middle-class families no longer viewed newborn infants as "temporary visitors" who might not live beyond their first birthdays (Ehrenreich and English 1978, 167).[9] Rather, parents regarded their infants as the "evolutionary vanguard of the race" (169).

With infant mortality rates declining among middle-class families, there was good reason to view an infant as more than a "temporary visitor" or "potential individual." There was more reason to have a gendered sign system in place for the public perusal of very young children. Such a system could help ease the anxiety over the fewer numbers of children being born to the dominant middle class. Still, it was apparently neither an easy nor a complete shift from a culture of preservation to one of preparation—of a focus on highlighting and enhancing "quality" in each and every child—when it came to gender and issues of innocence.

The sexually innocent image of the "romantic child"—represented in infancy by the gender-neutral, long white dress—endured symbolically from the late eighteenth century into the twentieth century. Higgonet and Albinson (1997) argue that this image offered a nostalgic reminder of a simpler and a more "natural" time and served to construct and maintain a separate domestic sphere or a "sheltered, mothering domain" (127). The popular literature of the late nineteenth century often described mothers as feeling traumatized when their sons had their first haircuts or donned their first pair of breeches (Earle 1895).

Period literature in the first decade of the twentieth century continued to advise mothers that "pure white" dresses were "sweet and dainty" and "symbolical of innocence" (Fox 1908, 27). For boys and girls alike, there was nothing "prettier... than white" (March 1905, 9). In 1914, it was still recommended that "for the first few months a little baby should neither be handled nor shown. Therefore, he needs no dress-up clothes...After the 5th or 6th week, for showy occasions, a white petticoat is needed" (Hitching and Lutes 1914, 26).

However, additional layers of meaning were complicating the picture of infant innocence. In addition to symbolizing a nostalgic past, infancy—especially male infancy—needed to represent modernity and the future. The romantic child became more gendered and more fashionable at an earlier and earlier age, perhaps in part to create and sustain the notion that children represent a progressively modern future.

Having a child reminds parents that their "own mortality is registered"; this child will eventually take their place and therefore represents the future of the family (Horrocks 1997, 18). In his treatise on "social hygiene," British sexologist Havelock Ellis (1912) discussed the need to abandon the old population principle ("increase and multiply") for the good of the emerging modern society. The mission of social hygiene was "to bring a new joy and a new freedom into life" by studying that which concerned "the welfare of human beings living in society" (Ellis 1912, v).

Much of the focus on the future of the emerging modern society still highlighted males:

> "The child is father to the man." Who wants to see a man with the smart hip drapery of the present feminine mode?" (1917, 29)

In many ways, the history of children's clothing can be traced to a series of negations, or various processes of "identity *not*" (Freitas et al. 1997). The initial demarcation of children's appearances from adults' occurred for relatively privileged boys, in a culture of preparatory education in the late sixteenth and early seventeenth centuries, as noted earlier; they were the first "specialized children." The prevailing concept seemed to be that childhood separated boys more from adulthood than it did girls. Without a proper educational system, girls were confused with women at an early age (Aries 1962, 58). The concept of childhood evolved as one that was different from dominant, adult masculinity: effeminate, influenced by the lower and working classes, and an archaized version of adult styles from previous centuries (Aries 1962, 59).

The negation of effeminacy was one of the later moves in the history of boys' clothing; Huun and Kaiser (2001) have shown how the emergence of infant gender-coding can be seen as part of a larger trend toward a flight from femininity in boys' attire. That is, the color pink and skirts of any sort have come to be associated with that which young boys cannot and must not wear. Their association with a complex of interrelated, negating concepts (i.e., femininity, homosexuality, and infancy in general) still precludes any conceptual connections with "normal" masculine development.

Between 1680 and 1780, strong middle- and lower-middle-class themes of self-improvement and self-education influenced a shift in thinking toward a culture of preparatory childhood (Plumb 1982, 308). The middleclass worried about excessive consumption, but it was still especially tuned into fashion, striving "to participate in the world of the great yet be free from its anxieties" (Plumb 1982, 269). Middleclass children became leisure objects in the eighteenth century, and a distinctive market for custom-made children's clothing—transitionally based on the uniforms of sailors, soldiers, highlanders, and milkmaids—emerged. Children became a target for capitalism, at the same time an attitude emerged that linked them with a preoccupation toward the family's future standing in society. Socialization, rather than salvation, became the operative concept as children became a "less risky vehicle for capital investment" (Plumb 1982, 287).

In the process of a culture of preparation and capitalism, the modern, masculine thing to do was to delineate: to engage in an Enlightenment logic of separation, distinction, and classification (Aries 1962, 188). And so much of the preparation, consistent with the masculine renunciation of fashion, was aimed toward that which modern, dominant adult masculinity should *not* be. Yet it was the twentieth century before a distinctive visual concept of infant masculinity took hold. It is interesting to reflect on the extent to which the idea of infant masculinity as identity *not* has been so remarkably enduring in the latter half of the twentieth century and into the twenty-first century. Twentieth-century anxieties associated with boys dressing "effeminately" have endured despite the feminist and gay and lesbian liberation social movements.[10] In many ways the visual, binary systems of gender-coding have foreclosed critical discourse on contradictions and complexities. As if to close off anxieties and ambivalences, these systems have become taken-for-granted visual realities.

The trend toward moderate to small families replacing larger ones continued in the twentieth century, although there was a slight reversal of this trend in the postwar baby boom of the late 1940s and 1950s (Glick 1957, 30–31; Schwartz and Scott 1997, 222). At this time, there was both a marked increase in the birth rate and concern about the care and development of small children (Glick 1957, 34). It seemed as though there was a pent-up demand to spend on infants whose births were delayed by the Second World War. The baby-boom generation was the first to be consistently "color-coded" in the system of pink and blue that has endured ever since. The idea of passing a long, white infant dress from daughter to son or son to daughter had become obsolete.

The project of investing "quality" in children was increasingly represented by gender-coded consumer goods. In part, this investment was viewed as a symbolic way of doing the "right" white middle-class thing; middle-class culture of the nineteenth century seemed "to place gender labels everywhere" (Rotundo 1993, 7), and this ethos eventually trickled down from manhood to boyhood. The eventual visual gendering of infants most likely helped to relieve middle-class anxiety over the future of the nation and its place in it.[11] At least some of this anxiety revolved around the changing role of middle-class women (Dean 1996, 36) and the institutionalization of homophobia (Spencer 1995, 318), as discussed in the following sections.

Modern Mothering, Teaching, and Consumer Capitalism

[T]he child in the hands of civilised woman is an accessory organ of conspicuous consumption, much as any tool in the hands of a laborer is an accessory organ of productive efficiency (Veblen [1934] 1964, 77).

If something goes wrong, it must be mother's fault (Margolis 1984, 259).

In the eighteenth century, there was "a growing sentimentality about the innocence of the child which needed to be protected at all costs" (Plumb 1982, 312). Yet, during those decades, the quality preparation of privileged children also involved their "contribution" to the economy through the consumption of new commodities (e.g., clothes, toys, furniture), designed and produced specifically for them but targeted at their mothers (Cook 1995). In the emerging, dominant consumer society, middle-class children were less likely to contribute to the family income (by contributing to the production economy) than they were to deplete it with expenditures. An urban-industrial society required that middle-class parents invest more than ever in individual children (Schwartz and Scott 1997, 222). Fashion was the "back door" through which middle-class women could enter the economy (Douglas 1977, 61), albeit vicariously.

Kaplan (1992) argues that a new "psychic relation" between mother and child emerged between about 1830 and 1970, as white middle-class families became smaller in size (27). Dominant mothering discourse became complicated by a shift from an "early modernist" reliance on the ideas of Enlightenment thinkers such as Rousseau, who emphasized the need to preserve innocence, to a "high modernist" focus on scientific thinking (Kaplan 1992) and "mothers as consumers" (Cook 1995). However, mothers retained the sacred task of preserving the moral innocence of children, who needed to be inspired to pursue the highest and most modern levels of "spiritual civilization" (Harris 1978, 51). The separate domestic sphere relegated to women after the industrial revolution made mothers responsible for the "evolution of the civilization" (Ellis 1912, 47).

How was it that women were supposed to take their identities from their husbands, when these same women "were expected to help shape male character" in their sons (Rotundo 1993, 4)? Further, it was assumed that clothes helped to "make the man" in middle-class society, but who had control over the clothes? There were a number of contradictions when it came to mothering young boys. Evolutionary thought hailed white middle-class males as the best hope for evolutionary maturity in society. Boys were expected to evolve away from femininity, which became framed as a kind of perpetual infancy (Russett 1989). Whereas the eighteenth century had expected a boy "to become a man by instinct, directed by his masculine nature, the late nineteenth-century parent was being told that masculinity could, and *should* be taught" (Paoletti and Kregloh 1989, 26). But who was to do the teaching? How could the nineteenth-century "separate sphere" ideology that placed women in the primary child-rearing role be sustained if boys needed to be taught how to become men, presumably *by* men?

One hundred years earlier, Rousseau ([1762] 1974) had argued that women should focus on mothering as their central occupation, but he wanted the "sweet task" of mothering to be one of nursing, not teaching. He complained about mothers who spent the first six or seven years of a young boy's life burdening "his memory...with things of no use to him" (16). He was especially concerned about mothers who were "slaves of fashion" (14) and encouraged artificial rather than "natural" interests in their sons. At the same time, he argued that boys and girls alike were supposed to look sexually innocent until adolescence, and this was to be accomplished by de-emphasizing gender difference. This latter focus shifted as masculinity became something that had to be taught, and clothes needed to help make the developing man.

By the latter part of the nineteenth century, however, the "feminization" of U.S. culture applied to the realm of teaching as well as mothering. Well-educated girls were trained to be the "teachers of America," and there were anxieties that the public literary culture as well was becoming feminized by women novelists and magazine writers (Douglas 1977).

Social Darwinism and other evolutionary theories of human development sustained thinking about the control of sexuality. They portrayed "unrestrained sexuality" as the province of less developed beings. Mothers were expected to play the role of repressing such sexuality for the good of the civilization (Dean 1996, 57), because manly self-discipline was required in an active marketplace. Ironically, the ideology of separate gender spheres fostered a "plan for the female government of male passions" (Rotundo 1993, 21–25).

Ehrenreich and English (1978) argued that the science of child development emerged as a "masculinist science, framed at an increasing distance" from mothers, who were ambivalently viewed "not only as the major agents of child development but also as the major obstacles to it" (166). Reminiscent of Rousseau, G. Stanley Hall (1908), a founding father in modern psychology, expressed concern regarding the "progressive feminization of the pedagogic force" in the instruction of children and suggested that boys, in particular, needed the influence of a man "for their best development, physically, mentally, and morally" (10238).

Anxieties about leaving the task of childrearing to women contributed to a cultural "free-for-all" in child-care advice in the late nineteenth and early twentieth centuries (Kaplan 1992, 21). Although the day-to-day work of bourgeois childrearing and, increasingly, teaching was left largely to women, the middle-class socialization of children was presumed to require the advice of experts, usually men, who knew how children should be raised "for the new world" in which they were expected to live (Beekman 1977, xii–xiv). Childrearing became "something of a collective endeavor: the province of scores of experts, psychologists, commentators, counselors, each feeding off parental anxieties, offering new 'solutions,' raising new alarms" (Ehrenreich and English 1978, 83–84). Multiple and often conflicting voices, in addition to the ideas mothers learned from their own mothers, contributed to an anxious condition about how to dress, feed, and nurture children (Cook 1995).

By the early 1920s, marketers were targeting working-class women along with middle-class women. The assumption was that regardless of family income, mothers could and should express their love and self-sacrifice by spending as much as they could possibly afford on their children's clothing (Cook 1995). A growing children's wear industry between 1920 and 1950 required an expanding market; yet, the size of the average U.S. white family declined by about one person during this period (Glick 1957, 23). As the children's apparel industry developed, producers and retailers stood to benefit by creating a demand for gender-specific clothing for young children.

Chauncey (1994) argues that many middle-class heterosexual men of the 1930s and 1940s were becoming increasingly concerned that "the gender arrangements of their culture were in crisis" (111). Anxieties about manliness intensified; the Kinsey reports documented that the middle class was least tolerant of homosexuality. Fears about the "feminization" of society had become a catalyst for discourse on male gender identity, which was framed around "assaults on an uncontrolled and uncontrollable femininity" (Dean 1996, 14). The image of little boys dressed in less-than-manly attire seemed to articulate cultural anxieties about feminization. Women were damned if they did and damned if they didn't focus all of their energies on childrearing. Even sexologist Havelock Ellis (1937), who tended to be progressive on many issues pertaining to sexuality and gender, expressed concern that the typical mother was "hampering and crushing her children's developing energies" (34–35).

By the 1940s, accusations of "momism" had become extremely common in popular discourse. Wylie (1942), a psychoanalyst, expressed concern about mothers "taking over the male functions and interpreting those functions in female terms" (200). The result of momism was the "mealy look of men" (Wylie 1942, 197). Added to the list of "identity *nots*" in the first half of the twentieth century were gay men, who were subjected to what Chauncey (1994) describes as "the worst part of a more general policing of the gender order" (28).

"Normal" Sexual Development: Boys Will Not Be Girls

> Joy to Philip! He this day
> As his long coat cast away,
> And, (the childish season gone),
> Puts the manly breeches on...
> Sashes, frocks to those that need 'em,
> Philip's limbs have got their freedom.
> He can run, or he can ride,
> And do twenty things beside,
> Which his petticoats forbad:
> Is he not a happy lad?
> (De La Mare 1935, 180)

The above poem captures the sentiment that boys' "normal" gender and sexual development were being hampered by overcontrolling mothers who were bent on maintaining male innocence, which became equated with infancy and femininity. Happiness in the young male became culturally constructed as a flight from femininity; pants came to represent the rowdiness of active, outdoor life. As Rotundo (1993) notes, active, outdoor masculinity became a pleasurable alternative to female domesticity and control. At the same time, parental anxieties about "normal" male sexual development translated into a fundamental change in the social role of the prepubescent boy (Bush and London 1965, 70).

Nineteenth-century popular and academic writers had depicted babies as "inherently good, saintly...asexual cherubs" (Paoletti and Kregloh 1989, 24–25). The assumption that awareness of sex was one arena in which adults and children had little in common endured into the twentieth century. At the same time, Darwin and Freud promulgated scientific thinking that was increasing anxieties regarding sexual development (Kaplan 1992). By the end of the nineteenth century, psychologists had become aware of the extent to which young children and babies were influenced by their immediate environments, and mothers had to deal with the conflict between accepting (especially) boys' "inevitable loss of innocence" and their "positive process of growth" (Paoletti and Kregloh 1989). The institutionalization of homophobia, beginning in the 1890s, intensified the semiotic associations among homosexuality, femininity, and infancy.

The use of boys' clothing styles that were still cute but had elements of manliness—including boys' kilt suits, Buster Brown suits, and Russian sailor suits (Huun and Kaiser, 2001)—helped to begin the early masculinization of boys without sacrificing innocence. Furthermore, similarities between boys' and girls' clothes (e.g., matching toddler sets in pants form rather than skirted outfits) may have helped to suggest a continuing sexual innocence, despite some gendering. For example, in a reference to Faust, Varron (1940) remarked that "identical dress for boys and girls [would appear]...to be most suitable, as it would prevent the children's attention from being drawn to the differences of sex, and would thus preserve them from self-consciousness in this respect" (1160).

Nevertheless, by the 1950s, when infants' clothes were first gender-coded systematically, homophobia reached hysteric proportions (Spencer 1995). Effeminate clothing came to represent something that boys needed to "grow out of" as quickly as possible. In a 1962 essay, "Appearance and the Self," sociologist Gregory Stone ([1962] 1965) expressed a familiar concern about the controlling mother who dressed her son in clothes that were not sufficiently manly and hence, presumably, hampered his road to "normal" sexual development. He based his analysis on interviews with men who recalled feeling "a revulsion against being a sissy" as young boys. He blamed the "ubiquitous mother" for the feminization of boys:

Dressed as someone he is not, by a ubiquitous mother, in clothing that is employed arbitrarily by his peers (and himself) to establish who he is, the American male may, indeed, have been disadvantaged very early with respect to the formulation of a sense of sexual identity. Advantages, rather, accrued to the female, who from the earliest age was dressed as she was by a mother from whose perspective she was provided with an adequate conception of herself in sexual terms (Stone [1962] 1965, 236).

In contrast to the discourse regarding the contradictions in male socialization and clothing, female socialization and clothing have been regarded as relatively less complicated. Although it has been established that girls learn quite early about the social rewards associated with being pretty and dressing fashionably (Kaiser 1989; Kaiser 1997), somehow the relationship between gender-coding and developing sexual identity has not been examined critically in either popular or academic discourse.

In the 1970s and the 1980s, feminist theorist Nancy Chodorow (1978, 1989) used a rather continuous model of identity development to characterize mother-daughter relations, based on same-sex identification. As Stone does in his analysis, Chodorow attributed the unresolved, ambivalent and repressed nature of socialization primarily, but not exclusively, to males. She critiqued and revised psychoanalytic thought to explain differences in gendered personalities and psychic structures. According to her explanation, mothers experience difficulty seeing a daughter as a separate person due to a complex internalized object-relational structure involving projection, narcissistic extension, and patterns of fusion. A daughter, in turn, may not feel completely separate from her mother (or later, others in general) and may have more permeable ego boundaries than a son does. Hence, a daughter is likely to define herself in relation to others and to feel ambivalence about being separate and independent from her mother.

Still, one gets the impression in reading Chodorow that, implicitly or explicitly, she prioritized continuity, fusion, and extension over contingency, ambivalence, and repression in the context of female socialization. Later feminist analyses (e.g., Braidotti 1991; Flax 1990) have placed greater emphasis on the contradictions and discontinuities that underlie feminine socialization. A host of contradictions and ambivalences surface in the fashioning of femininity. Concepts of creativity, pleasure, and even subversiveness become juxtaposed with those of oppression, obsession, and false consciousness.

In a study conducted with mothers in the late 1980s (Kaiser and Chandler 1991), there were both continuities and discontinuities between mothers' recollections of their own clothes as young girls and those of their daughters. Many mothers who where were born during the baby boom expressed frustration that their preschool daughters wanted to wear frilly, effeminate clothes that were impractical for various situations. Some (mainly white and middle-class) were surprised to find that they were not applying the gender-neutral principles of second-wave feminism as they had anticipated doing when it came to their daughters' clothes. As one mother relates:

> When I was pregnant and before I had my daughters I was very convinced that my kids would go around in jeans and tennis shoes and shirts, whether they were boys or girls. I was very committed to the idea that children develop their sense of identity and their sense of place in the world, not by what they are wearing but by how you treat them. But I've found myself succumbing to— whatever it is—the marketing, I don't know what—my past, when I was a little girl. I don't know what it is, but yes, I do find myself dressing her much more femininely than I would have thought.

Another explains:

> I told myself before she was born that it [gender] wouldn't matter, and I'd probably dress her in greens and yellows. She was born bald; she stayed bald for two years, and yes, she wore lots of pinks and purples and scotch-taped bows on her head so that we knew she was a girl. It hurt my feelings when they said, "Oh, what a nice son you have."

The mothers were well aware that they are judged by their daughters' appearances, and in that sense there were some continuities:

> Whatever she wears reflects on me. I'm sure people think, "Oh my God, this is how she dresses her child."

> People are going to judge me and my daughter based on how she is dressed. If she's dressed tacky, then it reflects on my capabilities of taking care of her and dressing her appropriately and teaching her.

> The reality is that when she looks put together it makes me feel like everything isn't falling through the cracks—that we kind of have it together.

So, where does femininity go from this idea of "having it all together"? In terms of a "disconnect" from femininity and infancy, in contrast to the symbolic framing of young masculinity in males, young femininity in females has become culturally understood as relatively continuous. Cook (1998), for example, found a relative lack of distinction among girls' styles between the ages of six and fourteen or fifteen in his study of the children's wear industry in the first half of the twentieth century. (One exception was the tendency for hemlines to grow longer as a girl reached her high school years.) A young girl of six, period literature suggested, should look neither like a fourteen-year-old nor a young child, so a separate retail department was created to fill the "growing girl's" void. Cook (1998) argues that the tension was one of sexual display; an intermediate age category (seven to ten or twelve) emerged to differentiate girls between the categories of young girlhood and adolescence.

The conflation between developing masculinity and modernity has made it difficult to visualize young, modern femininity. These issues become even more complex during adolescence. To the extent that adolescence is framed as a masculine discourse of rowdy rebellion from the norms of both childhood and adulthood, girls get caught between the discourses of adolescence and femininity. That is to say, they cannot easily resist the norms of childhood and adulthood without being perceived as unfeminine (Hudson 1984). It is not surprising, then, that they pursue modes of resistance within the discourse of femininity. Contemporary discourse offers a number of sexual signs with which girls can experiment to construct an exaggerated femininity (Hethorn and Kaiser 1998) that both articulates and represents cultural anxiety. The current industry trend toward apparel "downsizing" merely exacerbates this anxiety and leads to questions regarding the loss of innocence several years before adolescence.

Let's consider two examples of contemporary representations of such anxiety regarding girls' bodies. The national obsession with the murder of JonBenet Ramsey, the very young, blond beauty queen from Boulder, Colorado, is one case in point. Conservative cultural critics Medved and Medved (1998) remark that her seductive, made-up image and "posed pout, splashed like a coldly calculated fashion model's smirk across so many magazine covers, both captivated and disturbed us" because of the paradoxical "pairings of innocence and seduction, childhood and death" (9). Although she is older, the popularity of the (also blond) teen idol Britney Spears, a former Mouseketeer, may also be read as a juxtaposition of girl-like charm with the idea of taking young female sexuality to new levels. Her song "I'm Not That Innocent" also suggests a perceived need to mix a sense of transgression into her persona.

At first blush, images such as these, while generating anxiety, may seem to represent the end of innocence. Yet, viewing them within a cultural-historical framework reminds us about the ambiguity of symbolic childhood. In addition to symbolizing a nostalgic past, infancy has represented modernity and the future. The romantic child in the long, white dress was on its way in the early years of the twentieth century to becoming gendered and fashionable in order to create and sustain the idea that children constitute the future. In particular, as the long, white infant dress became increasingly perceived as effeminate, it became a semiotic synthesis of femininity, homosexuality, and infancy—a synthetic "identity *not*" from which boys had to flee in the context of homophobic, capitalist modernity. As Huun and Kaiser (2001) illustrate in their analysis of infant and toddler clothing depicted in the *Sears* catalog between 1896 and 1962, the idea that clothes "make the man" in a logical progression toward masculinity basically played out in the very forms and colors of the clothes offered for boys. It was generally boys' clothes that were the first to be "on the move" in new directions—almost always away from femininity. Femininity itself continued, inconsistently, to represent innocence as well as anxiety.

Childhood and Innocence *Not*: Concluding Thoughts

Part of the problem with the concept of modern childhood innocence is that it is an "anxiety-fed legend" (Kincaid 1998, 168). It is a legend that relies on an ambiguously negative construction; like "air in a tire," there is a lot to lose in an Enlightenment construction defined as what it is not (Kincaid 1998, 54). Fashion affords an outlet for the management of a number of unresolved, and perhaps unresolvable, issues surrounding innocence. And yet somehow the related anxieties regarding gender have been foreclosed, for the time being at least, by a dichotomous coding system that has been in place for over fifty years.

Some of the anxiety surrounding innocence involves its emergence as an object of desire. In the modern constructions of childhood and sexuality—"two new products on the market"—they somehow became mixed together (Kincaid 1998, 52), eventually surfacing in the imagery of the twentieth century's fashionable and "knowing child" (Higgonet 1998).[12]

Another problem with the romantic insistence on innocence was the "need to define children in terms of what adults were not: not sexual, not vicious, not ugly, not conscious, not damaged" (Higgonet 1998, 224). This tendency toward negativity also applies to definitions of young masculinity; as we have seen, modern masculinity has become defined as not effeminate. Higgonet (1998) concludes that "it might be a healthy change to substitute positive for negative, tolerance for denial" (224). To become fully effective, such a move would need to incorporate new ways of imaging gender and sexuality, as well as childhood *per se*. The relationship between early gender-coding and the idea that sexual innocence should be delayed still needs to be addressed critically and creatively. How and when can the line be drawn between gender and sexual identity? Similarly, one might ask: How and when can the line be drawn between childhood and adulthood? Perhaps a fruitful alternative to border maintenance is a recognition of the fluid and shifting nature of boundaries, as well as the tendency for appearance styles to articulate the contradictions among age, gender, and sexuality. The shift from representations of "identity *not*" toward more positive visual concepts of childhood requires an ongoing ability to grapple with these and other contradictions.

Even at second blush, innocence and anxiety seem to be diametrically opposed. After all, innocence is framed as something that is in the past; it becomes connected with nostalgia toward that which has been lost. Anxiety, in contrast, is framed toward the future—toward uncertainty with at least a tinge of angst. What is to come? In the realm of children's gender and sexuality, this question alone is enough to generate anxiety. Innocence and anxiety, if not exactly the *same* thing, at least bear a close family resemblance. They can be used heuristically, together with images of children's clothed bodies, to foster a collective sense of reflexivity about the interplay between continuity and change. Perhaps this is a lot of weight for children's bodies to bear. However, a discourse that moves the problem of children's clothing beyond "quick fixes" such as school uniforms just may provide an opening to respect children's agency in their developing identities, as well as to recognize the representational power of visual imagery.

NOTES

1   Throughout this paper, following Stuart Hall (1997, 3), we use the concept of representation to refer to the constitutive practices through which meaning is produced as individuals consume cultural "things" (e.g., clothes, images, education) in everyday life.

2   Aries (1962) marks the appearance of the portrait of the deceased child in the sixteenth century as an important moment in the history of feelings, because it indicated that the child was perceived as having a soul (40). In the late sixteenth and early seventeenth centuries, children appeared for the first time in their own portraits, separated from their parents (42). Childhood was becoming perceived as a life stage and a concept distinct from adulthood.

3   For further background on the shifting symbolism of pink and blue in the early twentieth century, see Paoletti and Kregloh (1989) and Huun and Kaiser (2001).

4   Although they do not specifically address symbolic childhood, see Davis (1992) and Wilson (1985) for helpful discussions of fashion, modernity, and identity ambivalence.

5   Anderson (1999, 234) notes that "these styles may just be a lark that they [young white males] can easily give up when they realize it is time to become serious about life." Furthermore, the judicial system treats black and Hispanic youths more harshly than white teenagers charged with comparable crimes (Butterfield 2000). Overall, despite tragic incidents of violent crimes—many of which have involved school shootings by white, suburban males—the dire predictions about increases in violent youth crime have not materialized (Westphal 1999).

6   There has reportedly been an increase in oral sex: "body-part sex" that the boys are receiving and the girls are later regretting (Cool 2001; Jarrell 2000).

7   See Hethorn and Kaiser (1998) for a discussion of cultural anxiety in relation to adolescence and issues of violence and sexuality for males and females, respectively.

8   Even rural white families, who were still likely to regard children as contributing to the productivity of the family farm, underwent a drop in the fertility rate. In 1900, their rate was 60 percent of that in 1800; disposable income allowed rural families to spend more per child (Easterlin, Alter, and Condran 1978).

9   Earlier, in the nineteenth century, it was not uncommon for frontier parents to leave their newborn infants nameless for several months (Ehrenreich and English 1978, 167).

10 It may be argued, of course, that a dominant backlash against these social movements has actually intensified the gender-coding of young children.

11 See Spencer (1995, 318) for a discussion of such anxieties regarding sexuality and population issues.

12 A systematic analysis of the contemporary "knowing child" in apparel advertising would be quite useful. It seems as though this child is often either white and female (with a model-like pout or in somewhat provocative attire) or nonwhite and male (wearing hip-hop attire and in an urban setting).

REFERENCES

Anderson, Elijah. *Code of the Street: Decency, Violence, and the Moral Life of the Inner City*. New York: W. W. Norton, 1999.

Aries, Philippe. *Centuries of Childhood: A Social History of Family Life*. Translated by Robert Baldick. New York: Knopf, 1962.

Beekman, D. *The Mechanical Baby: A Popular History of the Theory and Practice of Child Raising*. Westport, Conn.: Lawrence Hill, 1977.

Blumer, Herbert. "Fashion: From Class Differentiation to Collective Selection." *Sociological Quarterly* 10 (1969): 275–291.

Braidotti, Rosi. *Patterns of Dissonance: A Study of Women in Contemporary Philosophy*, translated by Elizabeth Guild. New York: Routledge, 1991.

Bush, G., and P. London. "On the Disappearance of Knickers: Hypotheses for the Functional Analysis of the Psychology of Clothing." In *Dress, Adornment, and the Social Order*, edited by M. E. Roach and J. B. Eicher, 64–81. New York: John Wiley and Sons, 1965.

Butterfield, Fox. "Racial Disparities Seen as Pervasive in Juvenile Justice." *New York Times*, 26 April 2000, sec. A1, 18.

Chauncey, George. *Gay New York: Gender, Urban Culture, and the Making of the Gay Male World, 1890–1940*. New York: Basic Books, 1994.

Chodorow, Nancy. *The Reproduction of Mothering: Psychoanalysis and the Sociology of Gender*. Berkeley, Calif.: University of California Press, 1978.

Chodorow, Nancy. *Feminism and Psychoanalytic Theory*. New Haven, Conn.: Yale University Press, 1989.

Connelly, Julie. "A Ripe Target for Web Retailers, Teens Keep Heading to the Mall." *New York Times*, 22 September 1999, 26.

Cook, Daniel Thomas. "The Mother as Consumer: Insights from the Children's Wear Industry, 1917–1929." *Sociological Quarterly* 36, no. 3 (1995): 505–522.

———. "The Commodification of Childhood: Personhood, the Children's Wear Industry and the Moral Dimensions of Consumption, 1917–1967." Unpublished Ph.D. diss., Department of Sociology, University of Chicago, 1998.

Cool, Lisa Collier. "The Secret Sex Lives of Kids." *Ladies Home Journal*, March 2001: 156–159.

Davis, Fred. *Fashion, Culture, and Identity*. Chicago: University of Chicago Press, 1992.

Dean, C. J. *Sexuality and Modern Western Culture*. New York: Twayne, 1996.

De La Mare, W. *Early One Morning in the Spring: Chapters on Children and on Childhood as It is Revealed in Particular in Early Memories and in Early Writings*. New York: Macmillan, 1935.

Douglas, Ann. *The Feminization of American Culture*. New York: Noonday Press, 1977.

Earle, M. "The Artistic Dressing of Little Boys." *McCall's*, April 1895, 124.

Easterlin, R. A., G. Alter, and G. A. Condran. "Farms and Farm Families in Old and New Areas: The Northern States in 1860." In *Family and Population in Nineteenth-Century America*, edited by T. K. Hareven and M. A. Vinovskis, 22–73. Princeton, N.J.: Princeton University Press, 1978.

Ehrenreich, Barbara, and Deirdre English. *For Her Own Good: 150 Years of Advice to Women*. New York: Anchor Press/Doubleday, 1978.

Elkind, David. *The Hurried Child: Growing Up Too Fast Too Soon*. Reading, Mass.: Addison-Wesley, 1988.

Ellis, Havelock. *The Task of Social Hygiene*. Boston, Mass.: Houghton Mifflin, 1912.
———. *On Life and Sex*. New York: Garden City Publishing, 1937.
"Fashions: Styles—and the Boy. "*McCall's* 45, no. 3 (November 1917): 29, 54.
Flax, Jane. *Thinking Fragments: Psychoanalysis, Feminism, and Postmodernism in the Contemporary West*. Berkeley, Calif.: University of California Press, 1990.
Foucault, Michel. *An Introduction: The History of Sexuality*. Vol. 1. New York: Vintage Books/Random House, [1978] 1980.
Fox, I. E. "For the Baby." *Modern Priscilla* 22, no. 10 (1908): 27.
Freitas, Anthony, Susan Kaiser, Joan Chandler, Carol Hall, Jung-Won Kim, and Tania Hammidi. "Appearance Management as Border Construction: Least Favorite Clothing, Group Distancing, and Identity… Not!" *Sociological Inquiry* 67, no. 3 (1997): 322–335.
Giroux, Henry A. *Stealing Innocence: Corporate Culture's War on Children*. New York: Palgrave, 2000.
Glick, Paul C. *American Families*. New York: John Wiley and Sons, 1957.
Hall, G. Stanley. "Feminization in School and Home." *World's Work* 16 (1908): 10237–10244.
Hall, Stuart, ed. *Representation: Cultural Representations and Signifying Practices*. London and Thousand Oaks, Calif.: Sage, 1997.
Harris, B. J. *Beyond Her Sphere: Women and the Professions in American History*. Westport, Conn.: Greenwood Press, 1978.
Hethorn, Janet, and Susan Kaiser. "Youth Style: Articulating Cultural Anxiety." *Visual Sociology* 14 (1998): 109–125.
Higgonet, Anne. *Pictures of Innocence: the History and Crisis of Ideal Childhood*. New York: Tames and Hudson, 1998.
Higgonet, Anne, and Cassi Albinson. "Clothing the Child's Body." *Fashion Theory* 1, no. 2 (1997): 119–144.
Historical Statistics of the United States: Colonial Times to 1970, part 1. Washington, D.C.: U.S. Department of Commerce, 1975.
Hitching, W., and D. T. Lutes. *Baby Clothing: Healthful, Economical, and Original*. New York: Frederick A. Stokes, 1914.
Horrocks, Roger. *An Introduction to the Study of Sexuality*. New York: St. Martin's Press, 1997.
Hudson, Barbara. "Femininity and Adolescence." In *Gender and Generation*, edited by Angela McRobbie and Mica Nava, 31–53. Houndmills, UK: Macmillan Education, 1984.
Huun, Kathleen, and Susan B. Kaiser. "The Emergence of Modern Infantwear, 1896–1962: Traditional White Dresses Succumb to Fashion's Gender Obsession." *Clothing and Textiles Research Journal* 19, no. 3 (2001): 103–119.
Jarrell, Anne. "The Face of Teenage Sex Grows Younger." *New York Times*, 3 April 2000, sec. B1, 8.
Kaiser, Susan B. "Clothing and the Social Organization of Gender Perception: A Developmental Approach." *Clothing and Textiles Research Journal* 1 (1989): 46–56.
———. *The Social Psychology of Clothing: Symbolic Appearances in Context*, 2nd ed., revised. New York: Fairchild, 1997.
Kaiser, Susan B., and Joan L. Chandler. "Gender Socialization, Appearance, and Stone's Ubiquitous Mother—A Feminist Critique and Revision." Society for the Study of Symbolic Interaction: Gregory Stone Symposium, San Francisco, February 1991.

Kantrowitz, Barbara, and Pat Wingert. "The Truth About Tweens." *Newsweek*, 18 October 1999, 62–72.

Kaplan, E. Ann. *Motherhood and Representation: The Mother in Popular Culture and Melodrama.* London and New York: Routledge, 1992.

Kierkegaard, Soren. *The Concept of Anxiety*, edited and translated with introduction and notes by Reidar Thomte in collaboration with Albert A. Anderson. Princeton, N.J.: Princeton University Press, [1844] 1980.

Kincaid, James R. *Erotic Innocence: The Culture of Child Molesting.* Durham, N.C.: Duke University Press, 1998.

King, Sharon R. "Where Does Generation Y Go to Shop?" *The New York Times*, 28 August 1999, sec. B1, 14.

MacGregor, Jeff. "Saving the World, One Sexy Teen at a Time." *The New York Times*, 16 July 2000, sec. AR 25, 26.

March, M. "Fancies for the Little Ones." *Modern Priscilla* 19, no. 5(1905): 9.

Margolis, M. L. *Mothers and Such: Views of American Women and Why They Changed.* Berkeley, Calif.: University of California Press, 1984.

Medved, Michael, and Diane Medved. *Saving Childhood: Protecting Our Children from the National Assault on Innocence.* New York: HarperPerennial, 1998.

"Not That Innocent." *Teen Vogue*, Spring 2001: 108.

Paoletti, Jo B., and C. L. Kregloh. "The Children's Department." In *Men and Women: Dressing the Part*, edited by C. B. Kidwell and V. Steele, 22–41. Washington, D.C.: Smithsonian Institution Press, 1989.

Phelan, Peggy. *Unmarked: The Politics of Performance.* London and New York: Routledge, 1993.

Plumb, J. H. "Commercialization and Society." In *The Birth of a Consumer Society: The Commercialization of Eighteenth-Century England*, edited by Neil McKendrick, John Brewer, and J. H. Plumb, 265–334. London: Europa, 1982.

Rotundo, E. A. *American Manhood: Transformations in Masculinity from the Revolution to the Modern Era.* New York: Basic Books, 1993.

Rousseau, Jean-Jacques. *Emile.* Translated by B. Foxley. London and New York: J. M. Dent & Sons, [1762] 1974.

Russett, C. E. *Sexual Science: The Victorian Construction of Womanhood.* Cambridge, Mass.: Harvard University Press, 1989.

Saint Louis, Catherine. "The Little Princess." *The New York Times Magazine*, 9 July 2000, 66.

Schwartz, M. A., and B. M. Scott. *Marriages and Families: Diversity and Change*, 2nd ed. Upper Saddle River, N.J.: Prentice Hall, 1997.

Slack, Jennifer Daryl. "The Theory and Method of Articulation in Cultural Studies." In *Stuart Hall: Critical Dialogues in Cultural Studies*, edited by David Morley and Kuan-Hsing Chen, 112–127. London and New York: Routledge, 1996.

Spencer, Colin. *Homosexuality in History.* New York: Harcourt Brace, 1995.

Stone, Gregory P. "Appearance and the Self." In *Dress, Adornment, and the Social Order*, edited by M. E. Roach and J. B. Eicher, 216–245. New York: John Wiley and Sons, [1962] 1965.

Tween Business. A Supplement to *Children's Business* (August 1999). New York: Fairchild, 1999.

Varron, A. "Historical Gleanings: An Ideal Dress for Children." *Ciba Review* 32 (1940): 1157–1161.

Veblen, Thorstein. *Essays in Our Changing Order*, edited by Leon Ardzrooni. New York: Reprints of Economics Classics, Augustus M. Kelley, Bookseller, [1934] 1964.

Westphal, David. "Despite Dire Predictions, Violent Youth Crime Falls." *Sacramento Bee*, 13 December 1999, sec. A1, 14.

Williams, Mark. "Once Trendy Abercrombie Looks for 'Shot of Newness.' " *Sacramento Bee*, 10 July 2000, sec. D1, 4.

Wilson, Elizabeth. *Adorned in Dreams: Fashion and Modernity*. Berkeley, Calif.: University of California Press, 1985.

Winn, Marie. *Children Without Childhood*. New York: Pantheon Books, 1983.

Wylie, P. *Generation of Vipers*. New York: Farrar and Rinehart, 1942.

PART FOUR

Making Childhoods with and through Media

Chapter 10

The Heterosexualization of Boyhood

Jeffery P. Dennis

On the sitcom *Third Rock from the Sun,* two intergalactic explorers disguised as a boy and his aunt go hunting for a new car. An oily salesman cozies up to adolescent Tommy and, with a lascivious grin, asks the question that, in past generations, preteen boys heard incessantly from out-of-touch uncles and abrasive family friends: "Sport, do you like girls?" Glaring at him, Tommy responds, "Yes, I do…sorry."

The joke hinges on conflicting constructs of sexual desire. The salesman believes (or pretends to believe) the traditional construct of preteen boys as "innocent," unable to experience or even understand the intense heterosexual desire that presumably will inform their adult lives. Sometimes their innocence allows them to spend childhood in a carefree homosocial Eden, but more often they are portrayed as poor handicapped souls barred from the only thing worth doing in life, "haunted by an absence," in the words of James Kincaid (1998, 16). Fortunately, according to this construct, heterosexual desire is inevitable: Once adolescent hormones kick in, the preteen boy will become a man, discover "the opposite sex" in a blinding Damascus Road epiphany, and subsequently spend every waking moment fantasizing about feminine smiles and bra sizes. The salesman is not asking, "Do you like girls?" but "Do you like girls *yet?*" He thus invites Tommy to share the secret of the lascivious grin, to acknowledge that he has been catapulted from asexual latency to heterosexual destiny.

Tommy disavows this construct of boyhood innocence. He has never lived in a homosocial Eden, nor has he ever been "cured" of asexuality by a glimpse of forbidden breast. A middle-aged information officer on his home planet, he is doomed by the caprice or ignorance of his superiors to appear on Earth in the form of a child; yet this form was desired and desiring from its very creation, already inscribed with a "sedimented history of sexual hierarchy and sexual erasures" (Butler 1993, 49); his single-minded pursuit of orgasm began at "birth." However, Tommy is aware (as the salesman is not) that men do not invariably derive their orgasms from relations with women; although his construct of desire omits any period of innocence, his experience could be either gay or straight. Tommy does not answer the question, "Do you like girls *yet*?" but instead "Do you like girls *or boys*?"

Neither construct, of course, fully interrogates the complexities of sexual desire in the social world. Deleuze and Guattari conceptualize desire as an dense and multifaceted lattice composed of "an infinity of different and even contrary flows" (1983, 351): many different "flows" (the desire for physical contact, sexual orgasm, social validation, even the desire to desire and to be desired) are directed at many different objects (individual people, types of people, physical or social character-istics, social situations, even theoretical ideas). Children are not excused from participation in this lattice of desire, though the intensities, objects, symbolic meanings, and levels of social validation evoked in them differ from those of adolescents or adults. However, at least since the eighteenth century (Ariès 1962), Euro-American mass culture has propagated an unproblematic construct of (hetero)sexual desire as universally absent in boys but inevitably and universally present in men.

During the twentieth century, when industrialization, urbanization, and universal higher education allowed childhood to be extended through the teen years and even longer (Palladino 1996), the construct developed into a discursive strategy resembling the narrative of a story, with introduction, crisis, and conclusion: The boy's bucolic homosocial world is disrupted by a teenage "discovery of girls," which results in several years of intense, undirected, and usually frustrated attempts at promiscu-ous heterosexuality. Eventually, in early adulthood, "the right woman" tricks, cajoles, or seduces him into marriage (and reproduction). His heterosexual desire abruptly vanishes, and he spends the rest of his life trying to regain Paradise with his homosocial buddies. Presumably, if he could evade being "hooked" in the first place, he could remain an adolescent, recklessly enjoying heterosexual liaisons with supermodels forever.

During most of the twentieth century, preteen boys in such diverse cultural products as movies (*Stand by Me*), newspaper comics (*Dennis the Menace)*, cartoons (*Jonny Quest)*, magazine art (Norman Rockwell's pastoral *Saturday Evening Post* covers)*,* and television sitcoms (*Leave it to Beaver)* luxuriated in a sexless homosocial Arcadia, enjoying "the daily small terrors of school; the aimless amusements of catching frogs and spitting off bridges; the disgustingly ambivalent emotions evoked by 'icky girls'" (Jones 1992, 124). Girls appeared only as adversaries, sisters, and maternal figures, and desire for them occurred occasionally, often in stylized, imitative crushes on female teachers. Anything overtly erotic was summarily rejected: When asked to comment on the attractiveness of a female classmate, 1990s bad boy Bart Simpson stridently replies, "You're asking the wrong guy—they all look alike to me."

Teenagers, conversely, were almost always portrayed as bumbling embodiments of heterosexual desire, television's Dobie Gillis whose Cartesian cogito was "I love girls!" or the comic book Archie Andrews who dissolved into a puddle of raw hormones whenever raven-haired Veronica favored him with a glance. After high school and young adulthood filled with enthusiastic hijinks in quest of the elusive orgasm (or kiss), however, their "carefree" days ended with the affixing of a ball and chain. Dobie Gillis transmutated into Ralph Cramden, Archie Andrews into Dagwood Bumstead, whose expressions of sexual desire were limited to guilty stares at secretaries and boss's nieces. The heterosexual coitus once so desperately sought became a trap, the marriage bed a Weberian iron cage to be escaped only briefly on nights of bowling or poker with the boys.

Through its fifty-year history, television has been particularly consistent in reproducing the asexual boy/hyperheterosexual teen dichotomy. Such boys as Ricky on *Ozzie and Harriet*, Nicholas on *Eight is Enough*, and Ben on *Growing Pains*, while astonishingly sensitive, intelligent, and mature in their evaluations of other adult concerns (Jordan 1995), were either utterly unaware of heterosexual desire or utterly unable to comprehend it. On the 1980s situation comedy *Who's the Boss*, preteen Jonathan grew up surrounded by heavy-handed sexual double entendres from his randy grandmother, repressed mother, and hunky housekeeper, yet he maintained an air of obliviousness; often he asked "questions laden with sexual implications, then stare[d] wide-eyed as the adults react[ed] with leers and snickers" (Jones 1992, 256). However, during one summer hiatus, his character "discovered girls" and returned in the fall fully comprehending and even participating in every leer and snicker; gay actor Danny Pintauro spent the rest of the series struggling valiantly to portray Jonathan as a horny heterosexual teenager.

In the products of mass culture, male adolescents are not only heterosexual, but absurdly eager; undesiring, minimally desiring, or desiring within reasonable limits is not allowed. They participate in sports, enroll in classes, volunteer for charities, and apply for college for no other reason than to meet girls. They lapse into jammering idiocy when a girl looks at them, hand over the keys to the family car in exchange for a kiss, agree to fight tigers or jump out of airplanes on the off chance that a girl might be impressed. When Dad hears of the latest mishap, he need only recall his own adolescence and ask, with a paternal chuckle, "What's her name?"

However, as Michael Kimmel observes (1987), hegemonic heterosexuality is often reified to demonstrate not heterosexual desire but the lack of homosexual desire; the depiction of an inevitable hormone-drenched "discovery of girls" may erupt in part from a refusal to depict a "discovery of boys," a disavowal of the possibility that the homosocial might evolve into the homoerotic. Hyperheterosexuality thus may be a negation of unstated homosexuality; absence informs presence, "ignorance and opacity collude or compete with knowledge in mobilizing the flows of energy, desire, goods, meanings, persons" (Sedgwick 1990, 4).

Certainly, products of mass culture, through their very construction, articulate both hegemonic and transgressive readings: Alexander Doty finds discourses of lesbian desire between the female duos on *I Love Lucy* and *Laverne and Shirley* present not in the script nor even (necessarily) in the actors' intents but in the dynamics of the interaction itself, in "a place beyond the audience's conscious 'real life' definition of their sexual identities and cultural positions" (1993, 15). However, a generation ago, these readings could easily be ignored. In a 1966 episode of *Gilligan's Island*, dowager Mrs. Howell begins to receive anonymous love letters. She and her husband interrogate the male castaways—Gilligan, the Skipper, and the Professor, but all are innocent. The Howells are dumfounded. "That's impossible!" Mr. Howell exclaims. "We've asked everyone on the island." They have failed to ask *everyone*, however; there are two women on the island, Ginger and Mary Anne. In 1966, the possibility of lesbian love need not even be raised to be dismissed: It was simply beyond conscious thought. It would never be so again.

Gay rights and gay pride movements in the 1970s and the AIDS epidemic in the 1980s increased the visibility of nonhegemonic sexual identities in the public sphere (Adam 1995), making it difficult for even mass-media products to present heterosexual desire as inevitable and universal without appearing impossibly naive. Rock Hudson's death from AIDS contributed to making it impossible. When the aging movie star was revealed to be "really" gay after two generations as a Hollywood heartthrob, many Americans felt curiously betrayed: Even though rumors of transgressive sexual inclinations had dogged Hudson's career and his films were often plotted around various hints of homosexual desire, Hudson had become emblematic of male hegemonic heterosexuality. In both his film personas and his private life, he exuded a "domestic iconography" (Meyer, 1991): He obviously liked women, felt comfortable around women, and rarely abandoned the wife or girlfriend to seek out homosocial adventures with his buddies. However, as Sturken states (1997, 151), "In the summer of 1985, we had to accept the fact that many of our fundamental, conventional images [of heterosexuality] were instilled by someone gay." The absent had become undeniably present, the unstated irrevocably stated. The question could never again be "Do you like girls *yet?*" but "Do you like girls *or boys yet* ?"

The mass media reacted quickly. Jughead Jones, a mainstay of the vast Archie comic book industry, had spent fourty years as a "woman-hater": He liked girls only as friends, vastly preferred the company of boys, and sublimated his sexual impulses into nonstop eating. Many stories of the 1950s and 1960s presented his resistance to compulsory teenage heterosexuality as mature and sensible. After Rock Hudson's death, however, *not liking girls* could be understood as *liking boys*, so the authors quickly gave Jughead a series of girlfriends. Still, the attractions seemed largely mediated on shared social interests other than on heterosexual, so one plotline in the 1990s demonstrated the penalty for articulating same-sex desire in bucolic Riverdale. On a bright spring day, while heterosexual couples are cooing at each other, Jughead feels overwhelmed by love for "his fellow man," and skips through town kissing his friends. Most of them are simply annoyed, but hulking homophobe Moose cries, "He kissed me! In public and everything!" and bashes him into an unrecognizable pulp.

In the 1990s, every homosocial friendship evoked the question, "Do you like girls *or boys?*" and the answer ("girls") was always implied, demonstrated, or even directly stated: The Genie tells Disney's *Aladdin* (1992) "I'm getting kind of fond of you, kid" but quickly adds, "That doesn't mean I want to pick out furniture." Timothy Burke calls Dr. Quest and Race Bannon, the adult males on the children's adventure cartoon *Jonny Quest* (1964–1965), "America's most attractive and stable gay couple" (1999, 115); their preteen male charges, Jonny and Hadji, also felt a homosocial attraction to each other that could easily be read as homoerotic. However, when a revised version of the program appeared in 1996, Jonny had inexplicably acquired a girlfriend, Race Bannon a daughter, and Dr. Quest a wife. Certainly, the inclusion of women adventurers was in itself a laudable move, but it also worked to destabilize the hints of homoerotic desire between the two male couples, providing an answer to the question that could not even be asked thirty years before.

Although the question "Do you like girls or boys?" must now be asked (and answered) for adults in mass media, it is conceivable that the construct of boyhood innocence could be retained; stories could still posit an asexual Eden and then a earthshaking discovery of "girls or boys." However, as Kincaid states (1998, 306), "children are being posed before us on movies and television screens in answer to deep and terrible cultural needs" that have nothing to do with their actual desires and everything to do with ours: The image of the innocent boy mirrors something the adult male wants to see in himself, either a bucolic world that validates homosocial bonds in the absence of women, or an eroti-cized world that validates heterosexual desire. If a boy no longer "dis-covers girls" automatically and universally shortly after his Bar Mitzvah, if he can eliminate the marriage bed altogether and set up housekeeping with one of his poker-playing buddies, why are any of us heterosexual? As Sedgwick states (87), "It is the most natural thing in the world that people of the same gender, people grouped under the single most determinative diacritical mark of social organization, people whose eco-nomic, institutional, emotional, physical needs and knowledges may have so much in common, should bond together also on an axis of sexual desire." But if none of us "discovers girls," who will produce and socialize the new workers essential for the continuation of capitalism?

In order to resolve this conundrum, the construct of sexual desire must be revised: heterosexuality must not be acquired, a theodicy enacted by a flood of hormones, but is instead innate, dispositionally active, and intense. In other words, like Tommy who fell from the sky heterosexually desiring and desired, men must begin their quest for heterosexual orgasm at birth.

The new construct of the boy as neither presexual or asexual, but actively and eagerly heterosexual, has appeared primarily in movies and on television. On *Married...with Children*, a flashback reveals that sexually frustrated teen Bud Bundy was a sexually frustrated baby, drooling over members of the "Swedish bikini team" while still in diapers. On *Sister, Sister*, the teenage twins find themselves on a "date" with an eight-year old boy, who leers at them, concludes that they are "his women," and congratulates himself on his ability to elicit the heterosexual desire of two women at once. On *Suddenly Susan*, the San Fran-cisco writer finds herself babysitting a ten-year-old boy who leers at her, boasts of the many women who have enjoyed his sexual prowess in the past, and invites her to "get horizontal."

A mere ignorance of the mechanics of heterosexual intercourse is no excuse for a lack of heterosexual desire. When eight-year-old Kyle on *Southpark* becomes attracted to his teacher, he rejects the romanticized, asexual crush usual in such plotlines and loudly asserts that he wishes to have sex with her. When she takes him out to dinner as a reward for getting an "A" on a test, Kyle misunderstands Chef's (a worldly, advice-giving adult character) innuendoes and presumes that they are indeed "making sweet love." The next day, he informs his grade-school cronies of his conquest.

Television commercials are not immune to the heterosexually desiring preteen. Gottfried maintains that commercials "nostalgically re-produce a world in which…gender works as a simple binary opposition, reproducing our cultural fantasy that gender is an unproblematic category of perceptual organization" (1994, 257); as such, they have increasingly abandoned the construct of the asexual, undesiring boy for one who is fully capable of feeling and even acting on the impulses of heterosexual desire. A boy of about eight years of age swaggers into a classroom, his sexual potency accentuated by gratuitous crotch and butt shots; he offers the teacher a can of soda instead of an apple and grins knowingly when she quakes in orgasmic enjoyment. A boy of about five, preening for a date, asks his mother to serve macaroni and cheese to increase his chances of romance; his girlfriend is indeed impressed by sophisticated culinary tastes, but the end of the evening is left to the imagination. Five multiracial boys grind and sway suggestively, thrust their crotches at the camera, and leer while singing "Girl, you got me going"; one wonders just what they are attempting to sell.

Sometimes the leer extends back even to the womb, or even earlier—it is interesting to compare Woody Allen's anthropomorphized but nonsexual sperm cell in *Everything You Always Wanted to Know About Sex* (1972), who awaits his suicidal leap with a mixture of resignation and despair, with the lusting heterosexual cowboy sperm cell voiced by Bruce Willis in *Look Who's Talking* (1989), who yelps and bellows his way up the uterus. Later in the film, the newborn Mikey seems to have backslidden into innocence: When his adult guardian sees a woman with large breasts and asks, "Are you thinking what I'm thinking?" (presumably about sex), Mikey responds with a hearty "Yeah—lunch!" In a contemporary commercial, however, a newborn baby in the hospital maternity ward is approached by supermodels who coo, mouth the words "I love you," and seductively caress their cans of soda; he grins, obviously appreciating the supermodels not as mothers or nurturers but as potential lovers, and becomes, according to the voice-over, "a Pepsi drinker for life."

Although the leering, posturing, heterosexually desiring boy occasionally appeared on some of the more "progressive" sitcoms of the 1970s and 1980s, such as *Taxi*, *The Mary Tyler Moore Show*, and *WKRP in Cincinnati*, he proliferated during the 1990s. *Caroline in the City* is chased around the room by a barely pubescent charge, and when Elaine Benes of *Seinfeld* offers her boss's young son a matronly kiss, she receives "his tongue" and a sexual proposal instead. A six-year-old boy adopted by the Bundys on *Married... with Children* brings his date home and, with the expected leer, invites her upstairs. She agrees, and the audience hoots its approval. One has to go back to the era of Louis XII to see such a blatant practice of "associating children with the sexual ribaldries of adults" (Ariès 1962, 103).

The multiplying ranks of horny preteens does not merely reflect the increasing celebration of sexuality of all sorts in popular culture (Cantor 1991) or Neil Postman's contention (1982) that the construct of childhood itself is eroding as the specialized knowledge that once set adulthood apart has become available to everyone. In such cases, heterosexually desiring boys would appear randomly across the universe of mass cultural products. However, the construct of the preteen boy as asexual and "innocent" has remained relatively stable in fiction, newspaper comics, television and film dramas, and all products aimed specifically at children (one cast member of television's *Barney and Friends* hit the age of fourteen before retiring, and still filled his life with sharing, toys, and nursery rhymes). Heterosexually desiring boys appear most often in products aimed at teenagers and young adults: comedy films, commercials, and especially on television sitcoms.

Within the genre of the sitcom, heterosexually desiring boys rarely appear on programs predicated on nuclear families. On *Cosby* and *Home Improvement*, for example, the goal is "to illustrate, in practical everyday subphilosophic terms, the tangible rewards of faith and trust in family" (Marc 1997, 191). The main male characters in such programs have successfully completed the reproduction required by the dynamic of hegemonic heterosexuality, and thus require no further validation—or even demonstration—of their heterosexual desire. Their children are either asexual preteens or hypersexual teens, with easy transitions between the two roles; plots involve sex-role conflict, petty ethical dilemmas, or the discontents of heterosexual marriage, but rarely do they dispute the traditional construct of boyhood innocence (Cantor 1991; Butsch 1992).

Heterosexually desiring boys, conversely, are endemic on progressive, adult-oriented sitcoms in which the main male characters are unmarried and therefore permanent adolescents pursuing enormous numbers of women either in an aggressive search for heterosexual validation (*Caroline in the City*; *Frasier*; *The Drew Carey Show*) or in resistance to the de-heterosexualizing implications of "the ball and chain" (*Seinfeld*; *Cheers*; *Two Guys and a Girl*). Since they have not yet reproduced, their heterosexual desire is still contingent and presumably open to a sudden "discovery of boys," a realization that they are "really" gay. A number of episodes play with this possibility: *Frasier* has erotic dreams about a male coworker; George Costanza of *Seinfeld* meets a girl who looks like his best friend Jerry and wonders if combining male friendship with erotic love might be "everything he always wanted"; *Drew Carey* tells a presumed male suitor that "It doesn't sound too bad, it's just the kissing that would bother me."

Heterosexualized boys, appearing on these programs as a validation of innate sexual identity, demonstrate that neither heterosexual nor homosexual desire appears as a sudden earth-shattering revelation or "discovery" of attraction where none was present before. Instead, male characters who identify as heterosexual (and presumably, heterosexual males in the audience) can rest assured that they always have been and always will be intensely attracted to women, that their dreams of breasts and bras began in the womb.

Generally, the figure of the preteen Lothario is not a regular cast member of the program he inhabits. He arrives in various guises—the boss's son who must be kowtowed to, a neighborhood kid who must be babysat, a prepubescent math tutor, or a grade-school student on a field trip. Left alone with a female character for some reason, he casts his leering gaze, brags about his many sexual conquests, and makes crude propositions. She responds with disgust—as she does with the sex-crazed propositions she regularly receives from adult men. A male character, arriving just in time to prevent a sexual assault, expresses disbelief, blame ("you know no man can resist you"), or feigned condemnation. In secret, however, he offers the offending boy a strong signal of approval and respect—a high five, a cry of "awright!", or a request for information such as "how was she?"

Jameson has argued that cultural products serve to "manage desire in social terms, negotiating between wish-fulfillment and repression, or to arouse fantasy content within carefully symbolic containment structures, which defuse the awakened (dangerous) desires (1992, 25). If the boy were "innocent," the desire evoked by the male gaze would be dangerous, an erotic penetration of asexual space; but as the boy is "experienced," already marked as irreducibly heterosexual, the desire becomes safely narcissistic, a mere replication of self. Indeed, it serves to validate the adult male's heterosexuality as essential and inevitable in an era which heterosexuality can be presumed neither essential nor inevitable.

On sitcoms in which the main characters are single parents, the constructs of the asexual and heterosexual boy often appear together, with playful permutations of the boundary divisions between the two. Little John, the eight-year-old son of the eponymous *Jesse*, bluntly asks his babysitting uncles, "Could you tell how to have sex?" Fearful of their sister's disapproval at finding Little John transmutated into heterosex-ually desiring Big John, the men frantically force-feed him candy; intriguingly, the typical "forbidden fruit" which, in myth, trench coat–clad perverts offer to entice boys into premature or transgressive sexual desire, here becomes a curative, deflecting the onset of sexual desire. When Jesse returns, Little John admits that he was really interested in candy all along; although "innocent," lacking in sexual desire, he is sufficiently cognizant of the effects of such desire to manipulate his uncles' panicked reactions to the possibility that he might have, at age eight, "discovered girls."

Frederick, the preteen son of radio psychiatrist *Frasier*, lives a continent away with his mother Lilith but visits occasionally. He constantly demonstrates heterosexual desire for the adult Daphne, insisting on hugging her and sitting on her lap, even peeking at her while she is showering. Most of the adults, believing that children are constitutionally asexual, find Frederick's "tiny crush" a pleasant attempt to garner maternal affection. Only Niles, Frasier's brother, treats him as a heterosexually desiring equal, a competitor for Daphne's affection. While embracing Daphne, Frederick sometimes gazes at the camera with the familiar leer, inviting the audience to share in both his erotic pleasure and his duping of the grownups with a façade of boyhood innocence.

On *Just Shoot Me*, fashion writer Maya meets Donnie, a twenty-six-year-old who is "slow" as a result of a head injury. A permanent child, Donnie is presumed "innocent" and asexual, but in private he confides to Maya that, like the extraterrestrial Tommy, he is really an adult disguised as a child. He has adopted the pretense of mental retardation to avoid taking on adult responsibilities; in fact, he is mentally alert, well-read, and as heterosexually active as his older brother (a fashion photographer who beds every female model in the business). Maya is horrified both by Donnie's deceit and his abrasive horniness, and she tries to trick him into revealing his "true" nature: She brings Donnie into her office, leaves the intercom on, and feigns sexual interest. However, he cannily reverts to his "slow" persona, shouting "Bad touch! Donnie scared!", thus leaving all of the other adults duped. The message is clear: There is no such thing as an asexual or presexual, undesiring or minimally desiring male; those who, at any age, claim to be innocent, uninterested, unaware, or less than manic about heterosexual orgasm are either gay and hiding in a closet, or lying.

I do suggest that the products of mass culture possess agency, volition, or motives, that sitcoms are suddenly exuding heterosexually desiring young boys deliberately to quell male homosocial panic or present an irreducible template for the production of tomorrow's capitalists. Queer theorists argue, however, that all cultural texts are structurally and constitutionally "queer," expressing "all aspects of non- (anti-, contra-) straight cultural production and reception" (Doty 1993, 3). However, some queer images are evoked only to civilize, control, and de-power the "homophobic, heterosexual desire for homosexuality" (Meyer 1991, 283); Judith Butler argues, for instance, that heterosexual-in-drag films such as *Victor/Victoria* and *Mrs. Doubtfire* provide " a ritualistic release for a heterosexual economy that must constantly police its own boundaries against the invasion of queerness" (1993, 126).

In this reading, the homosexually desiring adult and the heterosexually desiring boy must both be *queer*, in that they both displace sexual desire from the hegemonic goal of reproduction; however, the first also tends to negate and the second to replicate the presumption that everyone is, must be, or will be heterosexual. If these two images appear in tandem, they will likely be received as a structural unity, a disruption and subsequent validation of hegemonic heterosexuality, even though both are theoretically transgressive.

In fact, heterosexually desiring preteen boys have never, to my knowledge, leered at *The Golden Girls* or *Designing Women*, sitcoms in which mostly female casts celebrated horny eternal adolescence; nor have they lusted after the barmaids of *Cheers*, whose denizens could rest assured that "people are all the same," that is, unproblematically heterosexual. They have not appeared on programs with overtly gay characters in starring roles, such as *Will and Grace* and the Spanish-language series *Los Beltrán*. Instead, they usually appear in tandem with characters of ambiguous sexual orientation who claim to be straight but display "obviously gay" hobbies, interests, and mannerisms (Gill the food critic on *Frasier*), or claim to be gay but display "obviously straight" hobbies, interests, and mannerisms (Pete the mail boy on *Suddenly Susan*). That is, they appear in situations in which the available discursive strategies for demonstrating heterosexuality (or homosexuality) have proved inconclusive or contradictory, when *all* of a character's actions, words, mannerisms, words, interests, and self-identifications do not conform to expectations regarding gay or straight persons.

For instance, Josh on *Veronica's Closet* claims to be heterosexual; has a girlfriend, and has been shown engaging in repeated, energetic coitus with a woman ("wait—there's more!"). Yet the rest of the cast agrees that he is just fooling himself, that in spite of his overt heterosexual behavior (which, to be fair, is minimal compared to that of the other, indefatigably horny male characters), his swishy mannerisms and love for show tunes "prove" that he is gay. If even having sex with women does not demonstrate heterosexuality, what does? Could the ostensibly straight characters, with their leering, drooling, and alleged nightly bouts of kinky heterosexual sex be "just fooling themselves"? How can you "know" that you are really straight (or, for that matter, gay)? Enter, within a few episodes, the heterosexually desiring preteen, soul mate to the lustful postadolescent men, who, through mimicking at the age of ten their own behaviors at the age of thirty, has been essentially and irredeemably heterosexual since birth.

Other programs problemitize the universality and inevitability of male heterosexual desire by casting doubts upon a character's "real" sexual orientation. In many of the "progressive" sitcoms of the 1970s and 1980s, such as *All in the Family*, *M*A*S*H*, and early episodes of *The Golden Girls*, gay walk-ons initiated a sort of morality play (Henry 1987). Straight characters struggled to understand this bizarre phenomenon (rarely actualized through behaviors, desires, or statements other than "I am gay"), concluded that gay people could be permitted in their neighborhoods, mobile hospitals, or taxi cabs, and ended the episode by congratulating themselves on their tolerance.

More recently, when simply proclaiming a lack of homophobia on network television seems insufficiently noteworthy to warrant a "very special episode" (except on recidivist programs such as *Cheers*), the structural dynamic of disruption, the "struggle to understand," and the self-aggrandizing display of tolerance has become more intimate. Gay characters on *Taxi* and later episodes of *The Golden Girls* not only identify themselves as gay but express attraction to straight characters who are forced to negotiate the ensuing "threat to their sexual identity" and finally decide that they are indeed still heterosexual (Gross 1989). Sometimes, as on *Roseanne* and *That Seventies Show,* the gay characters skip the declaration of love and proceed directly to the kiss. In all cases, the heterosexuality of the straight characters is called into question; they spend sleepless nights agonizing over whether "the kiss meant anything," "maybe on some level I enjoyed it," or "maybe she knows something I don't, and I'm really gay after all." A plotline a few episodes later frequently involves a neighbor's plea to baby-sit, and a walk-on by a leering, lustful preteen.

In a less soul-searching permutation of the disclosure-ambiguity-tolerance structure, a gay character, through misunderstanding or deceit, interprets friendship with a straight character as romance. On *The Drew Carey Show*, delivery man Oswald begins to "hang out" with a truck driver, ignoring warnings from friends that "you're dating." *Frasier* plays matchmaker with his new boss and live-in healthcare worker Daphne, but the boss believes that Frasier wants the date himself; the truth comes out only at the end of an evening fraught with inadvertent sexual innuendos ("the view is even nicer from the bedroom"). On *Just Shoot Me*, Maya has dinner with a model who has been misled into believing her a lesbian; she discovers the truth only when the model suggests that they continue the evening at her place.

None of these situations precipitate a panicked flight: Oswald and Frasier are upset primarily about hurting their gay friend's feelings, while Maya says simply, "I'm really flattered, but I don't date women," and continues eating her dessert. However, an additional validation of essential heterosexual identity is evidently necessary: If "dates" occur regularly between men and men, women and women, and men and women, how can one really know how a dinner invitation will end? If the "discovery of girls" no longer inexorably divides the world into potential buddies (who can never be lovers) and potential lovers (who can never be buddies), how can we distinguish between the two? But if heterosexuality or homosexuality proceeds from birth, if the universes of friends and lovers inexorably split with that first splitting egg, then aside from a few minor misunderstandings, we will know instinctively whom to hang out with and whom to date. Heterosexually desiring boys often appear within a few weeks of the "gay date" episode to "prove" that sexual desire is instinctive and immutable, directed at either men or women but never both.

Hanke (1998) contends that a conservative ideology is at work in the sitcom genre, reproducing a compulsory heterosexuality that remains complicit within patriarchal structures of cultural capital and either masks or displaces attempts to recognize and validate marginalized sexualities. As a cultural product, the heterosexually desiring boy replicates hegemonic heterosexuality even while acknowledging diversity in sexual identity. However, as Mimi White argues, hegemony never restrains but invites; the same sign can be approached as a mark of domination or a hint of freedom (1992). The frantic posturing of the miniature Don Juans may presage a world in which diverse desires are tolerated, even celebrated, in which the question is neither "Do you like girls" nor "Do you like girls or boys?" but "Who are the important people in your life?"

REFERENCES

Adam, Barry. *The Rise of a Gay and Lesbian Movement.* 2nd ed. Boston: Twayne, 1995.

Ariès, Philippe. *Centuries of Childhood: a Social History of Family Life.* Translated by Robert Baldick. New York: Knopf, 1962.

Burke, Timothy, and Kevin Burke. *Saturday Morning Fever: Growing Up with Cartoon Culture.* New York: St. Martin's Press, 1999.

Butler, Judith. *Bodies That Matter: On the Discursive Limits of "Sex."* New York: Routledge, 1993.

Butsch, Richard. "Class and Gender in Four Decades of Television Situation Comedy." *Critical Studies in Mass Communication* 9, no. 4 (1992): 387–399.

Cantor, Muriel G. "The American Family on Television: From Molly Goldberg to Bill Cosby." *Journal of Comparative Family Studies* 22, no. 2 (1991): 205–216.

Deleuze, Gilles, and Félix Guattari. *Anti-Oedipus: Capitalism and Schizophrenia.* Minneapolis: University of Minnesota Press, 1983.

Doty, Alexander. *Making Things Perfectly Queer: Interpreting Mass Culture.* Minneapolis: University of Minnesota Press, 1993.

Gottfried, Barbara. "The Reproduction of Gendering: Imagining Kids in Ads for Adults." In *Images of the Child*, edited by Harry Eis, 255–272. Bowling Green, Ohio: Bowling Green State University Press, 1994.

Gross, Larry. 1989. "Out of the Mainstream: Sexual Minorities and the Mass Media." In *Remote Control: Television, Audiences, and Cultural Power*, edited by E. Seiter et al., 130–149. London: Routledge, 1989.

Hanke, Robert. "Redesigning Men: Hegemonic Masculinity in Transition." In *Men, Masculinity, and the Media*, edited by Steve Craig, et al., 185–198. Newbury Park, Calif.: Sage, 1992.

———. "The 'Mock-Macho' Situation Comedy: Hegemonic Masculinity and Its Reiteration." *Western Journal of Communication* 62, no. 1 (1998): 74–93.

Henry, W. "That Certain Subject." *Channels* (1987), 43–44.

Jameson, Frederic. *Postmodernism, or the Cultural Logic of Late Capitalism.* Durham, N.C.: Duke University Press, 1992.

Jones, Gerald. *Honey, I'm Home! Sitcoms: Selling the American Dream.* New York: Grove Press, 1992.

Jordan, Amy. "The Portrayal of Children on Prime-Time Situation Comedies." *Journal of Popular Culture* 29, no. 3 (1995): 139–47.

Kimmel, Michael. "The Contemporary 'Crisis' of Masculinity in Historical Perspective." In *The Making of Masculinities: The New Men's Studies*, edited by H. Brod, 121–153. Boston: Allen and Unwin, 1987.

Kincaid, James R. *Erotic Innocence: The Culture of Child Molesting.* Chapel Hill, N.C.: Duke University Press, 1998.

Marc, David. *Comic Visions: Television Comedy and American Culture.* Oxford: Blackwell, 1997.

Meyer, Richard. "Rock Hudson's Body." In *Inside/Outside: Lesbian Theory, Gay Theory*, edited by Diane Fuss, 259–288. New York: Routledge, 1991.

Palladino, Grace. *Teenagers: An American History.* New York: Basic Books, 1996.

Postman, Neil. *The Disappearance of Childhood.* New York: Delacorte Press, 1982.

Sedgwick, Eve. *Epistemology of the Closet.* Berkeley: University of California Press, 1990.

Smith, Corless. "Sex and Genre on Prime Time." *Journal of Homosexuality* 21, nos. 1–2 (1991): 119–138.

Sturken, Marita. *Tangled Memories: The Vietnam War, the AIDS Epidemic, and the Politics of Remembrance.* Berkeley: University of California Press, 1997.

White, Mimi. "Ideological Analysis and Television." In *Channels of Discourse, Reassembled,* edited by Robert C. Allen, 160–202. Chapel Hill, N.C.: University of North Carolina Press, 1992.

Chapter 11

Recognizable Ambiguity: Cartoon Imagery and American Childhood in *Animaniacs*

Chandra Mukerji and Tarleton Gillespie

In American society, there is assumed to be a natural fit between cartoons and children. The bright colors, odd characters, and strange narratives common to conventional animation seem ideal for kids whose attentions so often wander and who seem equally at home in their imaginations as in everyday life. Still, there is nothing natural about this association. The enduring popularity of cartoons among adults in Japan, and the proliferation (and success) of prime time cartoon shows in the United States belie this simple equation. Yet, cartoons continue to be produced "for" children—and dismissed by critics and scholars because of it. Why? What is the complexity behind this seeming simplicity?

The visual flexibility of cartoon imagery provides a particular opportunity for those who create cartoons to explore expressive gaps between the visible world and the cultural categories set in language. Cartoons are not constrained by the requirements of realism (reflections of and on perception) or by the linearity and structural rigor of linguistic formulations. In fact, the presumption is that the audience does not have sufficient knowledge of the world to even think realistically or enough mastery of language to see cultural categories as clean divisions within social life. This judgment makes it seem both unnecessary and perhaps unproductive to locate children's cartoons in a literal or real world. Between the possibilities of the medium and the definition of the audience, then, a space opens up for cartoons that allows unusual flexibility.

The problem with such flexibility within media, of course, is that uncharted innovation can easily become incomprehensible. Cartoons have the potential to be so surreal as to remove all reference points altogether. Some constraints are needed to produce socially shared systems of meanings. In live-action drama, realism provides this framework; but if not realism, upon what do cartoons rely? We argue that cartoon programs for children produce, depend on, and revel in a kind of "recognizable ambiguity." Cartoons create shifting worlds in which space and time become so distorted that realism drops away as a meaningful referent, at the same time partially stabilizing the imagery by using familiar artistic conventions and reflexive forms. This dual device makes the imagery seem recognizable, if not entirely clear in its intended meanings. Objects transform in shape and significance (elephants fly or toys come alive); storylines bring together characters or language from different times (a child goes into prehistory and finds an astronaut reciting Shakespeare; Chukovski 1968). Normal linguistic and narrative referents are undermined along with the realism, but the reminders of similar transgressions or transformations from past cartoons, and the expectation that cartoons will indeed contain jokes that the child can anticipate, help to place these images in a familiar context (Crafton 1982; Rowe 1995). There develops a *recognizability* in cartoons that does not depend on their meanings (or forms) ever being truly stabilized (Card, Mackinlay, and Shneiderman 1999).

With this recognizable ambiguity, and the transgressive possibilities it offers, cartoons can address in a particularly complex and interesting way the difficulties of being a child. Children begin their lives as prelinguistic creatures who don't know how to recognize (or name) themselves, much less anything else in their environments. Still, they immediately encounter a world in which they are already meaningful social actors. Their crying means something to their parents long before it means the same thing to them. They must learn their place as children within their culture; they must learn what their behavior means to others when they do things; only then can they have the intentionality to become social subjects.[1]

How do children manage this complex assignment? The simplest answer is that Western societies construct social spaces for children, particularly adapted to their "natures," in which children can learn what they are "naturally" supposed to be like. They encounter there the results of a long-standing tradition of Western age grading in which children have become (and have been for centuries) defined as first-and-foremost naturally *unlike* adults. In systematically engineered places and periods of social isolation (with other kids) in playgrounds, craft centers, sports leagues, and school rooms, they learn this fundamental distinction between themselves and their elders. They learn that they *ought* to be kept apart because they are naturally different. They also are confronted with their "natures" as playful, creative, physically active, and natural learners.[2]

It is not that this lesson should be so hard to learn, since it seems just a matter of mapping cultural categories onto physical differences related to age—children are like this, teenagers are like that, adults are like that. But in fact, the lesson is hard to assimilate because the world of childhood is far less coherent than we tend to assume. There are many definitions of children's natures—at least in the United States—that are often contradictory and have been accrued historically over quite different social periods (Mukerji 1997; Sammond 1999). Children find they must learn to fit into a social category whose dimensions are historically layered, whose contradictions are intentionally (or at least effectively) blurred, and whose existence is regularly naturalized.

The recognizable ambiguity in cartoons provides a means for addressing the complexities of childhood because it can stabilize unclear categories, making them recognizable without requiring them to have a consistent meaning. Children can see in cartoons cultural themes that describe the child's nature as well as how childhood works as a site of cultural conflict. The reflexivity within cartoons can be used to hold a mirror up against the contradictions of the culture, making a joke out of what could be seen as confusing or destructive to kids. Particularly those parts of children's cartoons that directly address what is culturally good for children can help make light of the fact that both what children are and what they need are contentious issues in contemporary America.

In this essay, we will examine segments from Steven Spielberg's *Animaniacs*[3] to see how they address some of the ambiguities in childhood that plague children, using laughter to reveal and lighten their burden. First, we will show how the program deconstructs definitions of children as natural beings as the fundamental opposite of adults and as creatures with special needs. Then, we will examine how this program reenacts the long-standing tensions between the European Great Tradition and American popular culture, implicitly contrasting school-based education with socialization into American cultural life. Finally, we will consider how the program dissects the moral significance of childhood and the purity attributed to (and expected of) kids, which burdens children with a responsibility for morality in ways never shouldered by adults. By exploring these (and other) fraught issues, we hope to demonstrate how cartoons like *Animaniacs* provide children with surprisingly complex cultural tools for negotiating childhood: on the one hand, understanding and managing adult stakes in childhood, and, on the other, learning how to be children themselves (in spite of the confusion) and to find some satisfaction—even humor—in it.

Genealogical Analysis of Childhood

To unpack these themes in *Animaniacs*, we consider their sources in a cultural genealogy of American childhood. We take seriously the notion that cultures have genealogies; that while they undergo change over time, old forms may still be reproduced even as new ones are elaborated out of them, resulting in a culture that carries its history with it—not in exact detail, but through identifiable (familial?) resemblances to earlier cultural constellations. The culture of childhood in the West has changed as adult preoccupations with children have shifted, resulting in new ideas about the nature of the child and the proper formation of childhood; this does not mean, however, that earlier notions of the child have died out. On the contrary, cultural conceptions of children build up in layers, new upon old, to form a kind of cultural laminate that seems singular but gains strength from its striate.

Genealogical threads between past and present find form in contemporary media not because producers necessarily know the history of childhood and want to tell and retell its story. When they think about what children will find funny, they generally remember their own childhoods and think about jokes that made them laugh as kids. In this intuitive, psychologized search for the child viewer, adult media producers unwittingly reproduce and refashion the sociocultural dimensions of childhood, "improving" on the past in ways that keep the lamination process of cultural accumulation active. With remnants of old views of the child finding new life in children's narratives, we can approach contemporary media for children—not to determine their aesthetic importance, psychological fitness, or commercial value, but to trace out some relations between these persistent definitions of the child and consider how contemporary media make those definitions available as cultural resources.

In Western history, the changing adult interests in children have articulated childhood as a cultural category and as a series of overlapping constellations of values and assumptions. Protestant reformers, worried about the vulnerability of children to sin while praising their Christlike qualities, helped to distinguish all children more clearly from adults by reference to their distinct moral position (Pollock 1983).[4] Enlightenment philosophers defined children as more "natural" than adults, arguing that they should receive an education that would allow them to explore the world through their senses, not just through books. By following their natural curiosity, they would be able to realize their natural virtue and use it to build a more utopian world (Plumb 1982). Moral reformers of the nineteenth century, still invested in the presumption of children's natural virtue, were horrified by child labor and the exposure of children to the dangers of urban streets during industrialization. They sought to protect children from adult corruption by more carefully delineating special spaces for children—especially through schools and playgrounds. They associated the goodness of children less with a moral nature and more in terms of their isolation from adult life—particularly from the economy (Zelizer 1985).[5]

In the twentieth century, social scientists translated Enlightenment views of children as natural learners into the psychology of child development, which focused on the acquisition of cognitive skills (inside child-friendly spaces). This work renaturalized children (and the distinction of kids from adults) but attributed slightly different natures to children of different ages (Cole and Wertsch 1996; Bettelheim 1971). This psychology of the child was partly paralleled and partly opposed by Freudian and post-Freudian accounts of the wild impulses in children—a secular version of persistent Christian anxieties about child vulnerability. These different psychological traditions can coexist in the culture of childhood (although not always in psychology departments) because childhood itself continues to be naturalized as an *obvious* time of life. The illusion of seamlessness is enhanced by the fact that all of these cultures of childhood emerged from their predecessors, without entirely supplanting them. As one part of the culture migrated in new directions, older parts survived in songs, stories, games, and the like—practices that held the corners of the culture stable over time. So, as the culture of childhood developed, it was refashioned and maintained (at the same time), producing surprising contradictions in cultural definitions of what is natural or special about children.

The result is a culture that is hard to see because it has been naturalized in our own time, but nonetheless a culture that children must *learn* in order to negotiate a way through this part of their lives. It is a culture whose contradictions are surprising but are practically employed to manage day-to-day variations in children. A temper tantrum can be explained away as the inevitable monstrosity of the "terrible twos," while surprising intelligence can be the result of a child's natural curiosity. Parents and teachers can highlight one mode or another to represent any given child, or they can describe the life of a child in naturalized terms that actually meander from one rationale to another.

Adults rarely notice the seams that hold this odd heritage together because they take them for granted, but cartoons often tear them open for the laughter that doing so produces. Images of the child, as they morph into animals here and robots there, raise questions about the very nature of childhood. Cartoons in their flexibility and sense of play provide their viewers useful information about the mixed messages they receive from adults, at the same time demonstrating ways to understand their lives, act in their worlds, and find pleasure in their confusion. Bringing a genealogical understanding of the history of childhood to media analysis helps reveal the historical depth of imagery that seems at first glance to be sterile and superficial. Held against older conceptions of childhood, many cartoons are revealed to be complex cultural artifacts, and lead us to entertain the unexpected possibility (nearly absent in the literature on children's television) that children in front of the TV are exposed not simply to vapid, exploitative nonsense but to a culture of childhood with daunting historical and philosophical depth. What children look for (what adults would never assume to find there) are representations of what it means to be a child, and layers of childhood that can make better sense of the experiences they find disorienting.

Learning to Be a Natural Child

Over the span of centuries, the child's fundamental nature, and the differences between children and adults, have been reworked in complex ways. Children are supposed to be defined by their nature—something that makes them a group apart from their elders (who acquire culture, bad habits, or affectations over time). By this definition, children have a simple task: to mature. But, of course, children do this in different ways in different cultures, because maturation is as much a cultural process as it is a physiological one. American adults are sure children in the United States are fundamentally natural and will grow up well in a good environment, but they may not be clear what the nature of the child might be. Sporadic shocks to this belief system, like the shootings at Columbine High School in Colorado, throw such presumptions into momentary distress; much of the cultural repair work that follows such events is precisely about recovering these beliefs by explaining away such "aberrations." And children are in an even worse position, asked to reconcile such beliefs with their lived experience each and every day.

The evidentiary basis for treating children as a natural category seems straightforward. Kids are small at birth and grow rapidly throughout childhood; they also begin with few skills and acquire them at an accelerating rate as they mature. Children who do not fit the normal developmental profile, however, are a problem in the United States. Those who refuse to learn naturally—particularly ones who are disruptive because they do not act as they should—are now diagnosed with attention deficit disorder and prescribed medication to help them recover their "natural" character. Those who seem prone to mischief are treated as unnatural (troubled), unless they fit the norms for "acting out" and "testing limits" that are associated with each age.[6]

The combination of the firm assurance about children-as-natural and an absolute confusion as to how to get kids to fit that category makes the nature of children in America an area ripe for caricature, and one powerfully (and playfully) deployed in *Animaniacs*. At the very center of the show is an unresolved contradiction about the nature of the main characters, the Warners—what are they?—that reflects the similar ambiguity about what children are or are supposed to be. These creatures must be what their name implies: fundamentally animal (all natural vitality) but also wildly maniacal (unable to act naturally). The contradiction, utilizing the particular aesthetics of animation to make it nearly impossible to classify and characterize them, is intentionally exploited.

While many popular cartoons offer characters that are "not exactly" what they claim to be (Mickey not exactly a mouse, Bugs not exactly a bunny), most are identified and identifiable as particular animals, an initial classification that is then troubled by the character's more human behavior. These creatures, representing children, locate them as natural beings, positioned somewhere between wild animals and real humans. But Yakko, Wakko, and Dot Warner do not offer even that level of clarity. Their very species is left ambiguous—purposefully, as we can see from a musical interlude called "What Are We? "

The sequence begins (significantly) in the office of a psychiatrist; Dr. Scratchnsniff, employed by the studio to keep the Warners in line, attempts to hypnotize the kids to make them less "zany" and more like "calm children." But the parlor trick fails (a deficit of attention, perhaps?), and the children happily bounce on his therapist's couch, assuring him that they are as normal as any other kid. Scratchnsniff, frustrated with their exuberance, insists they are "not normal" and demands that they tell him "what they are." The Warners, a glint in their animated eyes, "act naturally" and reply as *performers* (of their own nature) with a song that refuses to respond to the seemingly simple question. The song rhymes its way through various categorical possibilities—dog, cat, horse, skunk, flea, electric eel—and imagines the consequences. With each, the Warners visually morph into the animal they name; but before Scratchnsniff can respond, they have already leapt to another possibility. They turn the most fundamental of categorical assessments into a joke, eluding the kind of scientific certainty about their nature that American parents have relied on since the 1920s (Sammond 1999). The Warners become floating signifiers of seemingly endless ambiguity—until the song ends with what seems to be an answer. Dot proclaims "Hey, wait a minute, I've got it now" (like a scientist shouting "Eureka!" at the moment of discovery). Scratchnsniff answers skeptically, "You do?" to which all three Warners sing in unison, "We're not bees and we're not cats, or bugs or horses or things like that, what we are is clear and absolute! What we are, dear doctor... is cute!" The doctor, crestfallen that youthful charm has displaced scientifically verified character, can only respond, "I'm sorry I asked." [7] By emphasizing another aspect of the culture of childhood—their youth and innocence—they send the psychologist, who wants to tame their wild nature, headfirst through a brick wall.

The Warners pose both a challenge and an opportunity. Using the flexibility of animation, which frees them from real-world referents and corresponding cultural baggage, they pose the question to children about their nature. In *Animaniacs*, identity is up for grabs, and that categorical ambiguity is crucial to the pleasure of the text. The Warners offer child viewers the fleeting opportunity to experience life outside the categorical control of adults who use "what they are" as means of controlling them.

This experience might be disorienting except that the Warners stand clearly in a legacy of animated characters that traditionally escape the control of their creators. Well before Mickey Mouse and Donald Duck wandered off the drafting table, Koko the Clown slid down the drawing board to show his creator, Max Fleischer, how to be a better artist. The celebration of characters who exceed control of the authority figures that produced them is a tradition animation has explored for its entire existence as a cultural form. Knowing that the Warners resemble Mickey Mouse or Fritz the Cat in appearance and attitude does not solve the problem of their nature, but it does provide some benchmarks for recognizing them as tricksters on the drawing board. Leaving real categories behind through animation, the program replaces the lost referents with a world of drawings that defy laws of both nature and culture—but do so with relative consistency. The representational ambiguity in children's cartoons, including *Animaniacs*, opens up space to explore the conflicted meanings of American childhood; the legacy of animation holds the enterprise together.

Children are not only required to be natural, but also to be the opposite of adults. This categorical boundary is fiercely patrolled and reproduced with such vigor that the transition to adulthood is deeply disorienting for most teenagers. This cultural dichotomy is troubled not only by the dynamic quality of childhood when seen as a series of developmental stages (making it hard to counterpose a generic kid with a generic adult), but also by the contradictory purposes of the dichotomy itself. Do grown-ups need to be protected from children (to get peace and quiet or a serious workplace), or do kids need a safe world of their own separated from the corrupting influence of adults? Do kids need their own rooms, toys, and play areas in order to bring out their natural virtue, or do they need to be isolated and protected because of their vulnerability to dark forces? American middle-class children are sent to "their rooms" both as a form of punishment and to put them in an environment in which they can naturally grow.

Take, for example, the boundary between childhood and the "adult" world of consumption, a boundary American children are both urged to heed and invited to cross. Even though economic exploitation and corruption were presented as threats to childhood innocence in the nineteenth century, educational consumer goods for children have been part of the world of childhood since the eighteenth century. In fact, J. H. Plumb has argued that Enlightenment views of childhood actually depended on the growth of a consumer society. Children could have special needs and qualities only when there were consumer goods to supply them; their consumption of material goods became markers of the cultural capital of their parents. Still, concerns about commercial corruption and industrial pressures have been a central part of twentieth-century efforts to keep children and adults apart. No wonder, then, the role of commercial relations in defining childhood is explored in *Animaniacs*. In fact, it extends the fundamental ambiguity of the Warners as characters (McKendrick, Brewer, and Plumb 1982; Engelhardt 1986; Wartella 1994; Seiter 1993).[8]

The first episode of *Animaniacs* begins with a 1930s-style, black-and-white (but animated) newsreel that provides an origin story for the Warners;[9] in a classic "inside Hollywood" glimpse behind-the-scenes, the newsreel tells of the moment when animators, working in "Termite Terrace"[10] on the Warner studio lot, first came up with the Warner characters. According to this sequence, the Warners were first drawn back in these early days of animation, but were deemed "too zany" (childlike?) for the times; in the newsreel, the Warners begin as sketches on a drawing board but quickly leap off the paper into sudden three-dimensionality, bouncing around the room and out the door.[11] An authoritative voice-over reports that their nonsensical films were locked away in a vault, and the characters themselves were imprisoned in the water tower on the Warner Brothers studio lot. The studio has since disavowed any knowledge of their existence, until the present day, when the characters escaped their confines. Most *Animaniacs* episodes begin with the Warners escaping from the tower and eluding a studio security guard, yet another adult figure bent on containing them but unable to do so.

According to this sequence (fig. 11.1), these children are not born of parental characters within the narrative but instead are "produced" by the animators themselves, who stand in as surrogate parents.[12] It is important to note that the sequence does not shy away from acknowledging that this artistic conception is deeply embedded in a corporate context and industrial process. The studio is in some sense their parent, as their very names suggest. This blurring of corporation and family is extended and complicated by the recurring character of the studio boss, Thaddeus Plotz, who regularly provides a comic foil to the Warners. Plotz seems to believe that he has some authority over the Warners, but is in fact both enraged by and terrified of the children and their excessive play. The characters, who are products of the studio but cannot be contained by it, provide an analogy to the idea of children: produced both by family (literally) and by the culture (symbolically), they are, in the end, uncontainable by either.

The complexity of this origin story is further extended in the *Animaniacs* theme song: "We're animaniacs...we have pay-or-play contracts..." A dispute among fans centered on whether the words were pay-*or*-play or pay-*for*-play (it is somewhat difficult to make them out amid the orchestral cacophony).[13] In fact, the Warners are "players" in two senses—both as children and as performers/media celebrities. The

Immaculate Production

Fig. 11.1. The Warners are born from the mind of the studio, reflexively indicating their status as productions. ™ & © 2000 Warner Bros. All Rights Reserved.

ambiguity of their position as both excluded from the adult world and as necessary to the commercial relations therein actually points to some of the complexity of a child viewer's position in American culture. Paying or playing, or paying for playing, are actually meaningful differences in American childhood and point to different layers of social relations between adults and children. In this moment of the cartoon, two notions of the child are represented simultaneously and ambiguously—not as contradictions but as co-constituents of childhood.

Animaniacs allows children to work through the way consumer culture has complicated the relationship between children and adults. Industrial capitalism has for centuries included children as part of the commercial world—if not always a source of cheap and docile labor, at least a distinct consumer group. Changes in notions of labor, which have largely removed children from the workforce of the Western world and redefined them as valuable assets (Zelizer 1985), have not so much made childhood less commercial as they have confined children to a distinct social world of consumption. Children are urged to pay *to* play (buy toys, take classes, join sports leagues), and play *for* pay (get an allowance for being well-behaved or sell baked goods to fill their school's coffers); yet they have little or no power over the commercial world they encounter. When children are marketed to (as in the toy and breakfast cereal ads that accompany *Animaniacs*), they recognize their powerful position within the discourse of consumption; but this discourse regularly collides with competing cultural interests seeking to shelter childhood innocence from the contamination of commercialization. Children experience this conflict whenever they are addressed by adults: parents who distrust the commercial desires of their kids because they do not acknowledge their own, teachers who struggle to exclude commercial products and narratives from the intellectual world of the classroom, television that relies fundamentally on commerce even as it celebrates its attempts at educational content. Most representations of childhood assume a separation between these worlds that is rarely achieved in the lived experience of children. The Warners live out this contradiction when they, although valuable stars at the studio, find themselves continually chased and contained by the executives and guards of the corporation that carries their name.

Children enter a social world where these and other definitions of childhood are all made available, rarely explicitly, and never sorted out. The Warner characters dissect and confront the complexity of this world for children, allowing child viewers an opportunity to explore the implications of these different yet competing paradigms of childhood. The zaniness of the animation captures and satirizes the dislocating quality of this world, representing childhood as both relatively recognizable and explicitly ambiguous; rather than a coercive tool of socialization, animation helps here to generate a narrative vehicle suitable for children to navigate the uncharted waters of their own childhoods. In the sequences already discussed, *Animaniacs* confronts and playfully inverts the efforts adult society makes to classify, contain, and isolate children into a separate world of their own. The production of adult knowledge about children, be it parental, scientific, or corporate, cannot fully contain the meaning of childhood. The program is premised on the escape of these wild, uncontainable figures from that carefully designed world of childhood, invading the adult world and overturning, deflating, and revealing its expectations.

Cultural Identity and American Childhood

Children must learn not only how to act naturally as kids; they must also come to terms with a complex cultural field as part of being a child. Childhood is meant to be a time for learning, a period of socialization when natural learners confront a confusing mass of symbol systems employed in quite subtle ways. The difficulty of this task provides plenty of fuel for cartoon humor and visual reversals in cartoon imagery. Children's cartoons often have a particularly important relation to the learning process; many kids who spend most of their days in school come home to watch television as relief from it. They are quite prepared to laugh at what they have just finished experiencing, and to gain some perspective on what it means for them to learn.

The segment of *Animaniacs* called "Hooked on a Ceiling" provides a fine opportunity for some of this work. It is structured at first to look like an educational film strip. Over a map of Italy, a patronizing John Houseman look-alike describes the Italian Renaissance as a period of unprecedented achievement in art. We pan across a wall of paintings by various Renaissance artists, as Mussorgsky's "Pictures at an Exhibition" plays in the background; the narrator intones the great artists of the period, "Leonardo, Michelangelo..." But suddenly the Ninja Turtles (all of whom were named after Renaissance artists) pop up on the screen. The narrator reacts in horror, then banishes them from the screen, saying it is time to recoup the real Renaissance artists from an obscurity rendered by popular culture.

Soon, the educational film mode is revived as a static building calms the visual field, followed by the words: Rome 1512 AD (is it a history lesson, documentary, Hollywood epic, or all three?). The Mussorgsky piece begins again, and the narrator-teacher introduces the Sistine Chapel, its famous ceiling, and the great artist himself, Michelangelo. This sequence quickly locates "Hooked on a Ceiling" as a reexamination of the lessons that children face at school, and an opportunity to take pleasure in the struggles for cultural primacy between classical art and popular culture, education and entertainment, past and present. For all the children who have been reprimanded for being hooked on TV, the thought of being hooked on high culture, on the Sistine Chapel and its famous ceiling, is a tantalizingly subversive treat. Why are some cultural forms better than others, anyhow? How are they supposed to recognize the differences? And how are children supposed to use Renaissance art rather than cartoon narratives and characters to address their lives-as-children?

The narrator introduces Michelangelo as a genius, but he is depicted as a kind of small-brained, big-jawed, muscle-bound he-man in a toga, acting like a loud-mouthed lout. No sensitive artist, he is certainly temperamental enough, firing his assistants for being "incompetent fools." As he implores his muse for assistance, the Warners magically arrive, politely introducing themselves as though they were innocent sources of useful labor, not troublemaking kids. Michelangelo seems a testy but rather ordinary man with a deadline for getting the Sistine Chapel ready for a visit from the Pope. He may be the greatest artist of the Renaissance, but he is paying for pay too, and what he needs now is help. We know (and presumably he does, too) that young children are themselves supposed to be natural geniuses whose fundamentally creative impulses only need a little helpful guidance to come out. According to these cultural assumptions, his problem should be solved, so he lets them get to work. By cartoon conventions, however, children are wild cards; they can do anything, and he is in for trouble.

The particular nature of that trouble is interesting for understanding the complexity of the problem of cultural learning faced by American kids. This segment pits schoolbook learning and the European Great Tradition—here represented by Michelangelo, the Italian Renaissance, the Sistine Chapel, and the Pope—against the pleasures and excesses of American mass media. The Warners bring with them all the power and pollution of American popular culture to make up for the weakness of Michelangelo's work. He is too tormented to paint; he can't find good help; he runs out of ideas; and he can't meet deadlines. He is frozen, but they are all action. They are children; he is adult. He is the past; they are the present. Using a tune reminiscent of auto-painting advertisements run on late-night television, they sing, "To renovate your ceiling, come to us!" and offer their price: $29.95. To the Warners, it is just a ceiling to paint, something to do, not a crisis of "man" or culture. As if this "discounting" of Renaissance artwork were not disrespectful enough, their song cuts to a nightclub shot in which Dot sings "Ceilings" to the tune of the popular hit song of the 1970's, "Feelings." For sentimentality, popular culture has its forms, too.

The he-man artist summons up all the cultural authority of the Great Tradition to holler pompously back that he is the great Michelangelo and this is the Sistine Chapel. But it has little effect. They are kids, and he is just another adult yelling at them. Michelangelo finds himself shuttled out of the building, locked out. When he knocks, a Warner dressed in a green guard's uniform pops his head through the door, telling him (in a quote from the *Wizard of Oz*) that no one gets to see the Wizard.

American popular culture is too powerfully flexible, particularly in the hands of children, to overcome. Back in the chapel, Michelangelo finds the ceiling painted completely white: the Warners lament that they had "a heck of a time covering up the naked people." The artist howls that the ceiling was *supposed* to have pictures, so they are off again, energy incarnate, this time painting the ceiling with the most crass icons of American popular culture: dogs playing poker, Keene-type children with huge wide eyes, and a Vegas-style portrait of Elvis.

"Hooked on a Ceiling" ends as the Warners restore most of Michelangelo's masterpiece, but not before they have also revealed some common threads of hypocrisy behind both popular and elite culture—adult hypocrisies about teaching culture and protecting children. Dot reprimands the artist for painting nudes on his ceiling, in church and in front of kids, suggesting obliquely the hypocrisy of censoring contemporary representations of sexuality while celebrating classical ones. Then, the kids use paint-by-number outlines to restore the masterpiece, showing how degraded artistry has become for contemporary kids caught in the maze of consumer goods available to them. But these issues are not dwelt upon; more important narrative ones are at stake. The center of the ceiling is still empty, and "His Eminence," Michelangelo's patron, is due to arrive. The kids reassuringly tell Michelangelo to "go say hi" while they "finish up," and the great Renaissance artist grovels before his patron, turning his back on his own painting to do so. He has reason to regret the decision. When he looks up to the ceiling again, the Warners have filled the center not with the picture of God's hand outstretched to man, but ET's glowing finger stretched out to touch his young friend. Michelangelo is once again furious, but "His Eminence" likes the work. The Pope turns out to be none other than Steven Spielberg himself, who says to Michelangelo and the audience, "Painting is like show business; you have to know your audience."

The tensions between the European Great Tradition and American popular culture have collided and now become an opportunity to laugh at adult corruption and to marvel at the child's willingness to tolerate and embrace ambiguity. But it is more than that. It locates American children in a cultural dilemma in which they must manage to be both children and American. They must learn the Great Tradition in school, and absorb its values, but they cannot hold it as their primary sensibility. For Americans, the Great Tradition has always been partially suspect, a remnant of colonialism and a cultural game that Americans could only lose. Popular culture, on the other hand, has been a great success both in the United States and as an exported representation of what is distinctively American. Kids learning to belong to the world of the American child, then, are presented with an odd way of respecting and disrespecting both the Great Tradition and the United States' little tradition of mass culture. The Great Tradition is better, but not relevant. Mass culture is degrading but vibrantly alive and distinctively American.[14] This is not a lesson that most adults want to articulate, particularly because they often have interests in modifying it for their own purposes—depending on whether they are acting as parents, teachers, advertisers, or TV producers. This episode of *Animaniacs*, then, stands as a humorous guide to this cultural complexity; for children it is a revelation cloaked in chaos and laughter. In the way the Warners help erase, replace, refashion, and finally reproduce the ceiling of the Sistine Chapel, they also reproduce some of the contradictory lessons in culture American kids receive over the course of a day and make it recognizable, if not stable and clear.

Childhood as a Moral Category

While by Enlightenment standards the primary task of children is to realize their human nature (as natural learners), and according to twentieth-century psychology they need to mature and acquire the skills to take on their culture, by Christian tradition children are more moral actors. In fact, the moral status of children is just as central to the constraints placed on children and the passions driving adults to shape the world of childhood. The moral life of America is in many ways negotiated around or imposed on kids.

There are at least three competing views of morality and children that permeate American culture, and these have a role in *Animaniacs*. One is the tradition of *charivari*: the use of youth as moral regulators for adult society. Young men in late medieval and Renaissance Italy were given the charge of tormenting adults who violated the rules of their societies. They were seen as morally above adults and capable of enforcing rules that adults were too corrupt to impose on one another. In this Catholic tradition, older children had a moral virtue and social role that made them good judges of their elders. To this day, children, free from the passions that defile adult morality, are often seen as having a moral clarity that adults can no longer afford to keep. The Protestant view of children also defined them as morally distinct from their elders, but also as more prey to the influence of the devil. This meant that children could be conduits of evil into adult society. Children might be born more Christlike by nature, but they were potentially dangerous moral beings who could corrupt adults. The direction of moral influence is reversed in this second cultural constellation; the vulnerability of adults in Catholicism, and of children in Protestant theology, made these two perspectives on childhood and morality distinct though clearly related genealogically.

The Enlightenment view of childhood built on these notions of childhood virtue and vulnerability, but made it less a matter of heavenly order and more a matter of the child's nature. Children were vulnerable to adult corruption, so they required protection from adults in order to keep their natural virtue alive. But with education they could avoid the moral degradation born of adult passions and make a better future by sustaining their natural virtue into adulthood. With this turn of the culture, children were made repositories of hope for the culture. They needed to be moral and keep their virtue intact in order to realize the future dreams of their societies.

All these versions of childhood morality are reproduced in cartoons, sometimes in quite distinct forms that mirror quite accurately their origins, sometimes in blended forms that obscure the lineage but keep its complexity alive. We can see moments in *Animaniacs* in which the Warners confront moral issues and unpack their contradictions. It probably goes without saying that the Warners themselves continually challenge the moral as well as the social order in most episodes, helping to underscore in this simple fashion the centrality of childhood as a moral category full of contradictions and open to contest.

A more morally loaded view of children's education and the media is presented in an episode of *Animaniacs* that focuses on censorship and violence in children's programming. "A Valuable Lesson" follows the linked but dual problem of containing and controlling those ebullient cultural constructs—kids and cartoons—by keeping them both under keen adult supervision. As the episode begins, a familiar cartoon chase is already under way. Attila the Hun is after the Warners, using his looming rage and physical heft to frighten the resilient kids. They retaliate with those weapons still allowed in children's cartoons (weapons that kids could not possibly use aggressively in real life): a piano that falls from the sky, an anvil that follows, and an absurdly large cannon.

But as the cannon fires, the narrative is abruptly interrupted by a man and a woman in gray suits carrying briefcases: the network censors. They ask the Warners what child viewers are supposed to learn from this cartoon, and the kids respond, "Use a big cannon?" Horrified, the censors escort their young charges to see some "decent" children's programming. In a small theater they are shown a Disney-Smurf amalgam in which respectful animal-children sit in a colorful forest, listening to a lesson about the dangers of anger from their grandfather. The censors weep; the Warners snooze. This scene clearly demonstrates the way these adults idealize children, in hopes of stabilizing the boundary between adulthood and childhood. Purifying childhood through cartoons gives them a sense of mission; exercising power over children by managing the media gives them a sense of efficacy; letting out their childlike wishes for a perfect world evokes longings so profound they are moved to tears. The Warners recognize a cliché when they see one, and promptly fall asleep.

To continue the lesson, the network officials take the Warners to research labs where children are being tested for media effects. First, they are shown a boy and girl who have watched the officially sanctioned programming; they sit quietly, speak carefully, and spontaneously offer to share their toys. Behind a second window are children who have been exposed to *Animaniacs*-style programming; identical to the first pair (perhaps they are generic children?), they too sit calmly, smiling. But when a lab coat–clad researcher urges them to share, they smash him over the head with their toys, in classic cartoon style. The myth of media effects is reenacted—but the Warners know how to use this to their advantage. Asked if they learned anything, they request with the mock sincerity of model students a review of what they are not allowed to show on TV. The censors act these scenes out, hitting each other first with their briefcases, then escalating the violence until together they are squashed by a falling elephant. At this point Attila, who has still been pursuing the Warners, trying to complete his own narrative of cartoon violence, arrives. The censors try to stop him by suggesting he is really not so naughty, but he is infuriated and attacks the censors for their audacity. Safe for the moment, the Warners wisely stand aside, summing up the lesson they've learned from the show: Censors come in handy. Clearly, such supervisory figures transform violence between adults and children into conflicts among the authorities controlling the culture.

Attila the Hun is a historical figure, a real model of adult violence children learn not from TV but from "good" media objects such as history books; at the same time, he is a figure in a classic cartoon narrative, the oversized bully who must be outwitted by clever animal-children. As the first, he stands for a historical violence that cannot be denied simply by purifying the stories we offer children; everyday adult violence directed toward children remains unrelenting in spite of the cultural norms against it. As a cartoon character, he is pure id—more childlike than the children. He is precisely what the superego-censors are designed to stop. Untamed desire tangles with the institutional forces attempting to tame it, a narrative follows from the conflict, and our protagonists are left unscathed. The Warners have learned at least one valuable lesson. At the beginning of the program, they thought the solution to the problem of childhood vulnerability was to have a big cannon; now they know it is to compel adults to direct their passions toward each other so kids can be entertained by human weakness rather than be victim to it.

This story also suggests that children should recognize that powerful emotions are at stake when adults (be they Huns or censors) patrol the boundary between childhood and adulthood. Deep truths about human nature are supposed to be revealed when children are left natural, yet so much cultural work goes into saving them from adults and their corrupt peers (creating a separate world of childhood) that the category seems much more a cultural accomplishment than a fact of nature. The Warners treat the boundary as merely an interesting part of a game they play with adults. In the opening sequence, they are "caught" playing with Attila the Hun—obviously a very bad influence on little kids. Attila wants to restore the "natural" age hierarchy by regaining authority over the Warners, but he has only his physical superiority as an advantage, and the kids can easily outwit him with their imaginary weapons. They use him in a game of taunting and chasing, which he can play because although he is nominally an adult, he is as unrestrained as a child. The line between adult and child has been blurred, chaos (or is it fun?) results, and Attila is further incensed by the reversal of power relations.

All this chaos is too much for the censors, who also want to restore adult authority, but they have more complex cultural tools at their disposal: television programs. They hope to expose the Warners to a "better" world of children's programming in which Smurf kids listen to their grandpa, and children are quiet and polite and like to share. Ideal children clearly must inhabit a separate world of childhood where they are protected from bad models of behavior. For the Warners the lesson from this is not at all clear; children are both good and bad, quiet and wild, sometimes sequestered from adults and sometimes placed in contact with them. Enforcing a singular nature or way of life on children seems unnatural to them, a concern exclusive to adults.

The valuable lesson here is about the depth of desire and will that governs adult efforts to keep children separate from and subservient to adults. Attila uses force to keep the Warners under control and out of his hair. The censors expect to isolate children when they are young and train them to be good using idyllic fictional models of family life. The Warners recognize both strategies as familiar, if contradictory, adult techniques for constraining children—that kids themselves need to recognize and negotiate for their own well-being. In their cartoon world of identifiable narratives and unnatural environments, network censors can interact with Attila the Hun, demonstrating both the contradictory cultural constellations that each presents to children and the similar passions guiding adult efforts to shape children to fit childhood. This is, as the title of the episode suggests, a very valuable lesson.

Wheel of Morality

Fig. 11.2. The Warners close each show with a poke at the arbitrariness and conventionality of the "morals" of the story. ™ & © 2000 Warner Bros. All Rights Reserved.

In nearly a quarter of all the *Animaniacs* episodes, the Warners close the show by consulting "the Wheel of Morality" (fig. 11.2). Once again chased by the studio security guard, they abruptly interrupt the game to pause for the Wheel, a gaudy gadget they pull in from offscreen. The Wheel looks much like the one on the game show *Wheel of Fortune* standing on its edge, with colorful wedges representing various choices: numbered morals, dollar amounts, expensive vacations. The wheel spins as lights flash, finally landing on a moral, which is ejected as a printed message like an automated fortune-teller at a traveling carnival. Yakko reads the message to his siblings; they comment on it, shrug, then resume the chase as the security guard nears.

Closing the show with the Warners consulting the Wheel satirizes the common trope of closing children's programs and narratives with a moral—a trope as old as fairy tales and religious catechisms. But these are far from traditional morals. Spinning a wheel makes morality into something arbitrary, random. Fairy tales, and the children's television that has emulated them, always implied that the moral being taught was somehow connected to the story that had been told—the imposition of an interpretation for an audience of children presumed to be incapable of reaching the correct conclusions on their own. The morals that spew out of the Warners' Wheel of Morality have nothing to do with the preceding segments. In fact, they tend not to have anything to do with anything. Sometimes the morals are worn-out platitudes, vacated of any significance except as icons of moralization: "Don't be a fool, stay in school" (episode 66). Others subvert common sayings, often relocating them within popular culture: "If you can't say something nice, you're probably at the Ice Capades" (episode 24). Other morals are actually decontextualized commercial phrases, sayings that kids would have come across in their daily experience as received wisdom: "Lather, rinse, repeat" (episode 64) or "Do not back up. Severe tire damage." (episode 58). Occasionally there is no moral at all; in episode 47 the Wheel stopped on a trip to Tahiti.

This is not an educational lesson attached to a narrative for the purpose of the personal and moral growth of the child. Instead, it is an ironic representation of the hodgepodge of platitudes and pop culture expressions that surround American children, set in the context of a game show with all its glitz and its arbitrariness. The Warners are justifiably perplexed by the Wheel—while Yakko seems to think it is his duty to face this task, the others are reluctant to interrupt the chase, accepting it like an unwanted chore or homework assignment. As Yakko intones the moral with the dressed-up authority of an older brother, the others fidget and comment sarcastically on what they are being asked to learn. Only the trip to Tahiti garnered any real excitement; most morals elicit a wry remark before all three tear off, eager to be back in the game.

On one level, the Wheel is a clever jab at the various regulations recently imposed on children's television. Current concerns for the educational value of children's programming raised by parents, politicians, and regulators, and recently embraced by the FCC,[15] urge networks to include a specific number of hours of children's programming that serves some educational value. The FCC definition of educational programming, left intentionally vague, has been interpreted in a variety of ways by broadcasters. No doubt, the producers of *Animaniacs* would not claim that the Wheel of Morality makes their show educational (they may make such a claim, however, about the songs that are part of the *Animaniacs* repertoire, which often work history and science lessons into the humor); rather, this Wheel may be a scathing critique of those producers and regulators who believe that a vacant platitude appended to a cartoon somehow makes it educational. The quick fix is shown to be arbitrary, useless, forced, and empty—and *Animaniacs* suggests that kids see right through this, either ignoring the moral or using it as fodder for more humor, before dashing away to return to more childlike pleasures.

But the Wheel of Morality is indicative of the broader critique that *Animaniacs* is making about, and amid, American childhood. As a trope it is the ideal closer to the program, a program that works for its young audience by articulating and navigating the complex ways children are addressed by American culture. Just as the Warners' various adventures express a complicated array of definitions of child and childhood, so the Wheel combines contradictory modes of address—the commercial, the moral, the educational, and the disruptive—into a single mechanism. Morals pop out like magic from the inner workings of the machine, but neither the Warners nor the audience can predict whether they will be a moral admonition, a commercial appeal, or a sarcastic insight.[16]

The unspeakable truth of American childhood is that the relevant categories, while they are often treated as coherent in public discourse, are in practice fractured, multiple, and incoherent. Various definitions of child and childhood are at play simultaneously in American culture—often contradictory, rarely fully articulated, and sometimes hotly contested. When expressed to children, both in the way children are addressed and in what is expected and demanded of them, the ambiguity and complexity of these cultural meanings are overlooked. The problematic friction between different modes of address is erased from the discourse—though it is left for the child to sort out with limited available resources. Childhood as a coherent, singular category is a cultural fiction; the Wheel of Morality, with its polyvalent structure, its arbitrariness, its inexplicable intrusion into the narrative, embodies and exposes this cultural fiction for the sham that it is—as randomly random as spinning a game show wheel.

Children are treated, when they watch *Animaniacs*, to a kind of relaxation—a freedom from not intellectual demands, but from the force of cultural categories and any claims of their coherence or stability. They are given a world filled with recognizable ambiguities: childhoods filled with mixed expectations, child-adult relations fraught with contradictions, multiple cultural heritages that keep undermining one another. They are shown ways to laugh at the ambiguities and contradictions patterned into their lives, so they don't have to either ignore, refuse, or accept them. They are confronted, in short, with a clearer picture of the problem American children face in learning and navigating childhood, in which the rules of membership and definitions of the group are themselves confusing. The more clashes and contradictions in the cultural categories, scripts, and models for children, the more laughter for the program—because laughter addresses the problems children face that others seem to ignore. Cartoons hold children between the experiences in their lives and the words that are supposed to make sense of them, constituting a mobile space between language and the perceived world in which ambiguities in the culture of childhood, so hard for them to learn, are cracked open.

NOTES

1   See, for a good example, Michael Cole and Sheila Cole (1989). On children learning
    to fit their behavior (in this case, storytelling) to social categories, see Ageliki
    Nicolopolou 1997).

2   For background, see Opie and Opie (1987); Postman (1982); Berger (1971); Fine
    (1987); Thorne (1993); Seiter (1993); Kinder (1991); and Hays 1996.

3   The Fox Network first introduced *Animaniacs*, produced by Amblin Entertainment
    and Warner Brothers, into its Saturday morning lineup in 1993; in 1995, the
    program moved to Warner's new WB Network. During its five-year run, it was
    nominated for sixteen Daytime Emmys and won eight. Reruns soon appeared on
    weekday afternoons on the WB, and these later migrated to the Cartoon Network.
    Each episode was composed of several segments focused on an array of recurring
    characters. The most prominent were the Warners, who were often visibly marked
    as "the" *Animaniacs*; we will be using examples exclusively from their segments.
    Other segments included a group of mobster pigeons, a dog and a rambunctious
    little girl, and a giant chicken; the lessons drawn here, while not identical in the
    specifics, are applicable to the rest of the program—and to much of children's
    television. For more information about the program, see http://home.earthlink.net/
    ~wbwolf/beginners.html.

4   But compare with Ariès (1962) on the Catholic view of childhood in the same
    period. The differences in Christianity in this period had powerful consequences for
    children and childhood—literacy was pressed in Protestant sects, but child's play
    was cultivated more in Catholic sites as a means of learning. Still, both emphasized
    the need for children to have an education that would actively constrain the wild
    impulses of children and make them ready to enter adult company without such a
    disrupting effect.

5   This work was also connected to the politics of the material feminists who thought it
    was possible to build more utopian social worlds through design of places. See
    Hayden (1981).

6   As Sharon Hays (1996) has documented, keeping children within such "natural"
    definitions requires intensive parenting, placing a huge burden on parents and
    children in this culture.

7   In online discussions about the show, the regular participants put a moratorium on
    the question of what the Warners are, because the question had been debated
    endlessly without any means of resolution and perhaps in deference to the show's
    refusal to answer the question itself. The theory proposed at the end of that
    discussion suggested that the ambiguity of the Warner characters is a sly parody of
    the "inkblot" style of early American animation: solid black figures such as Mickey
    Mouse, Oswald the Rabbit, and Fritz the Cat, who needed their names to mark their
    species because visually they were nearly indistinguishable. Many programs aimed
    at children have provided archetypical characters as vehicles for their young
    audiences, most commonly by designing a motley array of personas, as in the
    Muppets or the Simpsons, to provide a typology of possible entries into notions of
    childhood. See Mukerji (1997). Instead, the Warners exploit the ambiguity made
    possible by animation to elide all categories. What begins as a joke on their
    animated ancestors results in a kind of purification of the animal-child archetype;
    left with few distinguishing markers of type, they are only children, or only animal-

children amalgams. Also, their gender is indicated, even emphasized, in their recurring introduction as "the Warner brothers and the Warner sister" and in the way the two boys regularly salivate over Dr. Scratchnsniff's curvaceous assistant. (The girl is emphatic about marking her gender, in a way that acknowledges an imbalance—perhaps in the world of animation itself—even as she attempts to correct it.) But beyond this, their "nature" is left ambiguous. This ambiguity offers an important space for children to experience these characters, and through them to experience childhood—a time when they are feeling quite ambiguous about their own "nature," unsure perhaps of what they are, and faced with often contradictory social definitions of what they are and should aspire to be.

8   For evidence of the ongoing importance of labor to the lives of children—even at school—see Willis (1981). Particularly for working-class children, the separate world of childhood can seem like a trap and lie more than a good description of their lives. For an historical perspective on this, see Whyte (1955). For the "adult corruption in the separate worlds of young people," see Katz (1988) and Macleod (1995).

9   This "newsreel" was then incorporated into many subsequent episodes as part of the program's introduction.

10   For those unfamiliar with the history of the animation industry, "Termite Terrace" was the nickname of the run-down shack on the Warner Brothers lot where most of the famous animated shorts of such character as Bugs Bunny and Daffy Duck were drawn. The name referred to the dilapidated quality of the building, and by extension the minimal interest the studio invested in animation at the time.

11   Interaction between animator and his or her creation is also a convention drawn from the traditions of early animation. Crafton (1982) describes how the earliest animators would include themselves, literally or representationally, within the diegesis of the cartoon narrative—Windsor McCay directing Gertie the Dinosaur to dance, Koko the Clown coming alive from the tip of Max Fleischer's pen. Crafton argues that the new aesthetic form was so striking and inexplicable that its "magic" needed to be secured by the visible presence of the animator. Crafton also notes that in most cases, the plot of these early cartoons has the animated character escaping control of the animator, a metaphor for animation itself, which always exceeds the cultural categories it represents. This convention has diminished over the course of the century, though the remnants can still be found (a famous example is "Duck Amuck," in which Daffy is being pestered by the brush of a mischievous animator who turns out to be Bugs Bunny at an animator's table). The fact that the *Animaniacs* uses a similar convention but represents the studio as the progenitor of the cartoon characters is telling—another homage to the traditions of early animation, and a further indication that the Warners exceed control in the very way that the medium of animation itself does.

12   In the online discussions about the show, animator/producer Tom Ruegger is commonly referred to as the creator of the *Animaniacs*, in classic "auteur" style. The patrilineage here is interestingly complex because Ruegger has acknowledged in interviews that the Warner characters are loosely based on his own children (his youngest boy has even expressed disappointment at being transformed into a girl in the representation). So, in a sense the Warners *are* the children of an animator/father/employee of Warner Brothers studio; the representation of (actual) children is not just brought to us by the corporate animation industry, but intertwined with it from the very start.

13   This lyric in particular provoked significant debate in online discussions. The debate seemed—on the surface, at least—simply a matter of fact; indeed, it was settled by participants familiar with the history of Hollywood (and thus the existence of a "pay-or-play" contract) and others who contacted producers of the show for confirmation. The vibrant debate could be dismissed merely as evidence of the meticulous nature of fans, but the dispute settled on a particularly complex and culturally telling phrase that highlights the contradictory status constructed for the Warners as commercial entities.

14   For the problem of finding and defining American culture in youth culture, see Berger (1971).

15   See, in particular, the Children's Television Act of 1990 and its overhaul in 1996. The definition of "educational and informational programming" cited in these documents is as follows: "Any television programming that furthers the educational and information needs of children 16 years of age and under in any respect, including children's intellectual/cognitive or social/emotional needs." The final phrase, appended in 1996, does not actually narrow the definition in any way, but instead provides more ways for broadcasters to successfully justify programming that offers the bare minimum of educational value. For explanations of the good reasons for educational television, see Lesser (1974) and Polsky (1974).

16   Interestingly, several fans noted in online newsgroup discussions that the actual animation of the spin is itself a fiction; to more efficiently reuse animation cels, the makers of *Animaniacs* use the same blurred spin for each sequence and draw new cels only for where the spin ends. Even the spin proves to be arbitrary. The security of believing that the spinner landed somewhere because of friction is proved to be a convenient falsehood, just as the security of believing that being a child is as simple as the culture claims is proved also to be a convenient falsehood.

REFERENCES

Ariès, Philippe. *Centuries of Childhood: A Social History of Family Life*. New York: Vintage Books, 1962.

Berger, Bennett M. *Looking for America: Essays on Youth, Suburbia, and Other American Obsessions*. Englewood Cliffs, N.J.: Prentice-Hall, 1971.

Bettelheim, Bruno. *The Uses of Enchantment: The Meaning and Importance of Fairy Tales*. New York: Vintage Books, 1971.

Card, Stuart K., Jock D. Mackinlay, and Ben Shneiderman. *Readings in Information Visualization: Using Vision to Think, The Morgan Kaufmann Series in Interactive Technologies*. San Francisco: Morgan Kaufmann Publishers, 1999.

Chukovski, Kornei. *From Two to Five*. Rev. ed. Berkeley: University of California Press, 1968.

Cole, Michael, and James V. Wertsch. "Beyond the Individual-Social Antinomy in Discussions of Piaget and Vygotsky." *Human Development* 39, no. 5 (1996): 250–257.

Cole, Michael, and Sheila Cole. *The Development of Children*. New York: W. H. Freeman, 1989.

Crafton, Donald. *Before Mickey: The Animated Film, 1898–1928*. University of Chicago Press ed. Chicago: University of Chicago Press, 1982.

Engelhardt, Tom. "Children's Television." In *Watching Television: A Pantheon Guide to Popular Culture*, edited by Todd Gitlin. New York: Pantheon Books, 1986.

Fine, Gary Alan. *With the Boys: Little League Baseball and Preadolescent Culture*. Chicago: University of Chicago Press, 1987.

Hayden, Dolores. *The Grand Domestic Revolution: A History of Feminist Designs for American Homes, Neighborhoods, and Cities*. Cambridge, Mass.: MIT Press, 1981.

Hays, Sharon. *The Cultural Contradictions of Motherhood*. New Haven: Yale University Press, 1996.

Katz, Jack. *Seductions of Crime: Moral and Sensual Attractions in Doing Evil*. New York: Basic Books, 1988.

Kinder, Marsha. *Playing with Power in Movies, Television, and Video Games: From Muppet Babies to Teenage Mutant Ninja Turtles*. Berkeley: University of California Press, 1991.

Lesser, Gerald S. *Children and Television: Lessons from Sesame Street*. 1st ed. New York: Random House, 1974.

MacLeod, Jay. *Ain't No Makin' It: Aspirations and Attainment in a Low-Income Neighborhood*. Boulder, Colo.: Westview Press, 1995.

McKendrick, Neil, John Brewer, and J. H. Plumb. *The Birth of a Consumer Society: The Commercialization of Eighteenth-Century England*. Bloomington: Indiana University Press, 1982.

Mukerji, Chandra. "Monsters and Muppets: The History of Childhood and Techniques of Cultural Analysis." In *From Sociology to Cultural Studies: New Perspectives*, edited by Elizabeth Long, 155–184. Malden, Mass.: Blackwell, 1997.

Nicolopolou, Ageliki. "Worldmaking and Identity Formation in Children's Narrative Play-Acting." In *Sociogenetic Perspectives on Internationalization*, edited by Brian Cox and Cynthia Lightfoot, 157–187. Mahwah, N.J.: Lawrence Erlbaum, 1997.

Opie, Iona Archibald, and Peter Opie. *The Lore and Language of Schoolchildren*. Oxford Oxfordshire; New York: Oxford University Press, 1987.

Plumb, John H. "The New World of Children on Eighteenth-century England." In *The Birth of a Consumer Society: The Commercialization of Eighteenth-Century England*, edited by Neil Mckendrick, John Brewer, and J. H. Plumb. Bloomington: Indiana University Press, 1982.

Pollock, Linda A. *Forgotten Children: Parent-Child Relations from 1500 to 1900*. Cambridge Cambridgeshire; New York: Cambridge University Press, 1983.

Polsky, Richard M., and Aspen Program on Communications and Society. *Getting to Sesame Street: Origins of the Children's Television Workshop*. New York: Praeger, 1974.

Postman, Neil. *The Disappearance of Childhood*. New York: Delacorte Press, 1982.

Rowe, Kathleen. *The Unruly Woman: Gender and the Genres of Laughter*, 1st ed. *Texas Film Studies Series*. Austin, Tex.: University of Texas Press, 1995.

Sammond, Nicholas. "The Uses of Childhood: The Making of Walt Disney and the Generic American Child 1930–1960." Ph.D. diss., University of California–San Diego, 1999.

Seiter, Ellen. *Sold Separately: Children and Parents in Consumer Culture*. Rutgers Series in Communications, Media, and Culture. New Brunswick, N.J.: Rutgers University Press, 1993.

Thorne, Barrie. *Gender Play: Girls and Boys in School.* New Brunswick, N.J.: Rutgers University Press, 1993.

Wartella, Ellen. "Electronic Childhood." *Media Studies Journal* 4 (1994): 33–43.

Whyte, William Foote. *Street Corner Society: The Social Structure of an Italian Slum.* Chicago: University of Chicago Press, 1955.

Willis, Paul E. *Learning to Labor: How Working Class Kids Get Working Class Jobs.* Morningside ed. New York: Columbia University Press, 1981.

Zelizer, Viviana A. *Pricing the Priceless Child: The Changing Social Value of Children.* Princeton, N.J.: Princeton University Press, 1985.

Chapter 12

Ghosts in the Machine: Postmodern Childhood, Video Gaming, and Advertising

Stephen Kline and Greig de Peuter

A mass-mediated culture is clearly an important factor in the formation of symbolic childhoods. As Joe Kincheloe (1997, 45) states: "childhood… cannot escape the influence of the postmodern condition with its electronic media saturation." To date, those who study children's culture have largely focused on the symbolic worlds conjured in television and films to advance our understanding of postmodern childhood. Often critics turn to the vivid representations of contemporary family life—from *Ren and Stimpy* to *The Simpsons* to *Home Alone*—to diagnose the crisis of mediated childhood (Kincheloe and Steinberg 1997). It is common for these critics to deride the prime-time fare as a force subverting traditional modernist values, aesthetic standards, and mores by eclipsing the distinctions between child and adult cultures. Echoing Neil Postman, Kincheloe argues that "boundaries between childhood and adulthood fade as children and adults negotiate the same mediascape and struggle with the same impediments to meaning-making" (45).

Although one may sympathize with these authors' fascination with the complicated and often bizarre representations of family life in prime-time TV programming, we find the conclusion that "children and adults negotiate the same mediascape" increasingly hard to accept in the face of the ongoing fragmentation of media audiences. The media-use patterns of children not only differ from those of adults (Buckingham 1996; Pecora 1998), but they also often happen in the isolation of the bedroom or with peers (Livingstone, Holden, and Bovill 1999). Our concern is that analyses that stop at the blurring boundaries between adulthood and childhood in our media-saturated world risk overlooking the countervailing social practices fostering divergence of adult and youth cultures in the postmodern cultural environment. In particular, it risks overlooking the growing emphasis on children and youth as a distinct media niche.

Video Gaming and Youth Culture

Since the early 1980s, when machine-mediated play first began moving from arcades and malls into children's bedrooms, the public awareness of video gaming as a youth media has grown. Witnessing the increasing penetration of "interactive gaming"' into American households and the fervent interest of those young players who spent up to an hour each day with these entertainment systems, Eugene Provenzo (1991, 8) foresaw the ascent of what has come to be called the Nintendo Generation: "This is the real significance of video game technology for contemporary childhood. It represents the first stages in the creation of a new type of television—an interactive medium as different from traditional television as television is from radio." Provenzo predicted "the remaining years of this decade would see the emergence and definition of this new media form in much the same way the late 1940s and early 1950s saw television emerge as a powerful social and cultural force" (105). Her study of virtual gaming communities also led Allucquère Rosanne Stone (1995, 26–27) to comment: "It is entirely possible that computer-based games will turn out to be the major unacknowledged source of socialization and education in industrialized countries before the 1990s have run their course."

By the mid-1990s, these prognostications seemed to be confirmed. Interactive gaming had indeed become the fastest growing and most profitable youth media. Dwarfing children's film and television industries, gaming has established a presence in 85 percent of American households with male children (Battelle and Johnstone 1993). In 1999 world sales surpassed $20 billion, with over $8 billion earned in the United States alone (IDSA 2000). A recent study indicated that millions of kids are now spending upwards of six hours per week playing video games, transforming boys' (mainly boys') bedrooms into virtual playgrounds (Nielsen 1999). One of the appeals of video games is that they offer an absorbing and intense simulation experience that goes beyond the conventions of realism and risk associated with the delimited "adultified" world of everyday life (see Kline and Banerjee 1998; Kline 1997).

In his critique of recent accounts of postmodernism, Sardar Ziauddin (1998, 10) suggests that video gaming provides the ideal metaphor for the new symbolic landscape:

> Postmodernism posits the world as a video game: seduced by the allure of the spectacle, we have all become characters in the global video game, zapping our way from here to there, fighting wars in cyberspace, making love to digitized bits of information. All social life is now being regulated not by reality but by simulations, models, pure images and representations. These in turn create new simulations, and the whole process continues in a relentless stream in which the behaviour of individuals and societies bears no relationship to any reality: everything and everyone is drowned in pure simulation.

The attraction of these digitally simulated worlds of action adventure and fighting games to boys between the ages of eight and fourteen has also fuelled what amounts to a "moral panic" about kids' cyberculture (Kline and Banerjee 2000). In an account of his experience testifying before the U.S. Congress on violence in children's entertainment, Henry Jenkins (1999) stated: "When the Littleton shootings occurred [calls from the media] increased dramatically." He goes on to worry that "Suddenly, we are finding ourselves in a national witch hunt to determine which form of popular culture is to blame for the mass murders and video games seemed like a better candidate than most."

Adopting a Foucauldian perspective, Valerie Walkerdine, Angela Dudfield, and David Studdert (2000, 198) remind critics that the "subjectivities" associated with video gaming need to be understood in relationship to "the discursive practices that make up the social world." Walkerdine and her coauthors examine these discourses critically, arguing that video gaming reveals itself as a "site of struggle" over values and ideologies concerning youthful sexuality, violence, and moral disintegration. In interviewing parents about video gaming, they found their attitudes oscillated between "'safe' production as rational mastery or its 'dangerous' manifestation as addiction or violence" (210). Such attitudes toward mediated childhood, they claim, are mostly "consonant with existing discourses projected onto children and onto technology" (210). Yet, as they go on to note, unlike television, most video-game play takes place within children's private space—beyond the surveillance of parents and outside the boundaries of their control. Among young players, there is widespread celebration of the pleasures of immersive experiences of game play—of exploring and problem-solving, of fighting and winning—as a quest for masculine mastery. Although both parents and players hold different points of view on the "mastery" motif of game play, Walkerdine and her coauthors go on to suggest that anxiety "is a central trope through which we might understand the fictions through which current fantasies of masculine childhood are produced" (207).

These divergent responses to cybermasculinity, however, do not fully capture the discursive practices that construct and position video gamers within the symbolic field of video gaming. Noting the growth of children and youth marketing, Stephen Kline (1993) has claimed that critics of postmodern childhood often overlook the fact that such struggles over children's media cultures are themselves precipitated in a commercial media environment forged by marketers' interest in selling various products to children. In 1998 in the United States alone, the child and youth market accounted for over $120 billion in sales, with kids spending at least a quarter of that money themselves (Lim and Turco 2000). An advertisement for Youth Television (YTV) in *Marketing Magazine* (1998, 16) reminds us of the specter of youth marketing that increasingly haunts the postmodern mediascape:

> Get Kidfluence working for you. Advertise on YTV. Canadian kids spend over a billion dollars annually on discretionary purchases. But their power reaches way beyond that to directly influence over ten billion dollars worth of household spending—on food, clothing, electronics, and even cars.

This children's marketing effort has matured as an ever-widening range of products aimed at children and youth—clothes, shoes, music, snacks, cereals, toys, and now video games—frame the discourses of and about youth-oriented media culture (Kline 1993; McAllister 1996; Pecora 1998).

The Promotion of Interactive Entertainment

Video-game marketing took flight during the early 1990s as Nintendo and Sega, the dominant console-makers at the time, began to vie for the millions of loyal followers by investing in sophisticated consumer research and intensive television advertising campaigns. As wars for a share of the youth entertainment market heated up, the video-game industry proved itself a dynamic leader in youth-oriented marketing, launching promotional magazines, Web sites, and a series of highly creative advertising campaigns (Hayes, Dinsey with Parker 1989; Sheff 1993). They currently outspend all other youth sectors on promotion, making game consoles and games the most advertised children's product on U.S. TV.

In her study of kids' media culture, Marsha Kinder (1991) noted how characters from children's video games were crossing into children's media culture. Kinder realized that video-game companies were forming corporate alliances with other media "to reach out to a larger audience by positioning the world of video games within other, more familiar contexts" (109). The cross-media marketing of video games has resulted in a steady interchange between popular films, TV shows, and the gaming industry (e.g., *Sonic, Mario, Carmen Sandiego, Mortal Kombat, Golden Eye, The Simpsons, Star Wars, Tomb Raider*). Their escalating marketing efforts have propelled video-game sales and established Nintendo, Sony, and Sega as household brand names. The recently achieved $3 billion of *Pokémon* sales has established a new high watermark for contemporary video-game marketers whose strategies seek to orchestrate this dense network of synergies—the promotional condition that defines the media-saturated universe of postmodern childhood.

Since children's lives are so bound up with the mediated marketplace, we see the necessity of examining another discursive practice within which the subjectivity of the video gamer has been constructed—the promotional messages of the game marketers that were developed expressly for expanding the youthful audience for gaming. In this essay, we aim to foreground the corporate strategies that haunt the children's media landscape by providing a critical diagnosis of the symbolic childhood of cyberculture through a case study of the television advertising of interactive entertainment products. We suspect that it is hard to find a clearer articulation of both the anxieties and pleasures underscoring postmodern cyberculture than the one found in the fantastical montages, cynicism, and frenetic excitement of the child conjured in video-game ads. To analyze the symbolic representations of video gamers and video gaming in these advertisements, we argue it is first necessary to account for the practices and contexts in which these representations are "designed." By illuminating the branding, positioning, and targeting of the youthful gamer, we hope to cast the shadow of the marketing ghosts we find lurking within this symbolic machinery.

Analyzing Hype: TV Advertising

Advertising is incredibly important, and understanding how games are
advertised can give you a better idea of how the industry operates as a whole.
—*Video Game Industry Analysts* (Sawyer, Dunne, and Berg 1998, 481)

Although a whole range of cultural products are synergistically linked in
the name of saturating children's culture with video-game brands, we note
that TV is the most heavily relied on communication channel used by
video-game companies to focus the branding of their systems because it
reaches the broadest swath of potential video gamers. Providing the most
direct contact with its consumers, TV advertising absorbs the lion's share
of promotional budgets in the video-games industry.

This advertising effort began escalating in 1992 when Sega invested
$45 million in thirty-five television spots concentrated in a four-month
campaign to launch its Genesis system to compete with Nintendo (Battelle
and Johnstone 1993). The ads were notable not only in the scale of the
budget, but also in their use of twisted humor, aggressive product values,
and music video production aesthetics to compete with Nintendo's
younger "family fun" positioning. These budgets have continued to soar.
The Sega Dreamcast, for example, was launched in 1999 with a $100
million advertising campaign. Similarly scaled advertising efforts
announce the launches of Sony, Nintendo, and Microsoft's new gaming
consoles, providing massive sources of new revenue for child- and
youth-oriented TV broadcasters.

For a number of reasons, TV has become the preferred medium for
marketers of video games to manage communication with gamers. First, as
one commentator explains: "Short of actually playing, the best way to get
a feel for a game is watching it being played—something that can only be
done on a TV. Thus advertising video games on TV seems like a perfect
solution" (*Next Generation* 1997). Second, TV affords cost-effective
marketing communication because children's media audiences are
concentrated in demographic niches. Third, advertising provides a
dynamic communicative space for constructing and hailing the video
gamer as an entertainment consumer. In combination, then, TV ads have
become an integral part of marketing programs, used simultaneously to
cultivate a brand identity for the console-maker in order to convey the
attractions of the game-play experience and to sketch a picture of the video
gamer.

In what follows, we offer a critical reading of ten years of video-game
advertising to bring to light the way marketing strategies and advertising

practices symbolically inscribe postmodern children's and youth culture and contour the meaning of this media experience and the subjectivities of those who play. The marketers' strategic thinking becomes encoded in the ad's design. Our reading is therefore intended to retro-engineer the marketing decisions, promotional narratives, and "structure of feeling" which guide these promotional designs. This chapter draws upon two hundred video-game spots produced for TV between 1989 and 1999. Combining a content analysis and semiotic analysis approach, our analytic protocol for decoding these ads focused on the industry's depiction of video-game culture. Our analysis started by detailing the representations of the player, the content of the game, and the experience of game play. But given the sophistication of youth advertising, we also had to investigate the themes and stylization techniques that gave the ads their deeper meaning: (1) masculinity, violence, and isolation, (2) power and control, (3) high intensity and immersion, (4) fantasy and escape, (5) the carnivalesque, irony, and twisted humor. We provide the following commentary on these narratives, characters, values, and situations we saw depicted therein by discussing ads that exemplify the predominant themes in our sample.

Constructing and Framing the Child:
Market Research in the Video-Games Industry

The starting point of the marketing concept is to identify and research the potential consumer for your product. Massive resources have been used in the pursuit of a fine-grained understanding of the video gamer—the consumer subject of foremost interest to the video-game industry. Industry commentators describe market research as the "secret weapon" in the business of marketing video games:

> They spend a great deal of money analyzing everything related to the entire game industry—from people's hobbies and interests to market research trends and driving technology factors, including hardware sales, software sales, and so on. They turn over every rock they can, and they use the information they gather to get a better understanding of the people who play games (Sawyer, Dunne, and Berg 1998, 380).

Consumer researchers probe the video gamer on everything from why they play games to what role games play in their social lives. A researcher at Electronic Arts, the world's largest independent video-game publisher, explains how they get to know their audience: "We listen to consumers, we read the reviews, we do hold focus groups, we review products, we run surveys internationally in a number of different cities, collecting information, getting feedback on our different brands" (cited in Stafford 1999). As a marketer at Sega makes clear, their consumer research doesn't simply involve "asking, 'What games do you like?' and 'Where do you live?' and that kind of thing. It includes things like the psychology of children and what their brains are capable of" (cited in *Next Generation* 1997). Gamers are also regularly invited to test new games to determine their attractiveness and playability before the production line starts to churn. The purpose of these research practices is to construct a "portrait" of the aficionado gamer, which in turn frames the design of games and advertising.

This research is vital for the precise targeting of consumer segments and for the design of the advertising campaign. Targeting, however, is a gradual process of narrowing and contouring your marketing strategy to the disposition of one's most lucrative consumers. For Nintendo, a brand that has become synonymous with video-game culture, consumer research played an important role in the positioning strategies for their systems. They had originally conceived of the Nintendo platform as a medium offering domestic family entertainment, initially even calling it "Famicom." But in the face of competition from Sega during the early- to mid-1990s, Nintendo increasingly focused on its "principal player," which research confirmed was a boy between the age of eight and fourteen. Although the industry has attempted to expand into a "girl-gamer" audience, video-game designer Celia Pearce (1998, 210) has noted that the prevailing target is "the world's most innocent and maligned victim of demographic opportunism, the ever-vulnerable, ever-receptive, ever-predictable adolescent male."

Echoing Pearce, commentator Diana Griffiths (1997) observes this emphasis on the masculine. "Conventional wisdom," Griffiths says, has long held that "most computer games are purchased by adolescent males." It's sound wisdom: Male consumers account for 75 to 85 percent of game-related sales (Cassell and Jenkins 1998, 11). The industry sticks to this predictable male audience because game development is expensive and stepping out of a guaranteed consumer market and stable design formula could be costly. As Griffiths explains: "Game companies produce games primarily for this market. This creates a positive feedback cycle so more and more games are written for this audience." Targeting concentrates product design and marketing communication on a distinct audience segment. It is not surprising that, in the attempt to target the video-game audience, gender and emotional biases are inscribed into this medium—whose traces are made visible in video-game advertising.

Video-game ads manifest a uniquely male energy. One of Sega's marketers astutely described his company's early-1990s branding strategy as "in-your-face, aggressive young male. We were all about testosterone" (cited in *Next Generation* 1997). Video-game ad-speak does indeed have the locker-room qualities of pumped-up aggressive talk. At the center of the ads is a gamer, mostly portrayed as a generic or "typical" teen user. Ninety-four percent of the visualized gamers in our sample of ads were young males estimated to be between the ages of eight and fourteen. Of these, 64 percent were playing alone—mostly in their rooms outside the reach of parents and friends. When male children were shown engaged in game play, 53 percent of the ads portrayed the gamer in a way compatible with the symbolic conventions for compulsive and addictive play; that is, they are often represented as "hard-core" gamers who have constructed a strong, often obsessive, bond with "gaming" as a way of achieving control and subcultural membership.

Streetfighter

Fig. 12.1. Through the cynical construction of the isolated male gamer, scenes such as this one from an ad for the video game *Street Fighter II* attempt to resolve the anxieties of "addiction" often attributed to gaming.

Ad-dressing the Male Gamer

Patterns in gender representation like this lead Pearce to claim that the gaming industry has been built on a cynical attitude to young males. According to Pearce, when the industry pictures a gamer, "The image that comes to mind is the classic pimply-faced video gamester who can't get enough of *Mortal Kombat* and *Street Fighter*, feeding quarters into an arcade game like a gambler at a slot machine or sitting at home shooting frantically at the television set" (210). A 1994 *Street Fighter II* TV ad offers us a glimpse of the marketers' concept of their core consumer. In it, a geeky boy sits, stooped over the edge of his bed manipulating the joystick between his legs, unable to sit still, groaning and grunting as he controls the fighting action on the screen (fig. 12.1). The ad is almost a literal portrayal of Pearce's remark that video games offer "boys...a form of electronic masturbation, a high-tech outlet for otherwise out-of-control hormonal oscillations" (211).

Listening outside her son's locked bedroom door, Mom, however, is getting worried. Holding the laundry in her arms, she tries to bribe him to come out and then threatens him to get him to stop playing his video game. "Mommy's got a gun," she feigns. She's clearly worried by the noises her son is making. Mom tries again to lure him out, telling him, in a mildly seductive and anxious tone, that the "new lingerie catalog is here." Immersed in the fighting, the boy shouts back: "Go away!" Alas, she gives up. Retreating, Mom says to herself, "I think I saw a chain saw in the garage?" It is through a humorous construction of the male gaming subject that these ads resolve the extreme compulsiveness attributed to video gaming. As well, in this promotional world, being lost in time is virtuous and losing sight of family obligations is simply evidence of a gamer's wonderful immersion in the flow of game play.

The story told in this ad is typical of the irony and twisted humor that is requisite in promoting video games to young males simultaneously questing for heart-pumping distraction and oedipal rebellion. Does Mom think her son is addicted to video games? Is he masturbating? Does the comment about the chain saw mean she's scared her son is dangerous? Or is she willing to use it to break into his room? Despite these interpretive uncertainties about the relationship between the characters in the ad or the overall message of the story, we get to see enough screen shots of action in the ad to know that *Street Fighter II*, like countless other games, provides the gamer with what Pearce calls a "repertoire of confrontational skills from characters who speak mostly with their fists" (211).

Nola Alloway and Pam Gilbert (1998, 97) interpret the gendered discourse of video gaming as a symbolic "field within which constructions of hegemonic masculinity dominate." Video-game promotional discourses, they go on to say, "align masculinity with power, with aggression, with victory and winning, with superiority and strength—and, of course, with violent action. They offer positions for young male game players that promise success as masculine subjects." Promoting Nintendo's home version for the kickboxing game, *Killer Instinct*, a 1993 TV ad makes clear the implications of these symbolic associations that "powerfully and seductively coalesces images of masculinity and violent action" (102). The ad shows four young males watching the graphics from *Killer Instinct* as the game is being played. They energetically identify with the action. As they respond to the game, a whistle censors their obscenities. They scream with surprise: "Same graphics, same (bleep)ing moves"; "It looks like the (bleep)ing arcade man!" The last gamer wails: "Sixteen bits! All I can say is (bleep)!" The game's packaging is then displayed while industrial music pounds in the background.

Yet as the next scene in this ad reveals, there is more at stake than the pleasure of fantasized violence. One of the boys is hunched over his desk in his bedroom playing *Killer Instinct*, only to be discovered by his mother who, in the classic irony of video-game advertising, screams, "What the (bleep)!" *Killer Instinct* is not just violent; it is also available to the gamer as a form of rebellion, censured and likely to be met with disapproval from adults. Indeed, this boy is even punished by having to wash his mouth out with soap. The gamer is again a rebel, willing to place himself at risk of getting caught and being disciplined. As the boy spits out the soap, the camera reveals it's engraved with the Nintendo logo. The captions "Play $%#? Killer Instinct!!" and "Now on $%#? Game Boy!!" close the TV ad. In this spot, young male dissent and the imperatives of branding are interwoven in the subjectivity of the brand-loyal male gamer.

This perhaps remains comic until we realize that Nintendo's "Now you're playing with power" slogan was in fact deliberately crafted to resonate with young males' deeper psychic and social issues. As a marketer at Nintendo told us: "This is basically a lot of kids' coming out period where they establish their individuality so when you are creating marketing programs you have to respect that—and appeal to that" (cited in Stafford 1999). And as Jörgen Nissen (1998, 165) argues: "A young man's feelings of insecurity and powerlessness can be compensated by a feeling of control over something—in this case a specific technology." It is with such insecurities in mind that Nintendo ads often construct the gamer as under siege by the adultified world while promising the young male gamer "empowerment" and "control" in an unlimited virtual world.

The cyberculture of game play is put in contrast to real life and associated with the experience of "true freedom" in a recent Nintendo 64 ad. Defiant phrases in the ad, such as "We won't zig when we can zag" are not just instructions for navigating a game space—they are the essence of the gamer creed. Gamers push limits rather than follow the beaten path, thus becoming dissidents engaged in the revolutionary act of overthrowing constraints. The joystick, as the narrator hails the gamer, is a means of being "in control of some place else"—an imaginary world of unbound exploration and fantasy. The Nintendo narrator goes on to make being in control of the joystick an act of ideological defiance: "We won't be told how to view the world." Many video-game ads hail the gamer with the delusion of male omnipotence—making such grandiose declarations as "Nothing is beyond my control" *(Total Control,* 1999, 132).

Screen Culture and Visual Assault:
Wiring Attitude into Game Machines

That parents don't understand or are opposed to gaming is more than a satirical trope; it also reveals the targeting strategies of the major console-makers. The industry knows that parents are not really in control of what games are being played. Even though many kids lack the financial resources to buy their own gaming systems, parents are often completely excluded from marketing strategies. Game makers found they didn't have to appeal to parents as buyers as long as they could activate the pressure of "kidfluence." "We don't market to parents," a marketer at Nintendo flatly claims, even though it is parents who supply the money:

> We market to our target group, which is teens and tweens. Parents may be highly involved in the purchase decision, but…it's the kids that are driving it. The parental seal of approval, while it is something that we like, it is not something that we actively encourage in our marketing because that might say to the kids that we're boring (cited in Stafford 1999).

Although television and video games are media in competition for youth's eyeballs, their point of convergence is the screen; both rely on visual communication to engage the youth audience. On reviewing a sample of video-game ads for the first time, viewers will be struck by the aesthetic of frenetic "hypersignification" that seems to permeate postmodern youth-mediated culture (Goldman and Papson 1996). These ads bear little relationship to the "reason why" advertising style discussed in marketing textbooks. In the TV ads for video games, it is not surprising that we find a symbolic childhood expressed through fantastic visual montages blending the frenzied excitement and visual irony associated with the MTV aesthetics of today's youth culture.

Contemporary games such as *Tekken, Golden Eye*, or *Soldier of Fortune* open with "cut" scenes that are that are cinematic in scope, style, and structure. The graphic and sensory sophistication at the heart of "gamer culture" was the starting point of Sega's early-1990s "Theatre of the Eye" TV advertising campaign. One spot opens in a movie theater where an audience of personified "rods" and "cones" are previewing the latest Sega games. The ad depicts metaphorically what is going on in the gamers' brains, eyes, and nervous system, as they respond to Sega's superior graphics. As the audience watches successive beauty shots of the console and game screens, a mounting sensory overload throws the brain into crisis. The brain, represented as a computerized office staffed by a group of males, calls on the optic nerve, asking of the graphics, "What's that?" The optic nerve responds, "I don't know!" A woman, presumably the "assistant" in the narrative of the ad, anxiously enters the brain chamber: "Nerve impulse on line two!" Then, in the nervous system office, the personified nerves frantically shout: "We're having a breakdown, we're having a breakdown, we're having breakdown!" The ad cuts to the theater where the rods and cones are going absolutely berserk from the "graphic intensity."

Indeed, visual intensity has grown into the valued affective state of good game play and the dominant production value in the ads. Advertisers know from their research that gamers hold good graphics, fast action, good characters, and good storylines as the requisite ingredients for an immersive experience. Julian Stallabrass (1996, 85) describes the offerings of gaming as "a palpable reality" in which the "gamer aspires to a phantasmagoric experience of total immersion." The immersion and excitement of interactive experiences is positioned as a therapy for boredom—perhaps one of the "problems" of childhood to which video-game ads offer a resolution. The ad designers must generate a symbolic connection between the narrative in the ad and the intensity of immersive game play—which, as Stallabrass says, "the player operates, by linking response, vision and sound" (85).

Ninety-three percent of the thirty-second ads in our sample include screen shots—full-frame glimpses of the onscreen action of the game. In just over half of these, screen shots filled the majority of the ad's time. The intention of these graphic blasts is to convey a sense of the "game play" as a graphic experience. Using this ad-design technique, the TV screen becomes the visual portal to the games themselves. As one Sony marketer claims: "In these new games, with 3D visual effects and CD-quality sound, I think TV works extremely well in conveying the experience of game play. It's all about the game. Everything in the ad is about the game" (cited in *Next Generation* 1997). Talking about the importance of graphics for conveying the essence of game play, he explains: "(In our research) one of the best comments we've gotten was that when they watch the TV ads they felt like they were going to feel when they play the games."

The advertisers' problem, however, is to communicate the emotions that good graphics bring to game play. Showing only "screens within screens" betrays a brand attitude that is less than exciting. For this reason the game screens must be placed in an emotional context. A rock music soundtrack accompanied the game screens in 30 percent of the ads. Fifty-six percent coupled the game screen with ecstatic vocalizations and screams. Perhaps this is why Sony's recent ad campaign has been described as "post-MTV style micro-cuts, (with) hidden information, and a harsh techno soundtrack" (cited in *Next Generation* 1997). Visual pyrotechnics and aggression seem to be the common elements linking these two visual youth forms.

Branding Attitude

Advertising is communication strategically designed to sell branded products—by making the qualities associated with those brands known to the targeted consumer. The marketers' goal is, after all, not to increase the number of generic gamers but to increase the number of those who are dependent on a single corporation's platform—Nintendo 64, PlayStation II, or Microsoft Xbox—for their game play. This is because revenue is derived equally from console and software sales—from games that are licensed to run only on the brand-specific gaming technology. Regardless of the specific design and narrative in video-game ads, one of the main branding goals is to convey what Sony PlayStation marketers called the "attitude to game play." To spark consumer interest, as in other youth sectors, designers must make the brand attitude both entertaining and cool. As a Nintendo marketer states, their key goal is to design ads that brand the Nintendo platform as "fun, irreverent, different, enjoyable, exciting and cool—without ever saying it" (cited in Mills 1998, 20).

A video-game brand is a symbolic field intended to connect the corporation, their console, and games with their loyal audience. One Sony executive explains their branding ambitions: "We want to have a consistent feel in all our communication, and to communicate the differentiation of our games versus the competition" (cited in *Next Generation* 1997). This leads to a surprising amount of comparative advertising, which, on closer examination, emphasizes brand symbolics rather than technological and pricing differences.

The marketers think long and hard about the specific qualities, tone, and styles that best convey the distinctive feel of their brand. As one PlayStation executive comments:

> We realize there is an attitude in the elements of game play and we have to recognize and understand that this attitude is the real motivator (that moves young people to both play games and buy them). That's the relationship we need to use to build Sony (cited in *Next Generation* 1997).

Because their marketing objectives span a campaign, it is difficult to account for a branding strategy from a single ad whose narratives interweave the brand image into a unified structure of feeling, subsuming references to the game-play experience, the target market, and the brand's implied attitude. But video-game brands do not just enclose symbolic fields; they enclose social ones too, hoping to prompt a long-term user commitment to the console. The successful labeling of contemporary young people as the "Nintendo Generation," in this sense, is a lucid "register of the power of advertising in popular culture, in and through which a simple brand name or marketing label comes into common usage" (Green, Reid, and Bigum 1998, 24).

Inherited from the "character marketing" tradition in the playthings industry, video-game marketers often use personalities from their games to communicate the brand attitude. Nintendo's Mario, Sega's Sonic, and Sony's Crash Bandicoot—a sardonic "in-your-face" Tasmanian devil-like smartass—were all carefully crafted and promoted to consolidate the brand's identity. And like Mickey Mouse before them, they have acquired the status of celebrities in kid's culture. Mario, of course, had movies and television shows to propel him to fame. Crash's more modest fame derives from starring in a series of brilliant PlayStation ads including one in which he holds up traffic at airport security because a metal detector responds to the "jet pack" strapped to his back, and one that depicts a sleepy, Midwestern small-town diner where he nonchalantly shares tall tales with a group of regulars about his *Jet Moto* adventures on the high seas. Sony clearly crafted Crash Bandicoot as a whimsical and sarcastic corporate mascot who can compete with Sonic and Mario.

In one of these PlayStation ads, Crash drives his shabby pickup truck to Nintendo's headquarters in a mock encounter between the fantasy world of video-game "bosses" and the corporate battle of brands. The back of his truck is jam-packed; its contents tower into the air, covered by a sheet. Bandicoot parks and jumps out, grabs his megaphone, and starts to taunt Nintendo's Mario. "Hey, plumber boy, mustache man. Your worst nightmare has arrived. Pack up your stuff. I've got a little surprise for you here. Check it out!" Crash tears away the sheet and unveils a pyramid of TV sets. Each screen displays his *Crash Bandicoot* game. Pointing to his digital image on the screen, he chides his rival: "What you think about that? We've got real-time, 3-D, lush, organic environments!" He continues to jeer Mario. "How's that make you feel, buddy? Feel a little like your days are numbered?" In the midst of the performance, a Nintendo security guard asks meekly if Bandicoot would please leave the property, which he does amiably.

This ad articulates an important distinction between the two corporate attitudes. Crash confronts the corporate giant Nintendo—and his counterpart Mario—with bravado, whimsy, and irreverence. Sony's Crash possesses a youthful arrogance—a quality that the aging and often bumbling plumber, Mario, will never have. Bandicoot's underdog persona therefore announces Sony as an "up-and-comer" in the market—a feisty little guy vying with corporate stalwart Nintendo. Though these multilayered references to brands, characters, games, and corporate attitudes may be lost on adults, the ad designers clearly assume their viewers are capable of getting the message: Crash represents a challenge to Nintendo's more familiar and sedate game-play universe.

In one of Sega's comparative ads, their pressured consumer is pictured sardonically as if they were faced with a life-and-death choice between competing consoles. In an overstated satire on "buyer's remorse," the ad opens with horror-movie, black-and-white footage accompanied by eerie background music and a solemn narrator who sets a funeral mood. Mournfully, the narrator remarks: "For those who purchased something other than a Sega Genesis..." In the next scene, a police officer is overseeing a mortician as he slides out a body tray whose contents need to be identified by a witness, none other than a gamer. A recognizable object—the Nintendo console—is revealed on the tray, beneath the sheet. As the mortician lifts the sheet, the camera turns to the gamer. In a baleful yet blunt tone, the gamer says: "Yep. That's it." The ominous narrator returns to complete his opening sentence: "...our sincere condolences." The gamer says frankly, "What a waste." The mortician asks the gamer to decide the fate of the Nintendo machine: "Burial or cremation?" The gamer takes one last look at the tray and answers: "Burn it!" As the Nintendo machine is drowned in a fiery blaze, the glass door of the crematorium is slammed shut—stamped with the surviving Sega logo. This ad would make little sense to those unfamiliar with video gaming.

This Sega ad exemplifies the carnival atmosphere that pervades the discourse of video-game advertising. Rather like the managerial hostilities in the World Wrestling Federation, the economic war between brands is referred to as a broad and mawkish jest. Some might say this self-reflexivity makes video-game marketing more honest and transparent. But the carnivalesque battle of brands reveals a deeper Catch-22 dilemma in youth marketing. Advertisers must entice promotionally overloaded viewers back to the screen through a pact of mutual pretense. Advertisers disguise their ads as hip entertainment rather than marketing, while savvy viewers submit knowingly to this sales pitch just so long as they are entertained by it. Even if youthful audiences recognize the promotional intent of the message, marketers know that they "will embrace—or at least absorb—a message that involves them emotionally" (Mills 1998, 17). This is why researchers at Sony are pleased when young viewers don't really understand these ironic ads fully:

> In focus groups and research when we play the ads we watch kids stop for a minute and think about what they've seen. They're going, 'I've gotta deal with this.' It makes them participate mentally and emotionally with our product, that's what we set out to do (cited in *Next Generation* 1997).

As another marketer states simply: "You have to entertain or make them feel" or you're not being effective (cited in Mills 1998, 20).

The Disappearance of Normalcy

The postmodern interpenetration of the "normal" and the "imaginary" is a common backdrop to video-game ads, as the discursive space within which games and gamers are constructed. For example, one early Nintendo ad opens with an aerial shot of a suburban subdivision house, a signifier so often associated with teen boredom and normality. The narrator asks: "What's it like to play the Nintendo Entertainment System?" The ad cuts rapidly between shots of the Nintendo console and two boys excitedly pointing to the video-game screen. The sound of thunder disturbs the scene and a strange energy begins emanating from the screen, startling the family's dog. The boys' facial expressions convey excitement more than fear, however, even though their home appears to be on the brink of explosion. The narrator intones authoritatively: "Now you're playing with power!" And the power is clearly that of the imagination as the Nintendo-energized house blasts off like a rocket into the sky. Similar fantastic scenarios of escape from the ordinary life of the teen permeate the scenarios depicted in game advertising; these narratives range from gamers being rushed to a hospital emergency room to be treated for playing too many video games to gamers being admitted and locked in a room of a psychiatric hospital while they deal with video-gaming withdrawal symptoms.

After Burner

Fig. 12.2. Illustrating the disappearance of normalcy, this scene from an ad for the video game *After Burner* is typical in its representation of the gamer being transported from a banal daily life to a fantastic level of reality.

The gamer is often positioned in the TV ads at the juncture of the colliding worlds of fantasy and daily life where these realms are either blurred together where he is elevated from the normal to the imaginary. In an ad for Sega's flight simulator game, *After Burner*, for example, a young boy is shown playing the game in his messy bedroom. The narrator exclaims: "*After Burner*: A game so exciting you can imagine you're in for the fight of your life!" Soon the console, the controller, and the room disappear as electrical impulses dynamize the boy's body, magically morphing him into the cockpit of a fighter plane. Transported, he is in full pilot's gear, waiting for takeoff. Then, as he launches into a game-fighting screen, the narrator intones: "*After Burner* gives you the real dogfight excitement of the arcade version: like barrel rolls, nose dives, supersonic speed, and radar lock-ons!" Closing in on his enemy, the gamer shoots and revels triumphantly as images of a real airplane explode on the screen before the aircraft spirals into the sea. Getting this revenge, the boy shouts: "Your turn to burn!" Cuts like this between multiple "levels of reality" were found in 62 percent of the ads in our sample. Sometimes gamers are transported and repositioned in the virtual world (fig. 12.2). In others, the video-game characters venture forth into reality. And in some, the game and real life blend in a unified field of a completely imaginary reality in which all distinctions between levels of reality have dissolved. The symbolic construction of this blurred ontological field is exactly what beckons the gamer with a promise of absolute intensity.

Of course, ads like these are not meant to be read naturalistically. Instead, they must be approached as layered symbolic fields embedding other cultural references that the ad designers assume resonate with the target gamer. For example, an ad for the Sony PlayStation game *Twisted Metal II* presents a dizzy intertextuality that exemplifies this postmodern ontology. Part James Bond film, part satirical car advertisement, and part video game, there is no reference to real players and imaginary games. The ad begins by following a tuxedo-clad Bond-like model, accompanied by a woman elegantly dressed in black and circling an expensive car admiringly. As the woman seductively slides her hand over its high gloss surface, the narrator, in a parody of advertising, recites its "standard" features. But soon we realize this is no ordinary car: "Style, sophistication, the ability to launch napalm into oncoming traffic. If these are the things you look for in an automobile…it's time you test-drive *Twisted Metal II*. Two rocket launchers, a little ATS flung-forty system—all standard." The man gets into the driver's seat, picks up the joystick waiting there, and begins to play the game on the screen mounted on his car's dashboard. The TV screen becomes a high-intensity joyride through a virtual battlefield as the car is shown blowing up whatever it encounters.

Reflecting on these promises made about the gaming experience, one is reminded of Douglas Rushkoff's (1996, 182) admonition not to worry about this confusing aspect of video-game play: "The games he plays are simulated drives through the very real data networks he will access later on with his computer and modem." Despite the optimistic arguments that these games simply socialize children and youth as agile users of new media, the implied collapse of distinctions between the normal and the unreal in promotional discourses on technology, according to Kevin Robins (1995, 143), requires us to problematize the underlying claims of postmodern cyberculture: "Through the constitution of a kind of magical reality and realism, in which normal human limits may be overcome and usual boundaries transgressed, the new technological medium promotes and gratifies (magical) fantasies of omnipotence and creative mastery." The problem, Robins argues, is that a "technological domain readily becomes a world of its own, dissociated from the complexity and gravity of the real world." On the highways of Los Angeles with gun-toting drivers, or on the playgrounds of Jonesboro, Arkansas, the site of a school shooting, however, parents can be forgiven for fearing the opposite: the more horrific consequences of these imaginary game spaces concern the reverberations of these fantasies of aggressive omnipotence within the normal world the avid gamer has left behind (Kline 2000).

Conclusion: The Commodification of Children's Media Culture

We have characterized the discourse of video-game advertising as a masculinized symbolic field and a supercharged imaginary world of virtual empowerment. We note too that this youth mediascape excludes and opposes the familial domain of normality as a restrictive, cumbersome, and oppressive domain. It is a branded universe wherein male fantasies are intensified by technology—involving violent and sometimes antisocial themes—aligning postmodern play with a screen-induced ecstatic state of suspended disbelief. The overriding message is a carnivalesque, yet somewhat whimsical, celebration of screen-mediated experience. Video gaming in the discourse of advertising is revealed as an antidote to the mundane—a superb way of escaping the stress and boredom young people experience in their everyday lives.

Yet, in looking at these ads as symbolic constructions mediated by strategic marketing protocols, we also bore witness to the broader commodification of children's media culture. By conjuring the marketers' ghosted intentions behind the fantastic gloss of children's virtual worlds, we have sought to remind cultural analysts that the symbolic child of video-game advertising has been forged amid strategic marketing decisions concerning brand identity, product positioning, and consumer targeting. Put simply, it is a symbolic childhood propelled and contoured by the bottom line. As one Nintendo marketer we interviewed confessed, his company makes use of "every marketing avenue possible to create excitement and interest about our games so that when we launch a game we see great sell through and great hype" (cited in Stafford 1999). We suggest that the pervasive role of promotional strategy within the video-game industry and marketers' inventiveness in conducting research and designing advertising campaigns makes its contribution to children's marketing a significant factor in the future of children's culture.

We know that marketers' plans for transforming the cultural landscape are, to the businesses that deploy them, simply cost-effective marketing strategies used to reach larger audiences, expand target markets, and prolong the shelf life of cultural commodities. We do not accept it as inevitable, however, that children's media and culture should be completely enclosed in the promotional mission. As the U.S. Federal Trade Commission (1999) recently noted, the targeted marketing strategies of the entertainment industry do have important implications for what gets communicated to children to the degree that kids accept and internalize these images and values. We offer this analysis to further document the video-game marketers' ongoing encroachment on children's culture.

REFERENCES

Alloway, Nola, and Pam Gilbert. "Video Game Culture: Playing with Masculinity, Violence and Pleasure." In *Wired-up: Young People and the Electronic Media*, edited by Sue Howard. London: University College London Press, 1998.

Battelle, John, and Bob Johnstone. "Seizing the Next Level: Sega's Plan for World Domination." *Wired Magazine* 1, no. 6 (1993): 74–131.

Buckingham, David. *Moving Images: Understanding Children's Emotional Responses to Television*. New York: St. Martin's Press, 1996.

Cassell, Justine, and Henry Jenkins, ed. *From Barbie to Mortal Kombat: Gender and Computer Games*. Cambridge, Mass.: MIT Press, 1998.

Federal Trade Commission. "Marketing Violent Entertainment to Children: A Review of Self-Regulation and Industry Practices of the Motion Picture, Music Recording and Electronic Game Industries." Washington, D.C., 1999. Retrieved 26 March 2000.

http://www.ftc.gov/opa/2000/09/youthviol.htm.

Goldman, Robert, and Stephen Papson. *Sign Wars: The Cluttered Landscape of Advertising*. New York: Guildford Press, 1996.

Green, Bill, Jo-Anne Reid, and Chris Bigum. "Teaching the Nintendo Generation? Children, Computer Culture and Popular Technologies." In *Wired-up: Young People and the Electronic Media*, edited by Sue Howard. London: University College London Press, 1998.

Griffiths, Diana. "The Gaming Gender Gap." *Games Domain Review*, 1997. Retrieved 1 November, 1998.

http://www.gamesdomain.com/gdreview/depart/rant7.html

Hayes, Michael, and Stuart Dinsey, with Nick Parker. *Games War: Video Games—A Business Review*. London: Bowerdean, 1989.

Herz, J. C. *Joystick Nation: How Videogames Ate Our Quarters, Won Our Hearts, and Rewired Our Minds*. Boston, Mass.: Little, Brown & Co., 1997.

Interactive Digital Software Association (IDSA) "Fast Facts." *Interactive Digital Software Association*. 2000. Retrieved 1 November 2000.

http://www.idsa.com/releases/consumer.htm

Jenkins, Henry. "Professor Jenkins Goes to Washington." *Red Rock Eater News Service*, 1999. Retrieved 30 March, 2001.

http://commons.somewhere.com/rre/1999/RRE.Professor.Jenkins.Go

Kincheloe, Joe L. "*Home Alone* and 'Bad to the Bone': The Advent of a Postmodern Childhood." In *Kinderculture: The Corporate Construction of Childhood*, edited by Joe L. Kincheloe and Shirley R. Steinberg, 31–52. Oxford, UK: Westview Press, 1997.

Kincheloe, Joe L., and Shirley R. Steinberg, ed. *Kinderculture: The Corporate Construction of Childhood*. Oxford, UK: Westview Press, 1997.

Kinder, Marsha. *Playing with Power in Movies, Television and Video Games: From Muppet Babies to Teenage Mutant Ninja Turtles*. Berkeley: University of California Press, 1991.

Kline, Stephen. *Out of the Garden: Children's Toys and Television in the Age of Marketing*, London: Verso Press, 1993.

———. "Pleasures of the Screen: Why Young People Play Video Games." *Proceedings of the International Toy Research Conference*. Angouleme, France, 1997.

Kline, Stephen, and Albert Banerjee. "Video Game Culture: Leisure and Play Preferences of BC Teens." Media Analysis Laboratory. Simon Fraser University, Vancouver, Canada, 1998.

———. "Moral Panics and Video Games." In *Research in Childhood: Sociology, Culture and History: A Collection of Papers*, edited by Jesper Olesen, Ning de Coninck-Smith, Flemming Mouritsen, and Jens Qvortrup, 147–170. Odense, Denmark: University of Southern Denmark, 2000.

Lim, Choonghoon, and Douglas Michele Turco. "The Next Generation in Sport: Y." *The Cyber Journal of Sport Marketing*. 2000. Retrieved 7 July, 2000.

http://www.cjsm.com/vol3/lim34.htm.

Livingstone, Sonia, Katharine Holden, and Moira Bovill. "Children's Changing Media Environments: Overview of a European Comparative Study." In *Children and Media: Image Education Participation*, edited by Cecilia von Ffeilitzen and Ulla Carlasson. Göteborg, Sweden: UNESCO International Clearinghouse on Children and Violence on the Screen, 1999.

McAllister, Matthew P. *The Commercialization of American Culture: New Advertising, Control and Democracy*. Thousand Oaks, Calif.: Sage, 1996.

Mills, Lara. "Chaos Rules: Today's Media-Savvy Kids Find Traditional Linear Narrative a Bore." *Marketing Magazine*. 20/27 July 1998, 17, 20.

Next Generation. 1997. "How Sega and Sony Try and Get In Your Heads,"1997. Retrieved 10 November 1998.

http://www.next-generation.com/features/marketing/sysmarketing.html.

Nielsen Media Research. "New Nielsen Media Research Study Shows Video Game Systems Not Just Kids Stuff," 1999. Retrieved 13 October 2000.

http://www.nielsenmedia.com/newsreleases/releases/1999/hometech.html.

Nissen, Jörgen. "Hackers: Masters of Modernity and Modern Technology." In *Digital Diversions: Youth Culture in the Age of Multimedia*, edited by Julian Sefton-Green. London: University College London Press, 1998.

Pearce, Celia. "Beyond Shoot Your Friends: A Call to Arms in the Battle Against Violence." In *Digital Illusion: Entertaining the Future with High Technology*, edited by Clark Dodsworth Jr. New York: ACM Press, 1998.

Pecora, Norma Odom. *The Business of Children's Entertainment*. New York: Guilford Press, 1998.

Pigeon, Thomas. "Packaging Up Coolness: What Designers Must Do to Capture the Attention of Teens and Tweens." *Marketing Magazine*, 20/27 July 1998, 21.

Provenzo, Eugene F. *Video Kids: Making Sense of Nintendo*. Cambridge, Mass.: Harvard University Press, 1991.

Robins, Kevin. "Cyberspace and the World We Live In." *Body and Society* 1, nos. 3, 4 (1995): 135–155.

Rushkoff, Douglas. *Playing the Future*. New York: Harper Collins, 1996.

Sawyer, Ben, Alex Dunne, and Tor Berg. *Game Developer's Marketplace: The Definitive Guide to Making It Big in the Interactive Game Industry*. New York: Coriolis Group Books, 1998.

Sheff, David. *Game Over: How Nintendo Zapped an American Industry*. New York: Random House, 1993.

Stafford, Brent, director. *Insert Coin: The Culture of Video Game Play*. Master's program project. Simon Fraser University, Vancouver, Canada, 1999.

Stallabrass, Julian. *Gargantua: Manufactured Mass Culture*. London: Verso Press, 1996.

Stone, Rosanne Allucquère. *The War of Desire and Technology at the Close of the*

Mechanical Age. Cambridge, Mass.: MIT Press, 1995.

Total Control, no. 5. March, 1999.

Walkerdine, Valerie, Angela Dudfield, and David Studdert. "Sex and Violence: Regulating Childhood at the Turn of the Millennium." In *Research in Childhood: Sociology, Culture and History: A Collection of Papers*, edited by Jesper Olesen, Ning de Coninck-Smith, Flemming Mouritsen, and Jens Qvortrup, 197–212. Odense, Denmark: University of Southern Denmark, 2000.

"YTV Advertisement." *Marketing Magazine*, 20/27 July 1998, 16.

Ziauddin, Sardar. *Postmodernism and the Other: The New Imperialism of Western Culture*. London: Pluto Press, 1998.

Contributors

Adriana S. Benzaquén received her Ph.D. in the Graduate Programme in Social and Political Thought of York University in Toronto, Canada. She is now assistant professor in the Department of History, Mount Saint Vincent University. Among her publications are "Vygotsky, Childhood, and Development: Revisiting the History of Developmental Psychology" in *Das Argument*, forthcoming in a special issue on critical psychology; "Thought and Utopia in the Writings of Adorno, Horkheimer, and Benjamin," in *Utopian Studies*, 1998; and "Freud, Little Hans, and the Desire for Knowledge," in *Journal of Curriculum Theorizing*, 1998.

Jeffery P. Dennis received a master's degree in English from Indiana University and taught for ten years at Old Dominion University, the University of Notre Dame, and elsewhere. Currently, he is a doctoral student in sociology at the State University of New York at Stony Brook, concentrating in queer theory and the sociology of culture. He has recently completed a book on cross-cultural articulations of transgressive and nonhegemonic sexualities.

Sara K. Dorow is a doctoral candidate in sociology at the University of Minnesota. Her dissertation is titled "Constructing the Spirited Child: A Multi-Sited Ethnography of the Transnational Adoption of Chinese Children." She has a master's degree in East Asian Studies from the University of Minnesota, and is author and editor, respectively, of two books on adoption: *When You Were Born in China* and *I Wish for You a Beautiful Life: Letters from the Korean Birth Mothers of Ae Ran Won to Their Children.*

Tarleton Gillespie is a doctoral candidate in the Department of Communication at the University of California-San Diego. His dissertation, "The Digital Renovation of Authorship," investigates recent disputes concerning the role of copyright law on the Net—considering how they both participate in and erase long-standing contests over the nature of authorship and cultural expression. His other work has investigated animation and consumer culture; the ideal of convergence in the study of television, music sampling and its challenge to principles of authorship, and the implications of interface design.

Janice Hill is a doctoral student in sociology at York University in Toronto, Canada. Her dissertation isntitled "Building a Nation of Nation Builders: Youth Movements, Imperialism and English Canadian Nationalism, 1880-1920." She currently teaches courses in qualitative methods and constructions of childhood.

Kathleen Huun received her Ph.D. in human sciences from Florida State University. Currently, she serves as an adjunct faculty member at Marylhurst University, Portland Community College, and the Art Institute of Portland. She is pursuing research on gender symbolism in infant clothing (in press) and variations in the style and meanings of men's neckties in the twentieth century.

Mark D. Jacobs is an associate professor of sociology at George Mason University, where he also served for seven years as founding director of the Ph.D. Program in Cultural Studies, the first interdisciplinary doctoral program in that field in the United States. He is the author of *Screwing the System and Making It Work: Juvenile Justice in the No-Fault Society* (University of Chicago Press, 1990), and is currently coediting *The Blackwell Companion to the Sociology of Culture*.

Susan B. Kaiser is professor of textiles and clothing and a professor in Women and Gender Studies at the University of California at Davis. She is the author of *The Social Psychology of Clothing: Symbolic Appearances in Context* (1997, 2nd ed. revised), New York: Fairchild. She has also published works in the areas of cultural studies; sociology; fashion theory; style and subjectivity; and identity ambivalence and negotiations. Her previous work has also addressed issues of gender coding and socialization related to children's clothing, and she is currently pursuing a larger project on "tween" apparel consumers and associated cultural anxieties.

Mary Lorena Kenny received her Ph.D. in anthropology from Columbia University and is currently assistant professor of anthropology at Eastern Connecticut State University. She is the author of "Hidden Heads of Households: Child Labor in Northeast Brazil" in *Human Organization*. She has also conducted research on citizenship and drought in Northeast Brazil, shifting patterns of drug use in Jamaica, HIV infection and AIDS among minority women in New York City, and the use of traditional healers in the Philippines.

Stephen Kline is a professor in the School of Communication at Simon Fraser University, Canada, as well as Director of the Media Analysis Laboratory. He is author of *Out of the Garden: Children's Culture and Toys in the Age of TV Marketing* (Verso, 1993). He is currently writing two books, *Paradox Lost: On the Interplay of Technology, Markets and Culture in the Making of the Video Game* (with Nick Dyer-Witheford and Greig de Peuter, McGill-Queen's University Press) and *The End of Play?* (Columbia University Press).

Kathryn Libal recently earned her doctoral degree in cultural anthropology from the University of Washington. Her dissertation, "Children and Nation-State Building in Early Republican Turkey, 1923–1938" traces emerging discourses on children as both subjects and objects of nation-building efforts in the 1920s and 1930s. She is currently a lecturer in Women's Studies at the University of Kansas.

Chandra Mukerji is Professor of Communication and Sociology and Science Studies at the University of California, San Diego. She is author of *From Graven Images: Patterns of Modern Materialism* (Columbia,1983); *A Fragile Power: Science and the State* (Princeton, 1989), which won the Robert K. Merton Award in 1991; and *Territorial Ambitions and the Gardens of Versailles* (Cambridge 1997), which won the 1998 Culture Book Prize from the American Sociological Association. She has published extensively on material culture in early modern Europe, as well as material analysis in both science studies and cultural studies. She has also written a number of pieces on American popular culture, particularly cartoons and childhood. Coauthor with Michael Schudson of *Rethinking Popular Culture* (University of California Press, 1991), she is currently working on two books, one on landscape engineering and the Canal de Midi and the other about war and American popular culture.

Greig de Peuter is a doctoral candidate in the School of Communication at Simon Fraser University, Canada, concentrating on the political economy of youth marketing. He is contributing to a forthcoming book, *Paradox Lost: On the Interplay of Technology, Markets and Culture in the Making of the Video Game* (with Stephen Kline and Nick Dyer-Witheford, McGill-Queen's University Press).

Roblyn Rawlins is Assistant Professor of Sociology at the College of New Rochelle, New York, and a Ph.D. candidate at the State University of New York at Stony Brook. In her dissertation, "Making Moderns: Discipline and Self-Control of American, English, and Irish Women and Children, 1870-1930," she utilizes a comparative/historical analysis of child-rearing advice literatures to investigate the architecture of the modern self and discourses disciplining the bodies, behavior, and emotions of mothers and children.

Harriet Strandell received her Ph.D. in sociology from Helsinki University. Her dissertation about daycare centers as meeting places for children was published by Gaudeamus Press in Finland in 1994. Currently acting professor in the Department of Sociology, Åbo Akademi University, she has authored "Doing Reality with Play: Play as a Children's Resource in Organizing Everyday Life in Day Care Centres" in *Childhood* (1997), and "*What is the Use of Children's Play—Preparation or Social Participation?*" in *Early Childhood Services: Theory, policy and practice*, edited by H. Penn Buckingham (Open University Press, 2000).

INDEX

Toby Miller
General Editor

Popular Culture and Everyday Life is the new place for critical books in cultural studies. The series stresses multiple theoretical, political, and methodological approaches to commodity culture and lived experience by borrowing from sociological, anthropological, and textual disciplines. Each volume develops a critical understanding of a key topic in the area through a combination of thorough literature review, original research, and a student-reader orientation. The series consists of three types of books: single-authored monographs, readers of existing classic essays, and new companion volumes of papers on central topics. Fields to be covered include: fashion, sport, shopping, therapy, religion, food and drink, youth, music, cultural policy, popular literature, performance, education, queer theory, race, gender, and class.

For additional information about this series or for the submission of manuscripts, please contact:

Toby Miller
Department of Cinema Studies
New York University
721 Broadway, Room 600
New York, New York 10003

To order other books in this series, please contact our Customer Service Department:

(800) 770-LANG (within the U.S.)
(212) 647-7706 (outside the U.S.)
(212) 647-7707 FAX

Or browse online by series:

www.peterlangusa.com